THE COMPLETE POEMS

OTHER BOOKS BY WENDY BARKER

POETRY

Those Roads, These Moons [a chapbook]. 2023.

Weave: New and Selected Poems. 2022.

Gloss. 2020.

Shimmer [a chapbook]. 2019.

One Blackbird at a Time. 2015.

From the Moon, Earth Is Blue. 2015.

Nothing Between Us: The Berkeley Years. 2009.

Things of the Weather [a chapbook]. 2009.

Between Frames [a chapbook]. 2006.

Poems from Paradise. 2005.

Poems' Progress [a selection of poems with accompanying essays]. 2002.

Way of Whiteness. 2000.

Eve Remembers [a chapbook]. 1996.

Let the Ice Speak: Poems. 1991.

Winter Chickens and Other Poems. 1990.

TRANSLATIONS

Rabindranath Tagore: Final Poems. 2001. Cotranslated with Saranindranath Tagore.

CRITICISM

The House Is Made of Poetry: The Art of Ruth Stone. 1996. Coedited with Sandra M. Gilbert.

Lunacy of Light: Emily Dickinson and the Experience of Metaphor. 1987. Japanese trans., 1991.

The COMPLETE POEMS
WENDY BARKER

EDITED BY **STEVEN G. KELLMAN**

INTRODUCTION BY **ILAN STAVANS**

LOUISIANA STATE UNIVERSITY PRESS
BATON ROUGE

Published by Louisiana State University Press
lsupress.org

Manufactured in the United States of America
First printing

Designer: Barbara Neely Bourgoyne
Typeface: Adobe Text Pro
Printer and binder: Sheridan Books, Inc.

Jacket and author photograph (on page 553) by Sue Hum

The poems herein were earlier published in collections titled *Winter Chickens and Other Poems* (Corona Publishing, 1990), copyright © 1990 by Wendy Barker; *Let the Ice Speak: Poems* (Ithaca House Books, Greenfield Review Press, 1991), copyright © 1991 by Wendy Barker; *Eve Remembers* (Aark Arts, 1996), copyright © 1996 by Wendy Barker; *Way of Whiteness* (Wings Press, 2000), copyright © 2000 by Wendy Barker; *Poems' Progress* (Absey & Co., 2002), copyright © 2002 by Wendy Barker; *Poems from Paradise* (WordTech Editions, 2005), copyright © 2005 by Wendy Barker; *Between Frames* (Pecan Grove Press, 2006), copyright © 2006 by Wendy Barker; *Things of the Weather* (Pudding House, 2009), copyright © 2008 by Wendy Barker; *Nothing Between Us: The Berkeley Years* (Del Sol Press, 2009), copyright © 2009 by Wendy Barker; *From the Moon, Earth Is Blue* (Wings Press, 2015), copyright © 2015 by Wendy Barker; *One Blackbird at a Time* (BkMk Press, 2015), copyright © 2015 by Wendy Barker; *Shimmer* (Glass Lyre Press, 2019), copyright © 2019 by Wendy Barker; *Gloss* (Saint Julian Press, 2020), copyright © 2020 by Wendy Barker; *Weave: New and Selected Poems* (BkMk Press, 2022), copyright © 2022 by Wendy Barker; *Those Roads, These Moons* (Alabrava Press, 2023), copyright © 2023 by Wendy Barker.

Previously uncollected poems first appeared in the following publications: *Banyan Review:* "Turning Eighty, Ruminations"; *Plume:* "On Silver Spoons"; *Rattle:* "In the Endoscopy Center" and "Stuff"; *Superstition Review:* "Bone Ash, Bone China," "The Bones Know," and "The Make-Up of Bones."

To avoid duplication, poems that appeared in both chapbooks and later collections are gathered here under the collection titles, except in the case of significant revisions.

LIBRARY OF CONGRESS CATALOGING-IN-PUBLICATION DATA
Names: Barker, Wendy, author. | Kellman, Steven G., 1947– editor. | Stavans, Ilan, writer of introduction.
Title: The complete poems / Wendy Barker ; edited by Steven G. Kellman ; introduction by Ilan Stavans.
Other titles: Poems
Description: Baton Rouge : Louisiana State University Press, 2025. | Includes index.
Identifiers: LCCN 2024047653 (print) | LCCN 2024047654 (ebook) | ISBN 978-0-8071-8391-5 (cloth) | ISBN 978-0-8071-8434-9 (epub) | ISBN 978-0-8071-8435-6 (pdf)
Subjects: LCGFT: Poetry.
Classification: LCC PS3552 .A67124 2025 (print) | LCC PS3552 (ebook) | DDC 811/.54—dc23/eng/20241011
LC record available at https://lccn.loc.gov/2024047653
LC ebook record available at https://lccn.loc.gov/2024047654

CONTENTS

LET THE ICE SPEAK
(1991)

BETWEEN FRAMES
(2006)

THINGS OF THE WEATHER
(2009)

ONE BLACKBIRD AT A TIME
(2015)

---

from SHIMMER (2019)

GLOSS (2020)

THOSE ROADS, THESE MOONS (2023)

UNCOLLECTED POEMS

INTRODUCTION

WENDY BARKER

'Tis Not a Different Time

ILAN STAVANS

Forever – is composed of Nows –
'Tis not a different time –
Except for Infiniteness –
And Latitude of Home –
—EMILY DICKINSON, "Poem 690"

For almost four decades, Wendy Barker conversed with Poetry as one does with the closest of one's confidants. The moment she figured out she wanted to be a poet for life, she made a pledge to devote herself to it with rigor and discipline. Her poems are sensorial as well as existential. Good poetry, she thought, "hits us in the gut, in the groin, changes our internal chemistry, even as it challenges or teases the mind." Barker liked quoting Dickinson, who believed poetry made her "feel physically as if the top of my head were taken off." Barker too had a visceral connection: it was the channel through which she processed the musical, visual, and tactile dimensions of "real" life, an art, she stated, "that can bypass the intellectual defenses often surrounding us like plexiglass shields." Volumes of poetry are seldom best-sellers, she argued, and poets seldom grow rich from their books. But, as William Carlos Williams believed, she stated, people "die miserably every day / for lack / of what is found" in poems.

At the time of Barker's death, on March 11, 2023, at the age of eighty, she left behind almost five hundred poems, some of them of astonishing beauty, the vast majority published in fifteen collections, starting with *Winter Chickens and Other Poems* (1990) and ending with *Those Roads, These Moons* (2023). There are also a number of unpublished poems, a few of them still in a larval state. Reading them sequentially, it is easy to follow Barker's stunning arc from a novitiate infatuated with the possibilities of language to a master in command with her crystalline style: empathic, capable of circumnavigating the daily chores of a sentient being in an age of hyperstimulation.

At the core of her oeuvre is an urgent theme: time. Anyone who wastes any portion of time doesn't really understand what life is about. For Barker, in every minute, every hour, every day she could find the inspiration for a poem. As a result, her poetry has the texture of a journal. She reacts to an event by letting herself be moved, rebuffing any stiffness, always surprised by what comes her way: love, friendship, marriage, childbirth, divorce, illness. Her work isn't solipsistic, though. The picture it draws is of a large canvas: a passionate American woman reacting to the achievements and excesses of her country since the fifties, from the civil rights era to the Vietnam War protests, the imperial decades when the United States "sold" democracy to other nations, up to the devastation of the COVID pandemic. She is interested in change, which, of course, is the paramount characteristic of time.

Her heroes were Dickinson and Williams, along with Walt Whitman, Robert Frost, Denise Levertov, Adrienne Rich, and Ruth Stone, members of the trend in American poetry she affiliated herself with, interested in the tension between the individual and society, ready to face the moral, religious, and ideological questions of the day honestly and without subterfuge. Stone described Barker's poetry as being capable, in the same breath, of making you laugh and breaking your heart. And Naomi Shihab Nye said that, if you were lost inside your own life, a Barker poem "could help you find your way home."

Through her verses, Barker established intimate relationships with objects, places, emotions. The examples are plentiful. These lines are from the poem "On Climbing Trees, for Louisa May Alcott":

> I am surrounded by live oaks. Small
> Texas madrones, leaves that turn
> golden in November, quiver in wind.
> I never did
>
> learn to climb a tree.

These are from "Swallow Watcher":

> Every house needs someone to watch the swallows,
> someone willing

to half close the eyes, lean the head back
against a tall chair
in a garden, on a porch, in a courtyard.

These from "On Salt," in dialogue with Pablo Neruda:

I wish I could erase
moments when I've been bullied, flattened
by comments that sliced through my skin. At times
those tauntings attack me in dreams,
like salt stinging a wound.

In these examples, time is the here and now as well as the forever. There is a line from Philip Larkin that Barker and her second husband, Steven Kellman, liked to repeat to one another: "Days are where we live." Even the time that presents itself to us in dreams matters to her. "When dreams go beyond the words you own," she states in the poem "Sounding Dreams," "it's best not to question them."

Mostly, Barker is intrigued by people: her music-loving son David, about whom she writes constantly, her friends, her husband, her students, other poets, even the dentist, a hair stylist, an IT specialist, a whore, a physician friend, a bus driver, an Orthodox Jew, and so on. For the picture of her encounters with them to materialize, Barker required an enormous amount of solitude. Not only that but silence, especially early in the day. "Morning silence is not a luxury, as far as I am concerned," she wrote. "It is a necessity." She practiced different scales of silence, because silence was the key to simplicity, a condition she sometimes explained through colors, or sounds—a condition "uncluttered by any pen or brush, this unframed shape—arresting / as a full breath." Several of her poems are an illustration of that simplicity, but they are never simple. Her approach has a hint of Buddhism: it provided her a way of walking into mystery, "a kind of harmony I do not experience otherwise," she stated. "It offers a way of seeing beyond the superficial, of making startling connections. It allows a way of living deeply, intensely."

In her own words, Barker was "wispy, pale-eyed, pale-haired, gangly, and, according to the general consensus, far 'too sensitive.'" Her full name was Wendy Wakelyn Bean. She loved her middle name and for a time considered calling herself Wendy Wakelyn. She was born in Summit, New Jersey, on September 22, 1942, and her family moved to Phoenix, Arizona, in the late 1940s. The family moved frequently within Arizona—from Phoenix to Tucson and back to Phoenix, living, as she put it, "in a succession of cramped tract-houses in various working-class neighborhoods." She counted thirteen different schools she attended in twelve years, because her father moved jobs but also because her mother thought there would be a better house, with a better school nearby, somewhere else.

Her mother was from England, and Barker was mesmerized by her accent, which appeared to change "on the rare occasions when her parents and a cousin visited us," turning them into "exotic creatures from another planet." The accent might have been one of the doors of perception for Barker to open up the room of language. She would later on say that "one thing all great poems share is some sort of play with language, with delicious sounds, some sort of music, a particular rhythm. And imagery."

Although Barker's father was "in most ways emotionally very distant," he introduced her to poetry—he would recite Frost at the dinner table, "Stopping by Woods on a Snowy Evening" being a particular favorite. As a girl, Barker "would sit listening on the sofa, rapt, and literally shiver" from her father's recitations. Later in life, as Barker's father neared death, she recalled the poem amid silence's absent cadences: "I wanted to recite that poem to him because I knew it was his all-time favorite, but for some reason, I just couldn't—uncharacteristically, I became speechless."

Barker wondered if she was adopted since no one in her family was quite like her. The feeling at times metamorphosed into an impostor's syndrome. Was she too tender, too raw? Could she write true poetry? In her scholarly book *Lunacy of Light: Emily Dickinson and the Experience of Metaphor* (1987), she looked at the poet though metaphors of lights and darkness. She was fascinated with the way Dickinson talked of an internally linked circle surrounding her writing—in Barker's words, "like a wall with no door." She discusses the possibility of Dickinson suffering from the genetic optic condition exotropia, a misalignment of the pupils that might have caused eyestrain and sensitivity to light. This, Barker believed, is why she might have been allergic to the outdoors, why she inhabited the penumbra of her own room.

A similar assessment might be made of Barker's work. As is clear, she pays enormous attention. And she is attuned to the tactile and auditive registers. Since early on, she had a penchant for writing. "From the time I learned to write letters," she wrote, "I was always jotting things down. Kept diaries as a girl. Wrote what I thought I'd develop into short stories in my teens and twenties. Always writing. Kept little bits of notes in the drawer beside my bed. It wasn't until I was in graduate school, in my late twenties, early thirties, that I realized those little bits were germs of poems. And that I wasn't wanting to write fiction, but poems." She wrestled with the perception that women are supposedly more in touch with their sentiments, yet she explored her emotions in their full complexity. That approach would remain steadfast throughout her life. In the poem "Crash," Barker chronicles, matter-of-factly, an automobile accident she was in:

> You thought it was
> the road home, and
> it was, till it
> wasn't, pavement
> slick from splattered
> rain, and flash, crash,
> you're smashed against
> a pole—car tilted,
> eighty degree
> angle, air bag
> flattened against
> your chest, glasses
> nowhere in sight,
> until kind hands
> open your door,
> "Are you okay,
> Ma'm? Now just breathe,
> here's a blanket."

But then, suddenly, she switches gear, relating—still in a direct style—the roller coaster of feelings that is overwhelming her and the chaos of recovery she might need:

> no blankets
> are warming me,
> still shaking from
> every pore,
> not a single
> road seeming safe
> even with no
> rain.

As an adolescent, her ambition was to become a fiction writer. She switched to poetry when she recognized her talent to tap a moment and turn it into an eternity. Yet, in truth, she never altogether gave up fiction. In fact, at one point she combined poetry and fiction in artful ways. To a large extent, Barker's verses are driven by narrative: in her verses, she concocts scenes, tells stories, and develops plotlines. Some poems feel like short stories. Others rotate around an action that hinges on a denouement and even a punch line.

She was fond of remembering when her mentor, scholar Sandra M. Gilbert, first expressed enthusiasm for her poetry but encouraged her to experiment with drafts. (With Gilbert, Barker coedited a collection of essays called *The House Is Made of Poetry: The Art of Ruth Stone* [1996].) Her husband would read every single poem, offering comments. Having studied in Arizona, Barker spent most of life in the Southwest, especially in San Antonio, where she taught at the city's branch of the University of Texas, first as an English professor, in addition to writer-in-residence. Living in San Antonio made her feel far away from the nation's gravitational poetry circles. Her early work was published in *The Atlantic* and other places. As editors left, she didn't pursue new relationships. Shy and self-effacing, she would decline invitations to poetry readings because they would distract her from her daily routine of digging the poems out of her consciousness. She had a small group of poet friends, some of them former students, who, along with her second husband, would read her poetry before publication.

Her love for fiction is abundant in *Nothing Between Us: The Berkeley Years.* Released in 2009, it is a novel in verse, or maybe a poetic memoir. Then again, every memoir, no matter how authentic it might strive to be, is fictional. Barker chronicles her erotic intimacies in the Bay Area in her extramarital affair with a Black lover called Ty, her friendship with her hedonistic friend Julie, her political awakening, her reading of Richard Wright's *Native Son* and Betty Friedan's *The Feminine Mystique,* and the empowerment she and others felt, realizing literature could denounce, could expand people's minds, could entice them to imagine alternative universes. Literature, too, was a means for women to regain control of their bodies. The plot is delivered in impressionistic, brick-like paragraphs. The cumulative effect is astonishing: it showcases the degree to which Barker was aware she was writing a testimony of the turbulent years of the United States from the perspective of an average young person. At the end of *Nothing Between Us,* Barker's affair ends and Julie, pregnant with an Oakland high-school principal's baby, commits suicide.

She also experimented, albeit sparingly, with essays. Her book *Poems' Progress* (2002) is an irreplaceable toolbox to appreciate how she put her poetry together. It displays almost two dozen poems written throughout her career, in finished form, along with one or more versions, and accompanied by a short essay in which she explains how each of them came to be. She discusses the countless rewritings each of these sometimes would go through, patiently, painfully, the ultimate goal being not only a complete draft—Paul Valéry said that "a poem is never finished, only abandoned"—but the unfinished versions as snapshots, iterations of the poet's self in constant mutation.

~

Inevitably, the most recurrent presence in Barker's later poems is her students. "Oh, yes," Barker told an interviewer, "students are like the birds! Coming and going in my life, entering it for a semester and then gone. And I have to let go. Let go and let go and let go." She saw teaching as a profession of enormous rewards, although "it can also be devouring." To survive, she said she had to learn "just how much of myself I can offer to feed others, and how much to withhold, to keep for myself." She thrived in the classroom, although the experience shook her to the core. A class for her was made of words and silences, the latter on occasion more meaningful than the former.

Teaching and writing, writing and teaching—the two went hand in hand. It is said that only the teacher ages in the classroom; the students are always of the same age. In Barker's classroom, she reflected on our numbing hyperconsumerism, the neglected needs of underserved groups, the apathy toward other people's suffering, and the curtailing of individual freedom on display as a result of societal blocks that amounted to censorship. The four walls turned the place into a microcosm of the larger culture.

In a poem titled "Waking Over *Call It Sleep,*" about teaching Henry Roth's novel *Call It Sleep,* which deals with Jewish immigration to New York, she was floored by a student's anti-Semitic reaction.

> I'm the closest thing to Jewish in the class even though
> at best I'm only one-eighth, according
> to my English mother, who insisted the shadowy figure
> of her granny was a Jew since nobody knew
> her origins and everybody talked as if something had been
> hushed up, shameful, and of course
> everything about her hawk-nosed face was unusually dark,
> especially the ringlets of her unruly hair.

And then Barker tells the students, in passing, that "only / 1% of our city's population is Jewish,"

which was when Heather quipped: "Of course, they're all
in Hollywood making millions from
trashy movies." I put down my book and didn't move—
you could hear the whirr
of the elevator down the hall. When I spoke, I said, "That
was a *very* offensive comment"—and
I realized I was shaking, after decades of holding forth
in linoleum-floored classrooms. It wasn't
like the times I've heard someone saying *wet* meaning
wetback which are both despicable
terms and I argue those too, but this time it was as if
I'd been slapped full in the face, called
sheeny, kike, and I swear that tears came to my eyes though
I couldn't cry out "*Gevalt,* help,
take that back, you ignorant little bitch."

The scene invites the reader into Barker's mind, her conflicted reactions, the upholding of standards of civility while recognizing that, at its core, distrust is palpable everywhere. Whereas the teacher wonders how to respond, the poet is certain: narrate the overall exchange, in the classroom as well as internally, reliably, without artifice.

Likewise, she is mesmerized when she teaches Emily Dickinson's poetry, witnessing the discovery the students make of her associative mind and idiosyncratic punctuation:

The students crack
their paperbacks, pressing
the valves of her phrases, working them
like bellows, determined
to ignite a fire with compacted air, evade
the cold that could razor the tops
of our heads. They want to illuminate
the shadowy dashes, the slivered
chasms, seal them for safe-keeping
under glass. She hovers
at the ceiling like an unfamiliar freckled
moth, like Jehovah—Yahweh—
a name we cannot speak aloud. She is
hovering like a breath taken

further and further until released,
a slip of thread lifted
by the wind. If only they could spread
their feathers, gain an arc,
know how neighborly, the invisible.

And she is shaken when, introducing Robert Frost's "Stopping by Woods on a Snowy Evening," a Mexican American student calls the poem *lovely.* Barker wonders if her own and the classroom's lexicon is the same:

Olivia wasn't saying she didn't like
the poems, but *lovely?* A word my mother detested as phony,
like someone holding a pinkie straight out while drinking tea,
the sort of word my grandmother used when vaguely praising
a Bartók piece, or a play she didn't understand. Like people
saying, "How interesting," when what they really mean is, "Spare me
the details," or, "Could we change the subject." So when
I asked Olivia what she meant by "lovely" and she talked about
the lush, long vowel sounds, I wondered why I'd felt stabbed,
until I remembered my father's lying in the ICU, the fat respirator
tube jammed down his throat, the whoosh of forced breath
fogging the glassed-in-room, and my stroking his forehead while
my father, whom I'd never seen cry, began to leak tears down
his chiseled face.

In *Poems' Progress,* Barker says that poets never know when the poems will come, "how they will find us. Or where. On the beach, in a city, in a garden, on a kitchen table, in a hospital, or even a classroom." Judging by the fecundity of the teaching elements, prominently in *One Blackbird at a Time* (2015), which in my impressions is where she is in full control of her craft, it is obvious the latter was her habitat. Poems "are all around us," she stated, "in the midst of our crowded lives," snapshots of the people, often those younger than us, that make us who we are.

~

Before I met her, in 2007, I was already a Wendy Barker reader. I admired *Way of Whiteness* (2000), with its reflections about learning a language, its depiction of the act of gestation, her recreation of places, and her "Liquid Poem" ("It is not true that water has no color. / Nor that milk is white.") And I treasured

Between Frames (2006), with its sweeping meditations on pain. Every time I would open one of her collections, I would feel close to her affinities, as if it was I who was in conversation with her. She would invoke a line from Shakespeare ("O, reason not the need!" from *King Lear,* act 2, scene 4), or a thought about Elizabeth Bishop's "One Art" ("a perfect poem, I say, and though no one /in the class is over twenty-five, everybody /nods").

I visited her and Kellman in their home in San Antonio. We also saw each other in New York, Austin, and other places. And she came to Amherst, Massachusetts, where Emily Dickinson lived and I do too. We talked about countless topics on our tête-à-têtes: food, poetry, films, politics, and translation. She read broadly in translation. I remember our dialogues about Pablo Neruda. I was translating some of his 225 odes at the time. I told her Neruda's simplicity reminded me of hers as well. And we talked about my efforts at translating Dickinson and Bishop into Spanish.

In one poem, "On Delta Flight #2164 from JFK," she talks about her passion for Whitman and Dickinson even as she finds herself like a sardine in the crowded airplane. Her old age and physical decline are tangible:

> Even now, whenever I
> leave home, I fear I won't return, will lose touch,
> become "Nobody." Maybe that's why I'm
> always bantering with strangers in our tangled
> strands as we board and deplane. If they're
> chatting with me, I could be somebody. Yet I
> must keep my own skin intact, and though
> I wish, like Walt, I could be "loos'd of limits and
> imaginary lines," I must hold to a few
> limits or I'd lose my whole self. "The Soul selects
> her own Society," says Dickinson, but
> who am I in this crowd? Always, as Emily laments,
> "the bewildering thread." I need to fasten
> my own threads the way warp strands on a wooden
> loom are tightened, so the weave will hold.

Actually, Barker was a translator herself. She rendered Rabindranath Tagore's last Bengali poems, a task she undertook with one of the Indian author's descendants, philosopher Saranindranath Tagore. The slim volume, *Final Poems,* came out in 2001. The poems were about illness. She wanted them to feel natural in English. One example is called "Recovery 6":

Distant, fragile, pale blue of sky
above the forest trees lifting
their arms, a silent offering of green.
Winter's tender sun on earth
spreads a shawl of clear light.
I am writing this down before
the painter, indifferent, wipes clean the canvas.

In one meeting, Barker and I talked about the differences between American and Hindu languages and cultures, the absence of an English-language word for a specific part of garments in India. Barker also reflected on Bengali words that convey multiple, at times contradictory, meanings. Needless to say, those are the challenges of any translator. In her case, these thoughts made her feel even closer to the English language.

Ironically, when Barker herself became ill, in her last decade, she too decided to trace her decline in meticulous detail while not surrendering to it. "I know I can't travel to seven continents any more. Maybe not even two or three. It's one of the realities of aging, knowing that one's energies are not what they once were, and that the time one has left is limited, and wanting to spend it carefully. (Interesting that I switched suddenly to using the impersonal and more formal 'one' rather than 'I'. . . .)" And: "[I am] getting at the realization that I'm no longer so interested in seeing far-away places superficially, but getting to know what's closest as deeply as I can." On her death bed, Barker asked her husband for her translations of Tagore. She read them aloud to him.

That switch from "I" to the formal "one" is indeed interesting. Barker's poetry travels from the "I" to the "we," and from there to transcendent "us" that is about infiniteness. She responds to Mary Oliver's famous question, "Tell me, what is it you plan to do / with your one wild and precious life?" with a rotund: "I shall turn the pulse of time into verses."

WINTER CHICKENS AND OTHER POEMS

(1990)

FOUNDATIONS

Once you're there, with the pickax,
over rocks, red clay, and saplings
high as your calves, it's hard to see
where the lines go.

You have talked all this out.
There will be every room
except the one you can never
remember, but it's too late
now, we are setting the strings,
applying the level.

These lines must intercept
at right angles. You try
to search the caves of your mind,
where was that room you have
forgotten?
                The house will go on
anyway. Strings, trenches, rows
of steel rebar over black plastic
over rock, this house
must not move once it's here.

The outline looks too big
without rooms. Where
will we butter toast, where
will we argue over the budget,
where will we stare
at the painted buntings that
drop their fire to the feeder?

You see all these trees? Can't fit
them inside. Windows, yes,
you can look out,
but what's inside stays inside
once the walls go up.

WANTING ANIMALS

My son reads about black stallions
mares, tails rippling like fish

in an ocean of wind.
He wants a horse, a gray one,

withers firm, nostrils wet,
whinnying blue air

by the stable he wants us to build
beyond the house.

But at the sliding-glass door
the neighbor's dog stares inside.

Won't go home. Won't stay in his yard.
Climbs over his chain-link fence

to lie on our porch.
Ticks swell the lines of his ears.

His ribs are long fingers pressing his lungs
his eyes fix on us.

We should take him in
add him to our collection,

rough-coated collies
Barred Rock hens.

His brown mottled back curls on our doormat
all night, a small, thin whine.

THREE POEMS IN DEAD WINTER

1.

I wait for birds.
Prepared. Old field guide
and the new one, slick photographs.
All around are tidelands,
reeds like giant nests
tangling with dried grasses,
seeding shrubs.
I study the drawings of Goldeneyes,
Buffleheads.
The water is the color of asphalt.
On the surface of this cold pond
I can't even see
the reflection of my own face.

2.

The knife blade is discolored.
Bread crumbs clutter
the edge, but it cuts clean,
cuts an orange right through.
The skin splits down
to the soft meat, juice, small tendons.
Seeds drop to the table,
we suck on the half-spheres,
leave them, orange, white, empty.

3.

Finches land in pairs
at the feeder.
You can hear small crunchings
as they crack
covers of seeds.
Their tongues are gray like gravel.
While their beaks work
their heads are upright.
Ready to leave.

DEER RUNNING

This is not brush weaving
in and out of wind.
The deer leaps
away from the cars, terror
explodes in her legs,
she hurls against the wire
webbing of the fence,
tangling through.

When she crawls
into the safety of cedar brake
she stands only to fall
on her side, and fall
again, again,
before she moves off
and loses us
among the dry leaves.

We're late
for David's piano lesson.
He says, "Well, we did what we could."

This morning, on the stairs,
it felt good, good to run
to the coffee, clean dishes,
you at the table.

I remember in southside Chicago,
you said when you saw them
coming, twenty or thirty,
moving straight for us,
you said, "Walk as fast
as you can, *walk.*
Walk like hell. Get out
your car key *now*
and slide in *fast.*

But I don't think
they were after us.
We were just there,
they were in a righteous
hurry, headed somewhere else.

She had no room.
She couldn't jump
because the cedars crowd so thick
and high near the fences
by the road.

For knowing the music
David's teacher gave him
a plastic bust of Brahms
She's teaching him to use
the right fingers
on the right keys,
not to rush the tempo.

SATURDAY KITCHEN REQUIEM

(for James Hathaway)

No dishes in the sink this time
just feathers and claws.
Plucking roosters, breasts still warm
soft as fur. No more crowing cuts
the air. Death smells stronger

than bacon in this kitchen, a smell of thick,
wet feathers. This morning
you are as far north
as I am south, and today, in Ithaca,
you bury your father.

Last night I watched my son sing
his first concert, third grade sopranos
gave their regards to Broadway,
Chicago, places they've never seen.
My son looked younger than eight,

as if he might forget the words.
On this steaming morning, I know
only feathers, black and white
feathers, plump thighs underneath
hardening to bone.

KITCHEN FEVER

1.

I try to hold the chard
flat on the table.
It billows around the knife.

The white stalks are obedient, even-threaded.
I cut them into squares,
fiber for the diet.

2.

Furiously cutting carrots.
Round slices.
You can see the sun inside, small
spokes yellow as butter in the pan.

3.

The clouds hurt with their whiteness.
They puff like poached egg water
at a hard boil.

Up there the wind blows.
Those clouds are traveling
over the whole picture.

DRIVE TO THE PIG FARM

Past clipped yards.
Nasturtiums hang over slat fences.
Fields rise out of wounds left by the road.
Jagged places, healed with lupine, poppies.

Drive toward hills.
Waves of wild carrot, yellow clumps
of wild mustard. Drive past all these,
past the small purple-bladed flower

opening in the shade of live oaks.
Past the farm with red stables.
Round the final turn
mud reaches to the horizon.

Hills of mud piled with pigs.
Hundreds of pigs, sprawled
on their sides, fat haunches limp,
stiff blond hairs rising

over the flesh like sparse fur.
One hunches dog-like,
two-toed foot under its belly.
Their feet mince through the stink, old

potatoes scattered like stones
over the ground.
They lift wet noses over barbed wire,
grunt quietly as we scratch their backs.

Swarms of pigs, half in,
half out of warm brown mud.
Noises from somewhere under their throats,
insistent as the buzz

of flies circling their eyes.
We turn from the fence, pull shut

the doors of the car and drive,
drive back to the rows

of houses, pastel colors,
pruned roses climbing the walls.

HOT FALL AFTER COOL SUMMER

The heat's on.
All summer we looked for it.
Looked in the lilac leaves crumpling
down, leaving stiff veins
clinging to branches.

Thought we'd found it in the faded
geranium blooms we pulled off
so the tart round leaves would flower again.
Thought the dahlias held the heat
in their strangely odorless perfect petals.

I even thought we'd found it at the Oakland Zoo
when I took you that Sunday
before school began, thinking
it would help for you to ride the little red cars.
But all we found were two drunk

teenage mothers whirling the cars
so fast their babies screamed.
I guess the heat came in with the corn.
Under waxy threads, tough skins,
rows and rows of milky kernels,

so tender they don't even catch
in our teeth. Eating corn brought the heat.
Picking corn, pulling off husks
boiling the water. The heat's on.
Close the house down by 9 a.m.

Pull the shades. Think of talcum
and sweet lemons as the sun curls roses
into parodies of themselves.
I'll keep eating corn. Next week
it may be time for apples.

MOVING IN, MOVING OUT

Young Mrs. Bailey has gone to live in her fridge,
the door closes so smoothly, she said, and there was room
between the cold roast chicken and last week's green
plastic basket of strawberries, only a little mold
fuzzing over the freckles.

she said she'd have a good view, needed time to stare
at the seven seeds floating in the empty pickle jar.
She'd thought about that jar, about opening
the yellow screw-top lid, picking out seeds, planting them
among the limp carrot greens.

Something might grow. Cucumber vines could curl
around the aluminum grid shelves, shove
open the rubber-sealed door, loll green tongues
like obscene gestures over the kitchen's vinyl tiles,
spilling the beans.

DISAPPEARING ACTS

We are so tired
there is no
cooking dinner.
In bed we share slices
of cheese and red apples.
We try
not to fall asleep.

When our boy comes home
from the magic show
he raves: the woman
in the shower
vanished!
                Just like that!
The thrill of such power,
the negative of creation—
to disappear someone.

Before he'd walked in
you had been saying
how upset you'd been
by the story in the paper
of the girl they'd found dead,
months had gone by,
no one had claimed her.
Who could disappear like that?
And no one know?

In Chicago last month
with five friends
after ten meetings all day
we joked so loudly
we began to drown out
the yelling of the Greek waiters.
Maybe there is no Self at all,
we laughed, maybe it's you
all the time who's the one
brushing my teeth in the morning.

We laughed and laughed while eating
moussaka, spanakopita,
and I forget what else,
joking about the non-existence
of the Self.

Under the blankets
I begin to blur.
Is it me these bread crumbs
are scratching?
If I could be like the *dolmas.*
Wrapped like that,
in a soft, green leaf.

If I were less tired
I might know who I'd be
when we wake,
when the bright lights
of morning shine on the shower,
show the magician's assistant
somehow back again, bowing
and smiling,
moist and supple
as pink spring lamb.

YOU, ARTHRITIS FUSING YOUR JOINTS

Rocking on wind the house sways,
the trees pelt shadows
into the rooms, shadows in the shapes
of leaves, of twigs, of stones.

You tell me your knee has fused now.
The doctor asked how you were able
to drive with your ankle so swollen,
how you were able to dress yourself.
Could the elbows move above the shoulders,
could the fingers still
pull a zipper.

How long does it take
to fuse bones, to tum this
fleshy interlocking puzzle
of 206 separate bones
into one piece,
something to fit a frame,
two-dimensional, flattened.

You have been told
to lie down
for twelve hours a day,
half of every day in bed,
horizontal, to stop
the grinding of the joints.
Stop the bones wearing
each other away,
bones that have pushed
against each other for thirty-six years,
infuriating the membranes
that have tried to hold them at bay,
tried to let them keep their distance.

This morning as the wind
turns the house inside out
I read in the paper

that two Brahma bulls
escaped from the packing plant,
plowed through a southside
neighborhood, running
and running, not even
gunshot could stop them.

I wish your bones could gather
like reeds by the creek,
clicking and singing in breezes,
hard and green but slick
from the water, smooth and wet,
gleaming from water.
I wish your bones could glide
easy as the twigs
of bones that let the sparrows'
wings work, let them fly
in all this wind.

Or failing that, let them rage
like the bulls, great muscles heavy with purpose,
dark with power, pounding the sidewalks,
running the streets, running
over the fused, flat ground,
breaking everything into stones.

THE NAVY BLUE CHAIR

Wraps quiet in its smooth chintz,
silent as a rabbit,
as the black dazzle of midnight.

Outside the kitchen a phoebe
sits on three eggs
while I rinse the omelet pan.

The chair's fabric
is slick as an egg, the chair
knows nothing of bloodshed.

Has no need for language.
Only—there is something
in the easy curve

of the firm high back
that might allow anything, anything
at all: hatching, feathering,

rising through dark air
with the lift of a Mozart sonata
the lilt of a perfect soufflé.

After the dishes are finished
I want to sit down. If I sit
long enough in the blue chair

I may know when the phoebe's young
will crack through to the air,
when the summer storms will break—

when the clashing of flesh and beak,
the loud pounding of hard rain,
of hard flight,

will have to begin.

LISTEN, WIND

Of course some people hate wind.
Rattles windows, reminds them
of the glass between their eyes and trees,
that the rhododendrons are framed

by sliding aluminum squares.
Makes eerie noises in the chimney,
doors suddenly slam for no reason,
you remember another room you had forgotten.

The same people who hate wind
Won't drink
the water in France,
insist on eggs for breakfast in Venice,

won't run on the beach at Morro Bay,
sand irritates their feet,
don't like tracking bits
into the house. You remind us

how easily we're blown over,
how eyes can learn to look inside
through to the curve of the skull,
read messages written in the middle of night,

secrets of darkness, waking our dreams
to wanderings of night clouds
veiling and unveiling the moon,
calling to those who belong to the breeze.

HOTEL PROPRIETOR, THE VILLA BETTY

At the station he oozes
from a corner, white fingers
plump around a card with a map,
arrows in red, pointing

the way to his hotel.
His nails are clean,
but in the crevices around his knuckles
there is soot as old as these trains.

His eyes blear, his English strains,
he dashes to the taxi, helps
the driver with your bags.
When you arrive

he's there already, hauling your heaviest suitcase
through gravel aisles cluttered
with hoses tangling the weeds.
In the morning, apron

covering his belly, he plops down rolls,
butter, one dab of red jam.
You tell him you are leaving,
you must get to the mountains.

MONTALBANO

The tower leads to the tower,
to reach it you climb twenty steps,
they are higher than they are wide,
there is no room for stopping.
When you get to the top
you are at the top, a square
platform, you can look down:
On the north side are trees,
yarrow mingling with bluebells,
to the west, gardens, roses
espaliered, arches of privet.
To the south, the valley,
towns, irregular fields,
corn and green hay. The house
lies on the east, sunlight
slices the windows, and the top
of the tower covers the sky.

SCANNO

Goat fleece dries on iron
railings, white against black.
Cheeses swell like udders,

hang in pairs
from braided ropes,
a mortadella is as big

as a man's head.
Old women hide their hair
under scarves, knit

in doorways,
look straight through you,
don't drop a stitch.

Their needles move
faster than children's
feet running after balls

on the church steps.
Houses are stone, streets
are stone, the mountain

against which they pitch
their lives is hard
white rock, and it goes

straight up, lines
unblurred by any leaves,
even in summer.

OVERNIGHT IN TARVISIO

Three men lift
a bread mixer the size of a stove,
set it on three steel pipes.

The old man pulls.
Bald, cigarette between his teeth.
The young ones push,

carry the back pipe
around to the front
after the mixer has rolled over it.

All through our pasta they work
from the kitchen to our table.
While we eat fish

they manage as far as the door.
After coffee we stretch, walk outside.
They're pushing the mixer

up a steep drive,
resting every couple of seconds.
We offer to help.

Five of us lift it
over a doorsill.
Everyone cheers.

We walk on, up the hill
where streams run like milk
over white stones,

where swallows are circling
the orchis and harebell,
the swallows, circling home.

WASHING IN CREMONA AT TEN O'CLOCK

Water runs into the sink
over crumpled shirts and socks,
splashes like water falling

on rocks in the mountains
high over grape-vined hills
the green of new peas.

Wring the socks, twist them hard
until they're furrowed as trees.
Hang the shirts in the window.

Water falls through the sleeves,
down the length of the cloth,
small rain on the window sill.

Warm breath of air
carries kitchen clatter,
women's laughter

over the cobbles, lulls
you to dream of clean
clothes that fit like new skin.

SCHÖNBRUNN YELLOW

The summer palace of the Hapsburgs is yellow
and inside, gilt climbs the walls like ivy.

Maria Theresa had sixteen children in this house.
To keep them she had 400 maids.

The yellow walls are the color
of the woman's apron in Brueghel's painting,

a woman dancing on village dirt,
dancing in an apron thick with grease,

an apron hard with scraps of dough.
Maria Theresa's favorite painting

was of three peasants, a family taking a walk in the hills,
a family of peasants like Breughel's, dancing

and drinking, filling their cheeks with cereal
and beer the color of gold.

WINTER CHICKENS

Not sure if the clucking is child's crying—
sometimes the sound winds out
through walls of wire mesh,
orange rinds, saturated leaves.
Red wattles hang from their heads,
eggs squirm from swollen vents,
still damp slick
and amazing as Meissen china.
Carry them inside

for the transformation:
eggs into water,
poached ovals on toast,
eggs in bowls before stirring to scramble,
eggs tossed in a smoking pan
sliding around like shoes on mud.
The shells go back to the hens,
grit for their old, hard beaks.

CUB SCOUTS AND YELLOW CORN

We figured they might run out of food
by the time our turn came,
but no, a drumstick and wing, skins
crackling fat, and bright yellow
ear of corn on styrofoam plates.

Award night for the Cubs
at Braun Station Elementary School.
Neckerchiefs folded, sleeves pressed crisp,
the members of Den 4 have earned
their transformations into bears,
Den 6 into wolves, small white teeth
stripping the rows of com.
The boys have not grown fur, only
tufts of hair that poke
and tangle under their caps.

No more woods in this neighborhood.
The few cedars left will be cut down—
rough, shaggy trees, they don't bend
to garden plans. This past summer
a bobcat came through these hills,
maybe driven down by the drought,
killed a Golden Retriever.

When the last raffle ticket has been drawn
from Frank Vargas' blue and gold cap,
we scrape back our chairs,
drive home in the cold blue night
with our boys who are wolves, who are bears.
We ask if their homework is done
before we make sure the dogs are in,
before we turn out the lights.

We sleep on clean sheets
and dream of corn—fields, miles
of corn stretching, chattering
under the moon, tassels spilling
feathery, yellow fur.

SAYING GOODBYE

You're in the kitchen slicing lemons.
Rain's quiet now, live oak leaves dripping.

The supper steams, you stir while you sing
glance out the north window.

No stars yet, maybe tomorrow
it will clear from this winter.

In the corner by the garden
your wife and I are culling words.

And as we talk, the sauce cooks down
you say it's time to eat.

When we look out the window again
the clouds have moved through

the evening, a clean new moon twists
into the sky, leaving a tang

on the tastebuds
a tart yellow that lights the night

so my drive home down the hill
is easy, quick as a swallow.

NIGHT SONG

The room lies vague
beyond the glare of the tensor lamp.
Two circles of light cluster like daisies
in the blackness beyond the window:

one's neighbor's porch light, one's down
further, by the road.
The darkness hums even-paced
under your snores irregular as a dripping tap,

jagged as thunder.
What is there to see in a dark house?
Refrigerator whirring and clicking,
two cars going past, one right after the other.

More for the ears than the eyes.
The dog shifts in his sleep, bumps the door,
our child rustles in his blankets.
Only the old hamster

creeps over to his plastic wheel
and starts the nightly run
on his red wheel
through Siberian fields of grain

that toss and quiver as quietly,
as edibly, as sleep.

LOST DOG

Rain has turned oak trunks
dark as strong tea and the ground
runs over with water.

Yesterday the rain hadn't come,
the dog was lost and the walls
of the house sharpened their angles
while I kept folding sheets and towels,
thirds, then thirds again, smoothing,
piling them into the closet, keeping
the hands and fingers going.

The horizon seemed too far. If he were
really gone, the trees would separate
from each other, spaces between
would lengthen. We didn't talk much.

And then when we looked up and the dog
was running toward us, panting,
we ran too, toward him, and I forgot about the hose
to water the bulbs, forgot the trash,
the blouse soaking in the sink.

Today the dog sleeps, sprawling
fur like limp feathers over the rug.
Rain pours and pours, the dog
stretches and rolls on his back
and I watch the rain, the laundry's done,
the dog is home, it rains, it rains.

RED CHAIR AT THE PIANO RECITAL

A red chair under pecan trees
outside the glass door. . . .

In September the children's notes
were single and slow,
songs so simple we could barely
call them music.

But now the first-year students
color the walls
with "Blue Danube"s and "Green
Boogie"s, while the chair
asserts its red space
in the April sun.

The children's curved fingers
find the white and black notes
steadily, accurately.
The lap of the chair glows
flame over the lawn.

When the kids are finished
the piano teacher plays
just one piece for us,
a Brahms intermezzo,

and the music becomes all the chairs
that ever held us, all
the chairs that ever waited,
all the chairs we ever
had to leave
without saying goodbye

while the red metal chair
under the new leafing trees
sits red, red in the green garden.
Even after we've walked out the door
for punch and cake,

no one sits in the red chair
that strums its own
upright, unrusted ostinato
steady as oceans, a pulse
around which we move.

EXPATRIATE

(for my mother)

Cockroaches crawled all night,
the boldest and largest
would still be there in the morning.
You whacked them,
cracking their backs against the wall.
During the day you found nests of black widows,
gummy webs protecting eggs.
You killed those too,
as easily as you closed the door
on the Fuller Brush salesman's face,
"I don't want any,"
the cords of your throat twitching.

Years later, when we drove up
to your childhood home
the green of the overhanging trees
and the green of the grass underfoot
colored your eyes,
you showed me the house,
bigger than you remembered it,
the lawns, the gardens, the roses.
In the hedge
we found a brown spider
spinning shining octagons,
feeding on blue water.

GRANDFATHER

We go to the park, to the "Little Farm" for children.
My father holds his camera like a portable microscope,
a way of seeing my son, seeing closely the small legs,
fingers, eyes, and hair, hair rising, falling, moving
in and out of focus in the glass, moving from the wind,
from running.

The camera is my father's way of seeing more
by seeing less, a way of framing, framing out hills,
eucalyptus, baby cows and pigs, the other children,
their parents, my husband, me. Through the long lens
my father follows his grandchild, clicking the shutter
many times a minute.

My son climbs a fallen log, straddles it and slides
down. My father is coming back to life, his gray hair
soft as a thrush's underside, his pale eyes squinting
in the outdoor noon. Through the long lens he studies
this child, listens to his own blood laughing,
framing the laughing.

NEEDLEPOINT

My mother has stitched
a bookmark,
pulled and pushed
A needle, silver-tipped
like my pen,
through canvas,
out, over, under,
prodding the point
into just the right place,
the same way she worked
a needle to lift splinters
from my fingers
when she was my young mother
and I was her young child.

My mother lives in the desert,
she has sewn
while breathing scorched air,
hands dry
from too much heat.
Holding the backing
taut, drawing through
small holes
the soft, curling yam,
spiralling over and
over the blue
and the green,
she has sewn,
so that I
won't lose
my place.

LOVE POEM

To talk about you
is to peel off parts
that stick to us both,
closer than clothes.

You knew me
when I was the puzzle
pieces scattered
on the Theta House card table.

We gathered all the pieces,
put them in the box
with the cover, "Forest Pond in Winter,"
carried them out to your car.

You told me not to worry,
I'd fit the pieces together sometime,
Couldn't do these hard ones on rickety tables.
Then you watched from a distance,

watering lettuce plants,
mulching potatoes growing hard underground.
You never interrupted
while the dark trees in the puzzle

found each other, lifted branches into sky,
while the ice thawed.
When spring came you brought home trout,
stocked the clear pond.

We eat well, both of us.
In the closet, old jacket
pockets lean against new shirts.
Something fits.

JULY

Up the street
the Ross daughters are home,
visiting with their babies.
Big women, hips

round as ripe peaches.
Their eyes glaze
as they nurse their children.
Anna's hummingbirds

Have found the new feeder.
They suck the sugar midair,
winged acrobats.
Next door the Sanfords

fill sacks with plums,
offer them around.
Pears hang
on the high branches

almost ready to yield,
and the fog
seeps down for the night
like sweet warm milk.

CANNING SEASON

Tomatoes are rolling
off the vines

tumbling out of bagfuls
over the kitchen tiles

until we lift them
into the kettle. Simmering,

skins peel off, expose pink
veins tracing over

glistening flesh,
seeds

surrounded in juice
like yolks of tiny eggs.

Sieving out
the pulp

we make sauce
save August for November.

I hold you now.
We're ripe.

THREE FOR FROST

1.

You never know whose woods they are.
Just as you think you've found out,
the trees shift
and the water unfolds another layer of gray.
You've no more miles to go,
this is it already, what did you
think you were waiting for, anyway?

2.

The sun takes the lake by surprise
in the morning, dropping its knives and slicing
until the water is no longer water
but fire and you turn
to aspen and fern for green, listen
for scratchings of chickadees, anything
to take the fire from your eyes.
Even your ears struggle
to sort sounds from a new roaring,
a roaring that comes when the rain beats
pebbles deep into soil,
beats through roofs until it finds
weak places, begins to pound
into the chinks between your own bones,
loosening the joints.

3.

On hot days the lake is still
cold. The ice from winter chills our drinks,
turns a glass of water into an instrument—
music as we drink.
Pages of the paperback mystery flap closed.
Doesn't matter, it's the pebbles
at the bottom of the lake that stay,
the granite and quartz the boys collect
in piles on the dock that always end up
back in the lake, that hold fast
under water.

COMING THROUGH DECEMBER

The rooms were no longer
ours, had lost definition.

Visitors do that. Their
needs turn floors into shapes

neither yours nor theirs,
spaces become no space.

Crowded kitchen, hard work
just talking, listening,

making your way
to the coffee,

table littered with crayons
and plastic teething rings.

The linings of the house
begin to sag, tear. I turn

from room to room, ask you
"Will it be all right?"

At night I wander through rooms
filled with sounds of sleeping

and stroke my hands over the walls,
rubbing smooth the names of the spaces:

kitchen, a room for one orange,
a black-handled knife,

and sunlight; *study,*
a place for each word cut perfectly

shaped with its colors and fiber
peppery, tart, intact.

Everyone gone but one sister,
and we go down to the coast

for the whooping cranes
that fly 2000 miles

to these tidelands
where the eye doesn't stop, keeps going

over watery grass and tide,
marshland both river and sea,

fresh and salt, neither one thing
nor the other. Water and sky

the same gray. Reeds and leaves
the same brown. Herons hunch so silent

the bank seems part of their wings,
grassy feathers. Over the wetlands

the cranes rise
tall as grown children.

Their necks curve like snow
lining the arc of an oak trunk

as they break acorn snails,
blue crabs in their beaks,

shell
and weed glistening.

~

Driving back to town
the world is divided in two:

navy earth and orange sky
and we are hungry.

We order oysters, they are hot
fried, so fresh their white flesh

glows blue. We talk about the snow geese
we had just passed, swooping

down to the black field by the road,
the water in the furrows

gleaming across the mud.
We say how there were hundreds

of geese clacking, lining
the field, quieting

as the dark
brought two worlds into one.

~

When a crane pulls one leg
from the water,

the leg shines a slim black line
on the yellow grasses.

Poised, the leg at that moment
belongs to the crane

until it pushes forward, down
again, toward the next bite of snail.

Back now in the house
from the market, I carry

the silence of white cranes
through every one of these rooms,

burnish them
silver and blue, salty,

fresh, from the long
pools of origin.

SWALLOW WATCHER

Every house needs someone to watch the swallows,
someone willing
to half close the eyes, lean the head back
against a tall chair
in a garden, on a porch, in a courtyard.

It doesn't matter if a cheap paperback
falls wrinkled from the knees,
a wine glass dangles
empty from the hand.
What matters is the watching:
                                                            following

the lifts and darts
of the small birds,
the racings and screechings over territory,
the jags and dips for insects,
the gliding on wind.

About the time
the neighbor's porch light comes on
and the sky
can't hold color any more
the swallow watcher moves inside

to the glare of living room lights,
but he turns, leans
against the cool glass of the sliding door,
and stares out at the dark sifting down,
quiet as feathers, as wings.

LET THE ICE SPEAK

(1991)

BAPTISM

Light dim as the crumbled leather
of old books, and Granny next to me
leaning down with her smell of lime cologne,
finger moving across the small black shapes.
She pointed to the clusters in their tidy lines,
barely stopping under each one, as the minister
kept on talking. My baby sister slept
as he held her, no one else
seemed to breathe.

But Granny's finger led
my eyes on and on, back and forth, down the page,
and then I saw: she reached *the* at the same time
the minister said *the,* and it happened again,
two lines down, and there were *the*'s everywhere
on those pages—"even unto *the* end of *the* world,"
her finger moved as he said the words
out loud, "*the* kingdom, and *the* power,
and *the* glory," naming.

PLAYING WITCHES AT RECESS

When we had recess at Encanto Elementary
the girls divided in teams.
                                        Ours would run
behind the pyracantha, berries all red on the outside,
but inside, gold as pumpkins, and we'd scream
as the Fairies flitted by, practiced
their dancing, leaping, arabesques.
Long hair bounced and fell on their necks
the way it was supposed to
and their voices never made the teachers mad.
Scratchy runners of Bermuda grass
never caught in their white socks
with scalloped edges.

But we Witches had power.
Saddle shoes scraped and stained
by winter lawns, one braid fatter than the other,
we held the talisman we all desired,
and we never let them get it.
My English granny had sent for Christmas
a leather diary smaller than a Hershey bar,
blue paper, gold edges, ribbon for a marker.
Flipping the pages made a sound like wind,
showed the days, months divided into squares
clean as the Arizona sky after a rain.

And when we flung out over our shoulders
a chant of Saturdays and Thursdays and October
the 31st crossed with the 3rd of July, we knew
we had it all over them,
that not even their skill at ballet
or tap could combat what we learned
from fingering those blank
pages of the year, from saying their names.
Maybe we knew even then we were tracing
steps to the longest dance of all:
neither curses nor blessings, only
the ways we would decide, fill in the days.

PLAYING THE GAMES OF STATUES

Whirling and whirling as the Tucson sun
curled down, we turned so dizzy
the purple mountains would set
firm in a wide stripe dividing the haze
of gray roofs from red sky
until, having spun ourselves
out of orbit like spent cops,
we fell frozen until the one who was It
gave orders., told us to *move.*
And move we did, a frenzy of leaping,
skating, arcing our backs for the high
dive and then letting go, over and over,
to land—*stop*—on the high wire
right there on the Bermuda grass
beneath our bare feet.

At the Galleria
dell'Accademia in Firenze, Michelangelo's
Four Slaves are still trying to separate
sinewy arms from the bulk of marble.
The David appears at the precise moment
he has become who he will be,
his head turned to one side, while we
circle around him, circle and stare
at such polished stasis, at the perfect
veins of his ankles.

How the rest of the body follows
the crisis of an instant—a freak pose
on an Arizona night
when the clouds boiled in the colors
of the High Renaissance Masters
and we whirled and flew and tried on other lives,
pirouetting or pitching, tight-rope-walking
for all we were worth,
still believing that, whenever you wanted,
you could always change your mind.

DANCING LESSONS

A white shirt pressed his shoulders
as he taught me how to let my hand rest
in his. "A good dancer
never feels heavy in her partner's
arms," he said, so I worked
at keeping my palm a little distant

while my father's arm held my back.
"You must anticipate your partner's
next move, he should feel as if you're part
of him, always let him lead," he advised
as he dipped and toed, looking off
somewhere beyond my head.

I stumbled backward around the room
trying to keep in line
with the tidy circles he made
avoiding the green chair,
the converted player piano, my sisters' toys.
I didn't mind the music, Cole Porter was okay.

But I could feel my sweat steaming
like the dishwater my mother stood over,
her red wool shirt
above the suds, the clatter.
And as the silver jangled
offbeat in the drainer

I dreamed of climbing up to the roof.
Might be hard to dance on sloped shingles,
but there'd be night air,
maybe a breeze, my body could breathe.

MY FATHER'S LIVING ROOM

Evening papers
crinkled in his lap,
his hands were clean,
nails trimmed short, his signet ring
had no initial.
I read the headlines from the floor,
trying to see inside, squinting to read
the little letters under the thick ones.
He turned the pages slowly.

"Don't bother your father," my mother
whispered. I learned not to. I practiced
quiet, practiced over and over
scales of silences,
learning as long as I didn't
startle him,
I could make my move
when the paper came down.

As we talked I would shiver
from holding in my words,
from not letting them out
too loudly,
from holding my ribs
close as piano keys
so I could sound
his fears.

MY PARENTS, IN THAT LIGHT

I see them in that yellow glow
of evening living rooms, beige linen
shades erasing shadow.
In that light

every thought could be curtained
among the well-upholstered arms of chairs,
easy greens and golds,
no colors allowed that might disturb

mellow illusions after dark.
When dinner would be exactly ripe was the question
asked and reasked in air thick
with the smell of lamb chops broiling.

Dinner was, after all, a matter
of proper timing, carrying
china plates, and thorough chewing.
They worked hard to digest the day,

trying not to remember
all those other dinners
when anger had jangled the plates,
when the talk would have carved the beef.

So they munched peas, mentioned
the dogs' new vet, spoke of the men
who every month pruned the natal plum.
After dinner, a return to chairs,

magazines, glossy, slick
as fat hardening in the pan.

THE FREEZER IN THE HOUSE

Shelled peas shone on the table
the creamy satin of my grandmother's
wedding dress.
After my parents
boiled them, they wrinkled like our fingers
when we'd been in the bath too long,
and they turned dark, dark as the shadows
under the leaves of the mulberry trees.
My mother and father scooped them into waxy white boxes,
piled them in the great white chest in the kitchen
closed tight with a silvery handle.

I'd spring on top of that freezer,
thump its slick white front with the heels of my sandals,
suck a lime popsicle pulled from its smoky depths
white as the clouds over the Rincon Mountains.
I asked my mother questions while she sliced carrots,
how to keep the boy with the plaid shirts
from teasing, how did it feel to have a baby.

When I'd licked clean the popsicle stick
and Mom said I should go outside
I biked three blocks down to Sandy Davison's.
Some days we sat out front in our bathing suits
with a tube of Prell shampoo and two razors
and practiced shaving our legs
in her little sister's inflatable pool.
The Davisons didn't have a freezer, didn't fuss
about food, they worked for the Phone Company,
belonged to the union. Sandy fixed their dinners.

Sometimes I stayed for canned corn and spaghetti,
except for the times Mr. Davison came home
with a face the color of muddy beets,
pulled his belt through the loops of his jeans,
and Sandy warned me, run, run while you can,

you can still get out, run out the back door.
I'd run as fast as I could
out to the leaves that spiralled and clung to the sky

but I took the back way home, through
acres of desert nobody had built on yet,
through creosote, palo verde trees, and I pulled
the leaves into my fingers, let them spring
into place on the branches
before I picked up the pace, headed
straight for home, hunger opening
a flat white box, empty inside.

MY MOTHER'S SEWING MACHINE

The rising whine and steady
freight train roar
of her sewing machine needle's bite

took the pale gray buds
that lined my bedroom
walls and ripped them, tossed

them on the table behind
her sewing machine,
behind piles of cut-out body parts,

arms, chests, waists, great
circular or gathered skirts,
heavy as tents. On the fabric

she sewed red rick 'rack,
rows and rows of glittering
purple braid, all

the brilliance my father
insisted she strip
from the living room walls.

If she couldn't dash
color over the rooms
of her house, she would drape

herself and her daughters
in her own designs.
She made sure that under

the crackling dazzle of those dresses
no one would hear our silences,
no one would know

that the pressure of my mother's foot
on the pedal of her sewing machine
all but split the house.

BLACK SHEEP, WHITE STARS

He'd appear like a bird
that wanders into a place
on its way between two continents.
Surrounded by houses
that sopped up sparkle like sponges
he'd roll out of a '47 black Cadillac

and wave a bottle of rum
shimmering in the sun like amber.
"Pam, darling," he'd call to my mother,
his voice so raucous
Mrs. Simonitch next door
would move one slat of her Venetian blinds.

His toes pushed from limp *huaraches*
and he grinned as if he knew
just how much acid
the sight of him
shadow-bearded, yellow under the arms,
produced in my father's stomach.

When he talked
our windows grew arches, opened doors
onto courtyards, lemon trees, parrots,
we could hear the rustling of green feathers,
the chirrings and cawings of orange birds.
Small on the sofa I said

"Let me come live with you,"
something in my lungs knowing
that in a place named Tlayacapan
people might swallow drinks
the colors of bougainvillea
and move at night

to music that had never heard
of a metronome.
And when Uncle Dick and his friend Pedro

sat me between them
on the Cadillac's dusty front seat
to watch *High Society* at the Frontier Drive In,

I held myself taut and sweaty, dreaming stars
thicker than sugar on oatmeal,
stars farther than heaven,
stars and hibiscus and mangoes
that could cluster around a life
as long as a laugh.

WHY WE WENT TO THE OCEAN

That screen door slammed on too much silence.
In the car we carried it with us.
It was Daddy who muttered and fussed
about the luggage, but only to Mom
when we weren't around, so all we knew
were the great sighs, my mother's solicitous
gestures, suggestions for where to fit
the big brown bag, the box with the extra towels.
He would never be able to get it all in.

My mother kept us quiet,
hissing to the back seat.
He needed quiet to drive. The roads
were harder then, two lanes, tricky
to pass, to keep your own speed.
The heat blew in from the windows,
mixed with our father's smoke, the smoke
from the Benson and Hedges that thickened
and stopped the air.

The desert stuck in my eyes
a great brown thorny silence
until we climbed up the mountains
before San Diego and the green
began its small damp murmurings.
We could stop for lunch, walk
around, find pine needles bundled
like tiny brooms, like the wire
brushes drummers use.

From then on the roads were wider.
From then on we stretched as tall as we could
from the back seat, waiting for that first
glimpse of the long breath
of blue stretching out beyond
the horizon, and it was downhill then,
as we sang out *the sea, the sea,*

and there it was, we could run
along its slapping hard breathing
body, we could laugh as loud as we
ever wanted because the ocean
had the loudest voice in the whole world.

SNOW WHITE'S FATHER'S SECOND WIFE'S TALE

The stories leave out the fact
that Snow White's mother and I
were sisters. That when she died
her husband the King
and I both wept.

I had never thought about
which of us was the more beautiful,
it was always the two of us, riding
bareback over the fields,
she would cling to me,

her white breath on my neck.
We thought we were lucky:
two princes, one
for each. But our husbands
were different as snow, fire,

and roses—white roses,
red. I still miss him. Running
through wide fields, the tall
grasses whispering
over our legs—midnights

on a blanket in the forest, the moon
pulling us, reflecting us,
until there was nothing we didn't
know about each other,
until we forgot who was who.

They never told me how he died.
My sister's child came,
white as new sheets,
and then my sister died.
I don't know why

the King insisted we marry—
he wouldn't lie with me outside in the night,
he said the leaves were damp,
the moss would stain. Why couldn't

I lie still in the pillows?
He stopped coming to me altogether.
I moved into the tower.
I am what happens
when you don't die young.

FROM THE ATTIC AT THORNFIELD

She did not want to burn
down the house because
she was in love with fire.

It was never that.
It was because of the closed
doors, the straight walls

that stopped any long breathing,
that told her, when she tried
to laugh, to stop.

And the chairs, the chairs
slim and delicate,
lined against the edge

of a room, lap sideways
to lap, no one facing.
Even the windows looking out

felt too slick and hard
to her fingers, nothing open
about them. How did she know

that what she saw
outside was really there?
That the hedges were any more

yielding than a locked door?
And the stones rose in walls so high,
so thick, she had never found

the way out.
                    In the first delicate
lickings of flame, the lovely

leafings of orange, yellow,
the prickings and twinings
of the snapping noises,

she could hear voices,
the click of new tongues,
the lap of loud breathing,

and she knew
that as the roar began,
with its great wind, blackness,

red over brightest red, flames
that took over the sky,
she knew she did love it

now, it was all
she had ever loved,
this sweet terror

that raced its own body
together with hers
over the terraces, the gardens,

out to the orchards, the hills,
its blazing voice
finally loud enough,

that the only way it would ever stop
would be when it had spoken
to everything it could find,

and there would be,
for the first time,
nothing left, nothing

left to say.

PERSEPHONE'S VERSION

My mother never
understood how, after that first time
(when the earth cracked and the blackness,
like a magnet,

dragged my feet down to the ore)
how after that, I went by myself, how
every October the pears rotting on the ground
blocked the way down, how

I burrowed under the brown fruit,
found my way, tunneling through loam
past bedrock, drawing nearer and nearer
to the fire. In the light of flame

veins of silver, clots of gold
fed my eyes,
my hands glowed scarlet
as I held them toward the hearth.

I never could explain him to my mother,
how I set up my own forge,
had my own hammer, tongs, built
circlets of rubies, diamonds, topaz.

He didn't nag like Apollo,
always saying "Look at me, look
up, look into my eyes when you
speak." I could carve all day.

Neither my mother nor her
brother ever understood
I went because I wanted to,
year after year. They never knew

that was how I was able
to return each April
to find Narcissus, and to feed
my brilliance to the breeze.

ON CLIMBING TREES, FOR LOUISA MAY ALCOTT

> Then Jo and Meg . . . set forth the supper on the grass . . . the lads were not required to sit at table . . . freedom being the sauce best beloved by the boyish soul. They availed themselves of the rare privilege to the fullest extent . . . and apple turnovers roosted in the trees like a new style of bird. . . .
>
> —*Little Women*

1.

In first grade the sun poured
onto the rough paper
flecked with embedded
slivers of pine.

The teacher bent
over our desks, told us to make
three dots in a vertical row,
guides to keep

our letters on the right lines.
She walked around the room.
My dots grew, my pencil drew
spirals, vines, twining

until she stopped at my desk
and said to erase
all that. She would tell us
what to do next.

2.

Too tall in the fourth grade
to be the heroine
of the Brownie play,
I was turned into

a tree, brown crepe
paper wound from my feet
to my glasses, arms
ordered to stay

upright for the whole thing.
I had my cues: when the star
of the show tripped in
with her basket

my branches were to wave,
and when she asked if I had seen
the Brownies, I was to say
in a wooden voice, *no, no.*

3.

A small tree growing from one
point in the dry ground,
my father had nursed
his Rhus lancea,

and our three-month-old German Shepherd
bit it off at the root.
Years later
I watched my three-year-old

son rustling its highest leaves—
in a dozen years it had grown
multiple trunks after its early pruning,
top branches lifting

over the Phoenix Mountains' caliche.
My father walked around on the ground
under his tree, shot dozens
of pictures.

In them our boy dangles
from a top branch, his chubby chin
sure, calm. He has climbed that far
up my father's tree.

4.

I am surrounded by live oaks. Small
Texas madrones, leaves that turn
golden in November, quiver in wind.
I never did

learn to climb a tree.
I press my cheek against the bark
of one of the old oaks, lean
against a splintering

cedar, my son's favorite
for climbing. In the crotches
of some of the oaks,
Virginia creeper, wild grape

twine around the hard crusts
of the bark, spiralling, gleaming
as they redden, even
as the light fades.

FOR WANT OF DOLLS

1.

A woman bends
over a blanket she opens
to offer a gift: Peruvian

dolls for the dead.
Formed from shreds, figures shaped
like family, friends, made

to keep the dead from loneliness.
Their yarn mouths grin
wide ovals, loose braids drift

down long skirts, the weave
ravelling, threads dropped
from the warp.

Some of the dolls hold
little ones, babies, faces
pale as the shells of eggs.

One lies on her back, swollen belly
covered with a tapestry of gold, red.
Three figures lean over her

as the baby emerges.
I gather the dolls in a row
in my room. Silent

color of berries,
doves, of rings
inside trees.

2.

Six years old, Phoenix
subdivision too new for trees,
too hot for flowers, I craved

the Story Book Dolls at the dime store,
full skirts that rustled
like petals pressed

into cardboard and cellophane boxes.
Dolls named after stories I read
in my room with the blinds

drawn from the sun, from the square yard
outside, bare except for the oleander,
castor beans we were told

never to touch with our mouths.
I saved my nickels
for months, but all I could buy

was a plain doll, short skirt,
not someone from a book,
Snow White, Sleeping

Beauty cost too much, their velvet
and lace, coiled hair, shining
crowns. I wanted them

to bloom in a row over my bed,
their wide skirts, petticoats
ruffling the bare wall.

3.
I remember in France, driving to Chartres,
how the cathedral
lifts the valley around it. I remember

our eyes rising to portals
where saints are gathered
in rows, where stone

has been carved into lace, stories
for people who couldn't read.
And I remember how we entered

in silence the vault of light
and faced the rose
window, its great round

ringing circles within
circles
          where doves wing

down to the mother
offering her child,
pale, oval faces blooming.

SNOW WHITE AT THE CONVENTION FINDS THE BEAR

> Snow White and Rose Red were going to run away, but they . . .
> stopped, and when the bear came up to them his rough coat suddenly
> fell off, and there stood a tall man, dressed entirely in gold. . . .
>
> —THE BROTHERS GRIMM

In the chromium palace of words,
the convention hotel,
she thought he would never come.
Sleek stairs, escalators running
like rivers of glass, the potted
palms lifting manicured hands
toward the quiet, well-mannered
ceiling that spoke only in hushed
tones: *would you like, of course,*
yes, we can take care of it
for you.
                              And in the elevator,
rising above restaurants, gift shops with displays
of earrings, paperbacks for insomniac nights,
she rose to the floor of her room, gray carpeted,
pad, pad, hush, on the carpet, the bags
carried for her, a quick click of the door
into her room: gray, white, a bit of coral, chintz
on the chairs, sweet air of expensive
soap clinging to the towels. Soon
there would be foam
in the bath.

2.

It happened downstairs: great
roar from the revolving doors,
arms outstretched toward her,
her name, her name, echoing in the chrome
lobby, and the wild
arms round her, his mouth telling
her what none of the meetings all day
ever could. And everyone watching,
who is he, who is he, with his

great beard, his gleaming
eyes, his huge shoulders and arms
around her so she could rest
like a pattern in the tapestry of his coat,
she could dance like a ballerina
on the center of his stage.
                                        She would never leave
the rough weave of his fur, the warm gray
silk of his silent belly.

3.

He refused to stay in the room.
Fussed. No fish in the bath.
He sulked, began to roar. Finally
she had to let him out, although
he knocked over the spindly-legged
tables in the halls. They had to go down by
the stairs.
                    The worst of it was that she began
to forget how to speak. His huge knees
were enough, his shagginess, the slow
coral of his wet tongue.
She found places she'd never
explored. They tried the roof, plenty of room
for him up there, no lines of chairs
crowding the air the way they did downstairs
in the meeting rooms, up here it was
all air, a wind through his fur,
and down below, the streets
like rivers, the cars like fish, his arms
almost long enough to reach
that far down.

4.

And then, on the last day,
when she knew she must go to at least one meeting,
he refused to be left, insisted she take him.
How would they fit? He would take up
five chairs, at least. And she,
she had forgotten how to talk.

When they arrived
the rows of chrome chairs were filled,
everyone faced the lectern, the mike,
the speaker's small glass of water.
No one saw them come in.
He stood, at the back, quiet, for once.
She was amazed, grateful.
She took a couple of notes.
She could feel
his breath, his fur, his heavy
presence. She listened.
She forgot him.

5.

There were no signs of him
in the halls, nothing knocked over.
But on the escalator down to the lobby
with old friends, laughing,
making plans for dinner, maybe red snapper, she saw
someone gleaming through the haze of tweed.
He came right up to her, reached for her arm,
and they moved off, whispering, they had
everything to say to each other—
his crown hidden in a thicket of
brown hair, just a glimpse of his coral tongue—
as they slid
into a slow dance, his thigh
moving between hers.
On and on
they danced through every floor, up
to the roof and down again, around
the lobby one more time, then
right on out through the glass
and chrome revolving doors, where
the streets swam silver, leaping with salmon.

HEAT, LETTING GO

(for Larry)

You held on to your rage
the way the heat held
this year, kept
the leaves in thrall,
unnatural green on the trees
all October, November.
There was no moving through it.
Heavy air, it wouldn't say
what it wanted. The smallest jobs
were more than I could bear.
Newspapers the dogs had strewn
across the field
stayed where they were,
and the dogs found more, a neighbor's
slipper, a garden glove.
Under the grasses
the trash grew.

Until the day I watched
your eyes turn and you saw it, for the first time.
Named it, your rage.

It was only
a coincidence that the heat turned then,
the nights chilled so that sleep was again
an easy affair with blankets,
as the sumacs, the Spanish oaks
flamed your fury, gloried in your raging,
the crisp air flaming until even the grasses
turned burgundy in the wind,
and we lived in a red land that said,
here it is, now, take it, take it,
and we knew that very soon
we would be able to see
even the tiniest twigs,

the shapes of everything underlying color,
the long thorns of the sweet acacia,
the small bare swelling where
the leaf end dropped.

SOUNDING DREAMS

The sound a guitar makes
in a room where no one knows
what to say.

Another oatmeal carton empty,
into the trash with yesterday's papers.
Time was we'd have saved it
for a drum, or cut a mouth
below eyebrows of yellow wool,
black paper notes would stream out—
a boy singing.

This weekend we looked at electric guitars.
A man who had been on the road seventeen years
was selling a limited-edition Fender
for half its value, and our son
was possessed by his desire to possess
this blue and white and gold lily of a thing,
its neck stretching out a long clear solo.

We have stopped asking why
his acoustic guitar is not enough.
When dreams go beyond the words you own,
It's best not to question them.
But in the car coming home, all of us knew
that we could not afford the guitar,
that the house would be gray, shadow—
filled without its shimmering
sleekness, a way to notes
that would dazzle even the heaviest air.

Through the warm husk of the car
come voices of a choir on the radio,
singing some mass. The words don't matter,
it's their voices, their human
sound filling the empty space.
We tell our son, "Maybe sometime soon.
We'll try, we'll try, if we can."

HURRICANE WARNINGS

Where is this wind that won't
blow through, that hovers
at the edge of weather
radio reports, the news. Predictions
drop brittle leaves on the roof.
We track the storm's path
on a map, collect water, decide
which room we will go to.

The satellite photo in the paper
swirls into a white breast, clouds
of milk surround a firm nipple
poised, ready for feeding.

I barely remember
nursing our son. The release
when the milk let down,
the feel of the fluid pulling
from some hot core, as if drawing
the whole body, the body swollen
beyond itself until it entered
the child, feeding.

When I was too tired the milk
Wouldn't come. We learned
to wait. His patient
sucking as I sat quiet, looking
out the window at the camphor trees
merged in fog, and then, there
it was, the hot sting, the flow,
and his eyes glazed.

Now in the mornings when we pull
the car up to school
he opens the door in a tall
breeze of legs, shoulders, and is gone
into the crowd of kids
gathering before the bell.

The storm swirls around us.
We watch bands of dark clouds
move the sky, drop a little rain,
a little wind.

There are times I want to lift
him back into my lap,
hold him like a lanky
stuffed colt, nuzzle
his soft hair. I want him to linger
in the car, I'd like to drive on
to a zoo, a playground,
where he would say "can you see me
now, Mom, can you see," and he
would want me to say
"yes, I see you, that's great,
great, you're really climbing now."

When he leaves the car in the morning
he yanks at the handle, breaking
the air between us.
I say "bye, have a good one,"
and maybe he'll say "bye," but
if he says too much
he'll be sucked back, he must move
into that crowd
of kids gathering their own
winds that will swallow us all.

YOUR 50TH, WHAT CAKE

(December 10, 1988)

For the birthday you said
you'd never see. Years
back I had said (in my 19-
year-old smiling) oh yes
you will, and more, and more,
I'll see to that, for I had read
of all the good
women who kept men alive
with fresh pink
cheeks by the fire,
their dainty
nibbles. Such sweetness
could not help
but keep a man going
long after he had
decided there wasn't
much point, long after
a dream had stretched
so far off the horizon's
edge his eyes hurt
from the strain of following,
had to look down, through
half-glasses, cry again
to follow the interest rates.

What cake. One friend said sweet,
sticky, the kind we never
eat any more, swirls of sugar
icing over layers
of puffed white flour.
But not your sort. Never was.

So when another friend told me
what he wanted to do,
I laughed until the sky
moved in under my heels,
moved the horizon

right next door.
Hire one of those huge
hollow cakes with a girl
inside, she'd leap right out,
pasties glistening
like strawberry glaze.
Maybe that would be all
it would take: one whiff
of such sugar
and you'd remember
that the white in your beard
is icing too, sweet, rich,
and still in the making.

14TH SPRING

We had taken winter into ourselves
for more than one season.
Shrivelled

stalks of grasses, seed
gone, our boy slamming alone
into his room,

locked. You and I
carried the weight
of the cold silence,

guilt pressing our shoulders,
why didn't we, we could
have, we should.

The belly learned
to live with lessened
expectation, made do

with memories of color: citron,
withered currants.
                                        Nothing much

moves in winter, a pair
of cardinals, bit of red, pinky
brown, a few jays, screeching,

cheeky blue.
Now in May, the bread rises
before I'm ready.

Thumb punches down,
and the hollow
navel, dark imprint, fills,

dough belly
swelling seamless
over the bowl.

Air so light, you and I might
as well be two
of the wine-cups, poppy

mallows, spilling
over the hills
covered with yellow

composites, hundreds of seeds
held in their centers,
gold as yolks.

And our son, a lead
in the 8th grade play,
brought down the house.

At night now he leaves
his door open, talks on the phone, at dinner
laughs at our jokes.

This afternoon, you call out:
beyond the deck, slowly
through the grass pulses

a hognosed snake.
It opens a wide glistening mouth
before it is gone, a wave

of muscle in the grass,
leaving us standing, trying
to digest all this,

yet knowing
it will take seasons,
years of long summers

to travel
the lacy intricacies
of the body, the belly,

as it fills.

SUMMER TIME

The days swim to a slow center.
Bean vines surround

their poles, zinnias
ruffle fatter and fatter,

heads rise to a yellow peak.
There are things I had meant to do.

Lists, the rectangles of calendars,
tidy grids, expectations.

The days start
hot, grow hotter, turn dark.

At night I read, tell myself,
tomorrow, I'll wake early,

get going, get to it.
But every morning the plants

want more water, the golden
fronted woodpecker nesting

beyond the house needs
watching when it comes

to the feeder.
And last night after we peeled

half the peaches
we brought down from Fredericksburg

sliced them small,
juice slipping off the table,

I had to watch:
my son's aunt, bent

over the old manual
ice-cream maker, turning the crank,

foot stomping, stomping, because
our son was out there on the deck

with her, his electric guitar
and his amp plugged in,

wailing on the strings,
the two of them singing,

singing, the handle turning,
the peaches and cream thickening.

GOING BACK, COMING HOME

We brought our week-old son
into that pastel stucco house
in Berkeley, wrapped most days in fog,

pale threads unwinding
as the day moved on toward noon.
Now on a gray day in August

we go back with our fourteen-year-old boy,
seven years after we watched
the moving van drive off

down the hill, and we stare
at the street, our old wooden
porch, the front door.

We visit the neighbors: Sandy, at ninety,
still cultivates orchids, and Ron, up the street,
has moved into astrophysics, observes

dark matter, whatever it is we can't see
that swirls beyond the orbits of galaxies.
They are all still there.

                                        Coming home,
the heat of our lives returns
in the first breath of entering.

Air conditioning turned off, bills
stacked on the desk,
newspapers coiled on a chair.

I have read that inside
the nucleus of the atom
are particles, tiny points

that, looked at from another direction, turn
into waves, the single point
loosened, changed.

I think of the knot on an oak branch
outside my bedroom window, a gnarl
I stare at trying to wake up.

Once, while working outside, I tried
to see where this bulge
lay along the line of branch,

but never could. It exists
only from one place on the bed.
We came home to the heat, relentless

pressure of the day's questions,
who will take
the old car, when will we

get to the dentist, who will
market, what time,
what time.

Until the rain let down
long blue lines that began
somewhere in the upper atmosphere

of clouds, ended in the parched
flat ground, single points rippling
puddles, spirals, waves.

ONCE MORE, SQUAM LAKE

The lake whitens in the hot light
of July. At Sandy Beach we see the sunfish
circling their eggs, rippling the water.
The sunfish do what they've done before,
will do again. I sit in a haze

of sisters, nieces, mothers, grandmothers.
When I was seven, Old Jane Noble was Young
Jane Noble. When I was seventeen
she was one of the mothers who knitted
argyles on the playhouse porch.

Too hot today for socks, for knitting.
But tonight the loons will yodel
and last week they counted
nine new chicks, three more than last year.
My son is learning to fish the lake.

My father will teach him
to let the line fall quietly
(only a small furrow of water moving
beyond the nylon thread),
to hear where bass live, to find the depth

of the lake. I watch from the dock,
the lake takes the planks and rocks them
backward, forward, I forget
how old I am, what year it is,
how it all matters.

IDENTIFYING THINGS

Is diabetes catching, he asks,
middle school braggadocio edged
this time with something else, I can't
quite put my finger on it,
until he tells about the needle,
that kid Jamie, jabbing a needle he had picked up
on the street, punctured far into the flesh
of my son's palm.

Trouble boils a greasy steam into the air.
Whose needle, what kind, whose veins
had it entered? My son, my son, only eleven
years old and the doctor over the phone doesn't help,
his nurse says you bet, plenty to worry about,
and it's not just AIDS we'd want to run tests for,
three strains now of hepatitis, find the needle,
bring in the needle, make sure those boys
find that needle.

Under the oaks
a new kind of bird flocks at the feeder,
I have no idea what they are, they swarm
and dart around the perches, on the ground,
they are everywhere, and outside their shrill
wheezing chokes out the drone of trucks on the interstate.

So he will teach us death, perhaps.
We will allow him the perfect death.
We will all work on dying
together, we will give him that, and maybe
it won't even happen, maybe the needle
belonged to Jamie, he's a diabetic,
maybe it was just one of his own insulin needles,
probably there is nothing in the world
to worry about, chances are slim, we mustn't
upset our boy, mustn't blow this out
of proportion.

I can't identify
the birds. They are too streaked
for goldfinches, they could be
warblers, winter plumage, but their beaks
are a little thicker, I'm just not sure
and none of these walls
line up straight.

When the boys find the needle and take it
to the principal and you stop by school
our kid is most upset because his father
is actually seen by his friends, only nerds have
parents who enter this territory,
he will never live it down, his own father
picking him up in front of his friends,
driving him to the doctor's. Just a little needle,
the kind for pricking a finger for small
blood samples, adults always overreact.
The doctor and the nurses laugh out loud,
at home the walls rise crisp
to the ceiling where the light dances.

And the new birds
are pine siskins, yes, they are,
just a little yellow on the wings and tail,
it helps, it always helps when you know
what things are.

FATHER'S FISH

I have seen them flop and heave
silver muscle on the boat bottom
and these were not those fish.

Rather they were feathers,
amethysts, sunsets,
clouds swirling and gleaming

in a rectangular blue world
he kept perfect: temperature,
pH, plants, clean gravel, all

perfect. And silent. Such brilliant
silences.
              Even the mouths
of the neon tetras, of the knife-narrow

black and white triangular angels
opened only the way a cry
in a dream clutches at silence,

the throat tries, strains
to be heard, aches to reach
the ears that stand

on the other side of the glass
but there is no sound, nothing.
And perhaps the ears would rather

watch, only follow with the eyes
the fishy sliverings, the tailings
and questionings round and round

in the water, and forget what it took
to keep it all going: emptying
the tubes, cleaning the white

gravel, replacing the charcoal,
never overfeeding. It may have been
too much trouble.

There is no longer an aquarium
in that house. Now
on a Northern lake I see him

bent in the boat, hands
trembling as he changes
the lure, prepares

to cast over
the lake's blue ridges,
hoping to reach

the mouths of small bass
as they shimmer
under dark rocks, cut

through dark water,
hoping their mouths
will open eye to eye with his,

yet knowing
that the only way
it will happen

will come in the sharp pull
they both hear,
silent, when the hook holds.

TRYING TO

As if under this wood a spirit could rise.
Rubbing and rubbing, I am unable to leave
the smoothness of tables, the cool
surface of kitchen counters. Fingerprints
on the bathroom mirrors I wipe away.
As if everything in this house
could gleam with its own right shape.

There are things that happen everyone says
could not be helped, there was nothing
anyone could do. I am trying to believe that.
I try not to say every morning when the line
of trees sharpens the bedroom window: If only.
If only I would have, he might have.

We have now had the dividing of spoils.
He would have said it like that, with a grin.
My son keeps his last four rolls
of Stick-O-Pep lifesavers, says he will
keep them unopened in memory of Grandfather,
maybe once a year peel back the foil
and suck just one, for good luck.
The brothers-in-law own more ties
than they ever thought they wanted.
Last month we sorted the books, shipped
boxes to each of the sisters.

When I rub and rub, the refrigerator
glows like a white shrine.
The sun folds clean stripes across the bed,
the sheets lie flat, unrumpled.
The bed sits squarely in the room.
This morning I had not wanted to leave it.
I sleep with his travel alarm
by my head, his silver bookmark
digging its delicate arrow
into the meat of my book.

REQUIESCAT, FOR MY FATHER

1.

No more travel
on this lake for now.
His boat has been stored and soon
the ice will begin to gather.
In the heaviest month
the men will come to cut the ice.
Great cubes. Lift them into the icehouse,
pile on pile, up to the roof.
Somewhere off Loon Island
his bones have been scattered.
Ashes, they call them, but
I know better. They will take a long time
to melt.

2.

Summer evenings on the screened porch,
breeze in the pines, clinking
of ice and sweet smell
of Scotch from their glasses
while we sipped
ginger ale, tried not to argue,
allowed to sit with the grownups.
I had white socks, blue barrettes
clipped over my braids
and was beginning to know
how hungry I was
for dinner.

It will be a long time
before I can hear
the jingle of ice in a glass.
I avoid groups, political
discussions, people who say
they've never been better.

3.

How many pieces of line left
at the bottom of the lake? Hooks
caught on rocks, lures
lost in the sand. And the last
great catch, eight four-pounders
he caught with Sam Howe,
a day in heaven they said,
until they found
that neither had secured
the stringer, the whole day's catch
gone back to the lake.
No story had ever been quite so funny,
and yet they had lost
the catch of their lives,
and it was my father's last.
But they'd had the day, he said.

All those soft places
under the lake, places he had only
found in the last few years,
his hair thin, silvery as the scales
of the small-mouthed bass
he had begun to learn
to bring up into the boat.
It tired him to clean them
down on the dock,
stooping over, but he wanted
to cook them for dinner.

4.

The ice is patching the lake
together, even now as I watch
cool shadows thread the fields.
We will leave the sandy bottom
alone for awhile, the tenderness
of moss on rocks.

Let the ice crust.
By June, when we take the metal pick
to the chunk of blue ice
cut from the lake and stored
under layers of clean straw
we will turn and face
the wide water that stretches
to Red Hill, to East
and West Rattlesnake Mountains,
and we will let the ice speak,
let the ice speak in the glass.

GIVING UP THE DEAD

1.

Is never easy.
Lines of folks there were, not only
moms and dads with young ones,
waiting to get in
to breathe for ten minutes
in a world so long defunct
we can't even imagine
the spaces between us.

The dinosaurs, titans before us,
lizardly mysteries, why did their time
come so suddenly, how did they go?

Their great necks
circle over our heads.
There was a time we had to crane
our necks just to look
into our fathers' faces.
We climbed the mountains of their knees,
sat quiet in their laps.

These are the largest creatures
we can imagine, old gods, great
grandfathers and grandmothers nobody
knows what happened to.

And yet when we touch their skin,
we find it soft as an old sofa,
soft as reading *Babar* in bed
before the light is turned out.

2.

The ice yesterday glazed the fields,
white glass heightening oak leaves,
thickened petals, a solid world.

Today the dogs tear
the bare dirt with their nails,
the leaves quiver after yesterday's
unanimous white, broad stretch of ice.

The trees are smaller without
all that whiteness, there is nothing
to look up to.

How the world shifts when the old
fathers are gone. We had always been
the small ones, living under the shadows
of the huge trees, the giants
among us.

Some say
dinosaurs had warm blood, were not
reptilian at all, these ancestors
of birds.

                    Outside my window the tiny
chirping sparrows gather. Dozens,
sweeping the ground. Barely
visible against the cold dirt,
the dried grasses, the colors
of winter. Sometimes I forget
to look, make sure
they are still there.

from

EVE REMEMBERS

(1996)

EVE REMEMBERS

It was his bending to the path I noticed
A deliberate dip, a sweep of his long arm.
Blind, we couldn't know what lay ahead.
He said he was picking up twigs, branches,
trying to clear the path. He didn't want
anyone who had to follow us to fall.

THE RIPENING

As we walked, our shoulders
met, a clustering, and gathering,
of hands, a swallowing of arms.

~

You didn't know the names of
the plants either. Our slow steps.
Did not use our tongues for naming.

TOUCHING ADAM

The surprise of his back
muscles—under my fingers
such a sweet declivity.

EVE ASKS ADAM

Where did you come from?
Always you were there.
Your eyes. A hand.
Our steps, easy,
even on the steepest,
the narrowest paths.
Your back, your hip
moving, mine.

PALM

Our small touchings.
Twigs, breezes. I
turned my palm.
You stroked a leaf,
cup, widening
bowl, lake, the whole
shuddering tree.

YOU HELD

my face, stroked, till
petal, petal
folded me. Close,
more opened as
nearest you were
all space around me.

YOUR NAME

opens and opens
petals: rose, lotus, lily—
one chrysanthemum, and still
unfurling. White mantle,
a crown, aureole surrounding
your seed-filled core.

MOVED

The rooms you opened.
I didn't even know
you were so delicately

learning the lock.
With every turn another
pane cleared. Walls thinned,

ceilings drifted. And when
you touched me, I crossed
over, into your house.

THE DIVIDE

I mainly remember a multitude
of leaves, seeds, twining things.
You say, quiet wrapped me.

You remember the day I led you
to the cave, curving dark. You kept
thinking of that peace, the damp.

I was, I am sure of it, noticing
mostly fruit, clusters, leaf shapes.
Where was that spot on the path

we were both so silent,
when air wrapped us, woven?

EXPULSION

Now you are nowhere.
I can't even remember
the cool kiss of your
hand across my breasts,
nipples, your hand so
delicate I became
one breast, four, and
more: rush of softness.
Mouths and tongues, all
petals, one full rose
opening after light
rain and not yet
yanked from the plant.

SPENT

Green stem of the calla
bursts its rounded mound—
the lily's white uncurl.

~

Milk trails the sweet
slope of you, softened
now from your flowering.

~

Even if I let them go,
nothing, nothing will
these tears nourish.

GONE FROM YOU

I am all ribs, thin cage,
so much space between bars
I am amazed I can't escape.

~

My jaw aches from closing
my mouth. To think
how you opened it.

~

The absence of your hands
presses into my breasts
a thick and bitter milk.

~

This peach is not your body.
The seed is hard on my teeth,
even after I swallow.

I AM LEFT WITH

a weightlessness of sun-
withered bones, splintered,
tossing in hot and fruitless
wind, not even a tree in sight
to land near, lean against.

YOU HAVE TAKEN

my whole face, the weight
of my small breasts, each one
of my soft places. My long

bones grow brittle, hollow.
No one but you will ever
move through me again.

OUT FROM PARADISE

Stretches of earth worked over,
fought over. Crops of rapeseed
here and there. Poppies
bleeding their centers.

The barns are tired.
Stones in the walls are missing.
I have forgotten
the language of the field.

WAY OF WHITENESS

(2000)

I. CEREMONIES

TAKING A LANGUAGE

I hear them, my husband and son, practicing
sounds in French I have almost forgotten.

La famille. Leurs mots. Deux, trois.
I don't join them. I have enough to do.

Every day the same steps to another day,
blinds pulled until the metal slats slide

to a tidy line above the window.
One bed made at a time, one side at a time,

my arms not long enough
to cross the space between us.

I have grown impatient with slow
progressions—with touch that may not lead

to love, the time it takes
to wait for the ends of sentences—and yet

in high school we couldn't even complete
a simple Latin sentence as

we followed our teacher through each
person of a verb, singular, *amo, amas, amat,*

plural, *amamus, amatis, amant,* present, past,
future perfect conditional. We didn't know

where we were going. I had no idea
in that class I would meet the boy whose

tongue was the first to reach to mine.
It took our entire sophomore year to translate

Caesar's accounts of the individual
customs of the tribes, the *Helvetii, Belgae.*

All Gaul was divided into single parts.
Evenings facing a new grammar,

nights in the back seat of a Chevy,
years before we were proficient

in the language of the country of love,
before we had entered

a French cathedral, to find the pattern
of small stones lined

to lead the devout to a state of prayer. Placing
the left foot one stone in front of the right,

heel and sole on stone,
one does not notice the rose window above

until, with an accidental glance,
light explodes, wheeling

spheres within spheres,
mother, child, man, innumerable

facets of glass. I had forgotten.
And below, a smaller window

where shoemakers bend to their task,
piercing the tiny holes lined in a row

to draw the laces through,
one, two at a time.

MATTER OF SINGING

> Why – do they shut me out of Heaven?
> Did I sing – too loud?
>
> —EMILY DICKINSON

> Her voice was ever soft, gentle, and low,
> an excellent thing in woman.
>
> —KING LEAR

I read in the papers that a woman
has been arrested because she sang
again at mass, the voice she says
of an angel who comes to her.
In fourth grade, on the school bus,
the driver told me to hush, no singing
on the way to school. Fall mornings
cooling, pyracantha berries
reddening. I had been happy.

~

Once in a sudden summer rain,
he had to put his Healey's top up,
for the first time heard my singing.
Said to stop. Every day he taught
people how not to sing like that,
didn't want to be reminded. The way
most women sound when they sing.
Too much breath. The smoldering
inside a throat, of notes wanting.

~

At the Vienna Volksoper, Mozart's
Queen of the Night floats to the stage
a cluster of stars, notes so high
they lift beyond the carved ceiling,
ranges of the Danube, Alps.
In the last act, she has fallen
to the floor, taken from the others'
reunion. We have lost her
high notes rising, resisting limits.

~

The voice that woke me in Berkeley.
Someone playing a flute, piercing
the night till I could not sleep.
A blanket in the hills, eucalyptus
rustling above us, their brown bells
around us, breath merging into breath
as he asked if I wanted to
sing again, again. Impossible not to.

SOME DAYS THE ONLY

horse in the field is the dull gray one.
Days when a husband of many years sags

into the upholstery of what might have been.
Days when I stare beyond his head

to relive the moments I have said no
to say yes to the familiar, keep intact

the tidiness of cupboards. For years
I have been sweeping, vacuuming dust

that refuses to settle. Even the grasses
of the field have turned drab as the horse,

beyond whose bulk may be nothing, not even
a gate leading to winter ground.

OF MICE AND MEN

1.

We are setting traps, packs of D-Con. Overrun
again by mice, rolls of paper towels chewed through,
soft nests of leavings
over the floor, bits of bird seed,
clumps of the litter left after the hamster died.

So old he could no longer move to his water.
You drowned him, our fourth hamster.
We decided not to replace him.

We set bait in every kitchen cupboard.
By the third morning there are no more sounds
of scuttling.

I sweep the floors of the closets, clean
down to the boards.

2.

We've been here before. The loyalty of parents
when their kids perform. High school plays
can have their moments, between the slow, jerky
changes of scenes.

This time we don't recognize our son,
bent with the weight of eighty years,
voice older than my father's before he died.
It's not so much the wig, the fragile silver hair,
as it is the tremor in the voice, the hand.

We have read the novel, think we know
what we are in for.
But when our son repeats
to the ranch hands who want to kill his old dog,
"I've had him from a pup," and when
the dog is shot and David's back jerks,
when we see him an old man turning to the wall
in a narrow bed before an audience of hundreds,
I am gripped by something harsher than stage lights,

darker than the farthest corner of this auditorium
after everyone has gone home.

In the glare of the lobby, I can't find him
among the kids accepting hugs and flowers.
Can this be my son? I ask him
to pull off the wisps of beard, I have to touch
his neck, his cheek, I have to know
it is still his young skin
under that white hair.

Driving home without him, we don't talk,
I lean on you the way I used to.
We thought we knew what we were in for.
We used to quote from Steinbeck's novel: I would say
"Tell me about the rabbits," and you would read
from Rodale's *Raising Small Livestock.*
You said we would build the cages
so the rabbits could be kept clean, dry,
well-fed, could tend their young.

3.

That fall morning we found
David out by the pool kneeling
over the edge, over a field mouse
he was lifting from the hose that floats on the water.
The mouse must have fallen in during the night,
must have swum to the hose and clung
until our son woke
to find him trembling.

We dried his fur with a garden glove,
carried him to a hollow in the grasses, brought
bird seed from the house, and left him alone.

At first when we went to check, he was still there.
But later, when we went again, there was only
the wind sweeping the grass.

STYLIST

He's been cutting my hair for six months now,
takes over an hour for a blunt cut
that I know could take half the time

but that would shorten the show.
Already I need him, one of his dependent
women who, he tells me between drags on his cigarette,

are much older than he, thank god, even though he is,
this very weekend (his booth bulging orchids and purple
ribbons), turning, god forbid, 36.

He would die cutting the heads of girls, would know he was ancient.
He stops, drops the scissors on the table, lights a new cigarette,
asks me, would I like to know the truth

about why he decided, after 4 wives and 2000 women, on men?
Because he watched them age, he said, and there's no
comparison, he said, moving in with the blades.

He liked the big ones, the ones with the huge cabangas,
and honey, they just don't hold up. Thank god
he found Joel, they're a perfect pair,

Joel's ten years younger,
a devoted husband, they've been faithful
for six years, Joel even makes their clothes.

He tells me to buy a teddy.
Four inch spike heels, we professional women have no idea
how sexy we could look, tottering around.

I should get myself some,
and I should get myself immortalized,
he has a friend who does portraits,

discreet, tasteful poses on a chaise,
my husband would love it.
Better do it soon, shouldn't wait much longer.

COLOR ANALYSIS

A fiftieth birthday gift.
Swatches of fabric held to my face.
I am a "Summer," am told
I mustn't wear winter, clear, sharp
colors of gems: rubies, sapphires, emeralds,
onyx. No mining black rock
for me. No snow, no black
branches of a naked tree.
Nothing too strong, definite,
I am semi-precious: amethyst, aquamarine, colors
of sky. I am probably an air sign.
Think of breezes, says my color counselor.

Then what are these wiry black
hairs that sprout in my blond eyebrows?
The dots of scarlet on my legs?
Pure white patches on my arms,
rents in the fabric of so many summer tans.
Flecks and cracks of shadow and blood
weaving now, my body.

I am told to have nothing to do
with the press of bright yellow, liquid greens
that rush the landscape in April and May.
No ooze of apricot.
Autumn would overwhelm me.
Crush of dark berry fruit.
Brown. I must not even think
of earth. Have nothing to do with rust.

To what season, then, am I linked,
apparently forever, floating
rootless on pale air? Am I simply
to sway here on wisps of gray,
pale cloud, a little gasp of pink,
fading lavender as the sun's face sinks?

THE BOTTOM

We knew she had lost it when she began to lift
the skirts of her silky I. Magnin dresses, twitch
her girdle side to side before she reached
the bathroom at the end of the downstairs hall.
They trembled as they moved beyond our vision,
largest parts of Grandma's little body, two great
flabby moons, drooping over her dropped girdle,
loosened garters, stockings wisping her thighs.
We tried to look the other way. Impossible

years later when our old friend the oncologist,
opera buff, beaming above the table's silver
at his fortieth, stood up at his place as if
to toast us all, then turned and dropped his
slacks right there, holding still so we could see
the small wisps of hair that shaded his two round
nippleless bottom breasts. I couldn't keep from
laughing—so hard my sides hurt. But I had no idea
what it was he offered, what he gave. Recently

mine have begun to drift below, beyond their
laundered, elasticized borders. A private
continental drift, as if the body is trying to
move beyond the narrow shape of itself, as if
each buttock were an outsized protoplasmic cell
dividing into a clump of overblown roses, giant
marshmallows held too long over the fire.
As if the body has become a low cloud building,
heavier and heavier with its own held weight.
The effort to keep it all together. The urge
of the body to move beyond geometry.

OLYMPIC TRIALS

Hip to hip last night we watched the Summer Olympics
on TV, the middle-aged Russian heavy-weight lifter
who came back after 12 years to win the silver.
Later, they showed the terrorists' slaughter
of the Israeli team in Munich, twenty years ago.
The pain of setting foot on that ground again.
The summer we lived in someone else's house
trying to rebuild our 10-year-old marriage.
Finding out about each other's lovers.
Separate rooms in the Phoenix heat.
Learning to touch again.

Tonight the divers are careening
heels over head, arms extended
to the deep water. One of the divers
opens his body too early, slams flat
against the surface. He had been close
to a bronze, now he has lost his standing.
When he steps from the pool, his back is
the color of exposed muscle. What is it
you and I keep trying to say to each other?
From the platform the water looks so far down.
After his next dive, a perfect slice straight through,
the crowd goes wild. Their palms must sting, burn
from such clapping, longer and harder than
for the 16-year-old who takes the gold.

ON THE SUBJECT OF JACKETS

Toward the last, my father asked for his tweed
jacket, described the tie, the striped shirt
he wanted to wear to the hospital, unknowing

he would be strapped to a gurney, dressed
in a short cotton gown for the winding
ambulance ride on New Hampshire roads

across the river. I followed in the car
with my mother, snug behind the wheel, sun
through the windshield. A thermos of tea.

He asked for his jacket in the voice he had used
to a secretary on the other side of his polished desk
when people signed their names to his words.

Today you tell me your grandfather, seventy years
ranching in the Texas hills, is dying. Matter of fact,
you say when it happens you won't know who you are.

Clean blue of a New England September sky
as my mother and I pushed through the glass
entrance from the shop-lined street where

I decided to buy a jacket. Soft, same blue
as the skirt I wore that he had touched,
saying, "Pretty, this is so pretty."

Every morning I pressed that skirt,
stroked the iron over the blue
cloth of the jacket, color of his eyes.

Wore it when I walked into his room
unable to talk because he couldn't.
Wore it for weeks after

as I met my classes. And then forgot,
left it in the room where I met you
that fall my father died. Your blue eyes, like his.

You talk now of the way your grandfather
wielded a knife for castrating calves.
The jacket's cloth was smooth from all that ironing.

I never got it back. I have nothing left to prepare you
for the cold, except what I cannot give. Stroking
of skin on skin. The clothes we can never wear.

CEREMONIES FOR THE DEAD

1.

I have never learned the right way
to say goodbye. Friends drift
to another section of the river
and by the time you look up from your own
thrashings to stay afloat, they are so far
even a shrill call won't find them.
All you can do is keep up with the current
that pushes you cold on to the river's mouth.

2.

When that student died to me he was holding
a flask of olive oil in his hand, his gift.
In the car, we said goodbye
to the people we had been.
I don't know who he is now.
I don't know who either of us is becoming.

3.

So little warning. The grizzled friend
whose jokes we are still trying to retell
died after successful prostate surgery.
In Tuscany together we had all walked
through the Etruscan museum, studying
cinerary urns. Who had fashioned the statuary
of the dead whose cinders lived inside?
Who decided the shape that determined
how one would be remembered?
A man reclining, leaning on an elbow,
other arm pointing to a ship.
Was this the gesture he wanted us to know?
Perhaps, instead, it would have been
a kiss on his daughter's forehead.

4.

It takes four handwritten pages
for my old friend from college to say
she is ending our friendship
and I am not to write back.
She must be no longer
the woman I have loved and yet
I will do as she says, I will not write.
But neither will I destroy her letter
and when her birthday comes round
again, I will not forget.

5.

This is what it comes to. The air that passes
in and out of pores until it is no longer
your air or mine, simply the woven threads
of our lungs' shuttles, all of our
heavings, exchanged. Whose is whose?
To continue the small regular breathings.
There will be no cinerary urn.
No one will be commissioned.

II. ANNUNCIATIONS

GENERATION

The eggs that have dropped alone into the womb
over the years, hundreds
of millions of sperm that have shrivelled
in their struggle up through the soft plush
to reach the great sun, ovum, be the one
who makes the successful stab at the vast arc,
pierces the envelope.
                              And the ovum, embracing
the one who finds her, the sleek
one who pillows himself so surprisingly
determined under her covers, this tiny whipping
pulse that plunges upriver
to reach her or die, she is so moved
she lets him
break her tight closed circle,
wave and rock through her entirety
until she finds herself multiplied, two
in one, four of two, eight from four,
till a face takes shape, fingers
separate from the palm of a hand
that assumes a shape like the hand of
the woman who surrounds all this,
who thinks she has caused all this
while a hand strokes her abdomen, her hand
pulls him down to her again
                                        and again not thinking
of all the eggs yet stored
that will never be opened, never have
the chance to lose
whatever it was they had been.

IN VENICE THE TRAVELLERS

lighten, they have left behind
London, rectangular landmarks,
neighborhoods of the famous

novelists, upholstered homes
of Dickens, Carlyle. Have left
the clacking of their jet-lagged heels

dragging through Bloomsbury, through
the floors of the National Portrait
Gallery, lines of public faces.

Ready for Venice, for water
that lures them over bridges
whose names they can't pronounce,

lures them into shops glistening
with glass swirled into vines, petals, swans
shimmering like the canals

that dazzle silver flowers in the afternoon,
the water that blazes, crackles gold
blood loosed to the tide

in the evening. When they stop, catch
their breath, they stare down into the chasm
lengthening shadow that shapes

the under arch of a bridge
and their eyes fix on the water
beneath. Nothing is reflected.

They no longer remember
what they had forgotten to tell
the neighbor who is watching the house,

no longer notice who stands next to them
on the bridge, or the moment
they let drop with no splash

their memory of maps,
the way to go back,
the shapes of their own faces.

ITHACA, ON THE LANDING

How was it Penelope waited
upstairs all those years,
before he finally

found his way back?
Every night unravelling the weave,
her fear of fixing to the wrong one

knitting her nerves.
But the wool kept the shape of the warp,
she could not straighten the strands

after so many nights.
All day weaving with more and more
wrinkled skeins, all night pulling out

threads with her fingers,
all that winding
and rewinding, back and forth

across the loom after breakfast,
the sound of the soft
contact between wool and wood,

the rhythm, meshing
color upon color, and then
at night the whole thing in reverse,

everything pulled apart
until blue and silver
strands turned dull, lost their sheen.

Sometimes she would stop, try to see
beyond the window's flat shadow.
She could not know him

through that space, she could not know
who he would be
becoming in those years

of sailing, slipping into fern-
lined coves, dashing his prow
against headlands so splashed

with sun and spume
that at first he couldn't even tell
who lived there.

And who was it
he would come home to
after all her nights unravelling?

Sometimes during those
unfinished years, sometimes under
the weight of a blunt moon,

she thought she heard music,
one of the men on the ground floor
singing, so softly singing,

and once she leaned down
over the upstairs landing to see
how they lounged in her chairs.

She travelled their faces:
not brutes, not swine, but men,
beards curled across their cheeks.

Some young, smooth
as the rubbed wood of her loom.
And the lean one with the flute,

long thighs relaxed
in sleep, smiling in his sleep.
What if, at night,

she left her weaving alone?
Let it grow, become whole?
What might the tapestry become

if she stopped saying no
over and over, refusing
the downstairs of her own house?

FACING MASKS

Venice closes down early. By ten
the alleys have blackened, so narrow
the travellers walk single file.

Magic how they emerge
into the lighted campo, face
the mask maker's shop where they had

lingered that afternoon.
Hundreds of masks, their eyes
open to a dark wall,

silky, gleaming faces
of queens, demons, fish.
One of them, enormous:

silver and gold, a sliver of moon
kissing a full round sun
billowing flames like a halo.

One of the travellers
had opened her purse,
bellissimo, she had said.

But not like her to desire
something so big, expensive,
difficult to pack.

Face to face she stood
with the man who made the masks
and told him no, grazie, no.

                Late that night
the moon will silver
the shutters of her window.
She will not sleep but think

back over a dozen canals, shadowed
bridges, and her desire will rise
for the mask,
                        the mask maker.

His faces, hundreds
of colors, some with lines
like blood running through them,

some made of lace, delicate
as expensive underthings.
The gold and silver one,

sun and moon, embracing.
What kind of man is he
to know so many faces?

He would live behind the front
of his shop. Halls would stretch
back into rooms opening

to a balcony, to the dark
water. Cushions on a tile floor.
Pillowy chairs, he might even have

one chair for every mask
he has ever made. If she could
let herself down

in them. Take her time.
And if he—with his long fingers—
would loosen

all her old tight masks,
take them off. What would she do,
then, with such lightness,

her own sun and moon
rising liquid to the zenith
of the sky she is breathing, he is

breathing her hair
into feathers, tendrils, flames that uncurl,
burst the lines of her face.

THE FACE THAT

She didn't launch anything. Only herself,
when she left Menelaus, snoring, every
couple of weeks grabbing her, poking
a jagged fingernail, stinking ale. Always
she had known, from her swan-feather youth,
she herself made only half a broken egg.

The loveliness of the one who had come
for her. Black eyes like meteors, peonies.
He didn't say he was a prince. Come down
from the high mountains where he had slept
with the wind that swept through the trees
like desire, like the way she wanted him.

So they left. That simple. She chose to
leave the stale place that kept women inside,
kept tedious track of children's last names.
She remembered the stories of the old women
who spoke from their tapestries of a time
when it hadn't mattered who fathered a child

as long as there had been delight. After their
first pleasure, couldn't they have returned
to the mountain, arms around arms, unnoticed?
Couldn't they have launched a new people,
lovely as black and white swans, fire-red
shooting stars, whole unbroken eggs?

THE JUDGMENT, APHRODITE SPEAKS

As usual, unless it involved masquerading, cross-dressing
as a bird or bull, old Zeus avoided conflict. Let someone else
decide which way we'll move on it, he said. You're all
coming at me at once. I can only do one thing at a time.

It wasn't any of us who wanted a decision, it was Eris
who always insisted on pinning everything down, this or
that, you or me, one or the other. Three of us, for so long
we had been three, none of us could imagine any less.

That flash, flame in the loins, moist rapture—I came first.
Second, Hera: promise, long term. And then, with time, Athena:
wisdom, patience, spinning, building beyond a generation.
We'd worked together as long as any of us could remember.

Then Eris insisted on ranking us. We should have seen it coming.
Divide, conquer. And old Zeus after a few beers never was very swift.
How could they blame the boy? Not even out of his teens,
all he'd known were lambs, that little river, and his mother.

At his age, of course he chose me. And we all three loved him.
Could have settled in for the long haul, me with my feathers,
amber honey, Hera with her cupboards and shelves, herbs, flannels,
babies, and Athena with her mind like a map, a grid, a star chart,

a proof. She would have organized the entire neighborhood, built
a market square, and the villagers would have filled our temples.
We could have made that mountain sing. I tried to make him happy
with a woman of his own kind, mortal, but as you know, that backfired.

MERMAIDS, THE SINGING

He leaned over the balcony, let his eyes
touch the edge of sea where birds dipped
in the afternoon, cries across the water.
Pelicans, gulls, not much color.

The mockingbird at home had sung outside
his room every morning, so many songs.
As a boy, he had planned to shoot it
until one day, silence, absence

glaring into the light as he tried
to wake. Maybe he had killed it.
Cried in his room. Never told.
Blurred, the line between sea and sky

out there. At first he thought they were
birds, bobbing on the swells.
He reached for binoculars. Were they women?
And naked? They couldn't be

mermaids. If they were, then under
the water they would stretch
glistening green, silver, quivering
glints of gold as they whipped up foam.

Down the wood steps, across the sand,
he ran. He could see their heads, hair,
loose. The surf curled over his ankles.
Arms, pink and dark, pale and brown.

His feet locked on wet sand. Here
and there a faint crest of a bare
breast and arms pulling toward him.
The salt spray of their splashing.

Waves caught his knees, chest.
The tide rocked him in foam
that frothed the swelling of so
many sudden breasts, round stroking.

So beautiful he thought he'd drown.
But they held him, so many ways
they held him, and he found himself
with every one of them. He even

swam right up to the oldest, flesh
of her belly rippled as the currents
beyond them. He shivered as he saw
the chasm of tears between her long

breasts, as she bent down to him,
as he gave her his own tears,
salt water into salt, warm
rocking, the wise cave of her.

When another lifted
nipples like scallops, supple
as if fresh from white shells,
he opened his mouth to her,

dove far into her, with her, through
layers of deeper and deeper water
until he fell back in her arms, asleep.
And woke. Pulled himself, limp,

from the water, dragged himself
over the sand, up the steps
to the evening sky, feathered
with every bird song of this world.

ANNUNCIATIONS

1. THE DOVES

The day the doves began to roost on her roof.
Their curdled calls, a sound of something boiling.
Odd, the fog that crept so cool, mornings, around the windows,
that by noon cleared for only a couple of hours,
returning mid-afternoon to blanket the house
so the murmuring of the doves seemed louder.

She refilled the feeder that hung
outside the kitchen window. The rush
of tiny kernels of millet into the long tube.
Rush of the small wings of finches, chickadees
landing on the metal rods. When the doves flew down,
smaller birds, frightened, flew away.

Neighbors fussed about the doves, too many,
they tore the roofs. The couple next door trapped them.
Evenings she would creep outside, let the birds loose.
Would come back into the lighted house, finish
the dishes, place them, dripping, into the white drainer
as the doves fluttered into place
under her eaves, settled on her roof, quiet now,
so all she could hear as she slept were the fog horns
calling from the wet black bay, the fog horns,
their low, incessant calling.

2. THE OWL

In Max Ernst's painting, she is struggling under
the heaviness of a feathery red cape, thousands of
feathers gathered, drifting from her frail shoulders
like ripples on a dark lake, like the waves
that gripped her in seizures of desire.

Why do her breasts push away from such splendor?
Her nipples harden, refuse to be flattened
under the yoke of this mantle.

Her head has been taken over
by the strange bird. She cannot get away
from the close-set yellow eyes, the way they stare
into the empty tunnels of her body.

3. THE SWAN

It wasn't sudden. She'd been going down
to the pond most evenings, when
the pink flush rose over the water.
The pond had been spilling over its edges, grasses so wet
she was muddy to the thigh now when she walked there,
evenings, as the light changed.

The night he glided to her she wasn't frightened.
Even with the fierce black marks over his eyes.
At first his whiteness barely brushed her legs, but then
every one of his long feathers touched her.

Waking, she slid under
floating pads of lilies, ripples.
The pond opened when she dove down and again
when she lifted white
feathers into the night sky, scattering
stars that pierced the fog.

III. WAY OF WHITENESS

ECLIPSE

1. SAN MIGUEL DE ALLENDE

Walking to the market for a chicken and carrots
I could barely keep my footing.
Rain flooded cobbles, pulled at the stones
round as eggs, breaking.
Nowhere to walk and stay dry.

On the way down I had driven through forests of yucca,
trees so tall they could barely sustain their own
weight, height, spines bent
to the clay underneath.

When the rain stopped I entered the Church of Carmen,
stone figures filling the chapel, crowded
intricacy of the human knife: faces of angels.
High above, the single father, sword lifted.
Farther down, bleeding feet close to her eyes,
the grown son, stretched beyond suffering.
And between them, the mother, head bent
to her shoulder.

2. ASSISI

The strange flooding a year ago in July, hot afternoon,
shock of finding my skirt suddenly soaked through
the way it had first happened at twelve.
And the pain, waves of cramping
that would not go away so that all I could think about
was sorrow.

The friends whose lives had swollen
until they cracked open. The woman
whose marriage could not hold, brittle
shell no longer able to contain the yolk
held too long, putrid when it finally broke.
Wet mess, the slippery floor, traitor
to feet exhausted from trying
to keep the shape of the house.

And the friend whose black hair had shone
through a whole concert hall as she played
Liszt, Liszt dances, rhapsodies,
hair braided above her black eyes or
dropping to her spine, falling like a mantle
until the week of the sick headache, until
her head was shaved bald as a stone
and she was gone, her sixteen-year-old son
playing his cello at the service.

The bleeding kept on through the week in Assisi.
I was unable to walk down the hill
to the Basilica of Saint Francis
or even to the nearer Church of Saint Rufino,
its stone Madonna of Tears.

3. SAN ANTONIO

Home by the time of the eclipse,
light under the trees so changed
it could have come from another country.
The stories behind eclipses: punishment from God.
Conjunction of evil with good.
Sun and moon making love.
No longer either/or. Both/and.
All of it.

Only thing to do is bathe, ease
into water, deep bath under the window under the trees
as the moon moves into the belly of the sun. At the peak
of the new light's coming,
I step out of the bath, leaving the towel on the rack,
and walk through every room of the house
until outside, I stand under the trees,
drop clean water over the grass
in this umbral light, diffusion
of shadow that will last
only another hour.

LIQUID POEM

It is not true that water has no color.
Nor that milk is white.

During the years I nursed our son,
sometimes when I leaned over you in love

the milk let down and rained
warm over your chest, rippling your hair.

From how far inside it had come.
We could never describe its translucent

clarity, fluidity, digestible sweetness.
And the cologne in this bottle

is lighter than even a petal of jasmine,
easier to smooth

across the inside of my elbow
than anything I know except your mouth.

AT 50, CHOOSING NEW MAKE-UP

The world asks, how are you, and I never know
what to say. A word, a phrase won't do it.
Cosmetics at the counter—bottles, tubes, liquids
to cover the face. Ivory Beige. Tawny Glow. Porcelain Rose.
I could say, I'm fine, I'm Ivory Beige.

Eye makeup I gave up long ago.
The times I used to cry and the mascara
ran black, even when the label said Light
Brown, tunnels staining my cheeks.
Pain of not knowing who I was.

Shopping for skins can drive you wild.
How much does the world need to know?
When my father died I wore the first pink I ever owned.
The folds of the skirt hung in the closet like an azalea, new lips
opening among the dark flannels and tweeds.

If I could decide on one of these shades, cover
the red clusters, broken vessels of my face.
I have found my breathing spaces.
How it feels to look you straight on skin to skin.
This business of artifice

when the ache to connect drives
deeper than it ever did at twenty, the tide rushes
swifter than anyone told you it could. On my hand
veins rise, blue as water from a distance. Rivers
through the body, all that has passed and passed by.

PRACTICALITY, FOAM, AND NIGHTIES

Not very practical, you said, when I brought home
the satiny lace nightie, won't hold up. Funny:
this pale shimmer takes to suds as if it were
made for water. Pale green foam

of ocean, pearl bubbles of white lace.
Sometimes when you're floating in the shallows
and a wave folds in, pushes you under,
you gasp at such sudden immersion.

When a breast spills from a slipped strap,
when we sink down under the sheets,
sometimes I would like (wickedly) to whisper
we are not being very practical.

REASON OF LACE

Sudden, these cravings
for black lace. Slips,
nighties, bras of lace

loosed from tight
windings on the spool.
No heaviness of fingers

determined to fold
fabric to a cuff, collar.
Crushed in the palm,

lace reveals nothing
but blackness, stiffness.
Only when loose

across flesh, expanses
of flank, undercurve
of a breast, drifting

over belly, pubis,
does black lace show
its wandering threads,
                                        mazes of dark

canals, veins, running
vines among the lattice
work of November leaves

that drop, unveil
the further lace of
branches, twigs, intricacy

of the spaces between
thin stems that let
wind shiver

grasses in the field,
sway them as if to music,
the way a hand brushes

the lover's thigh, slowly,
over and over the same
place, yet never the same.

Threads of black
lace like winter
branches stripped to sky

shape regions between
stars, constellations,
pauses in the embroidery

of baroque ornamentation,
exhalation after
a long breath

as the legs begin
their lacing that leads
to the places where fern-

shaped cells spin
gloss, liquid
threads that part,

make way to receive
the small darts that piece
everything together.

PERENNIAL

We are alone in your car driving across
northern California hills greener than
any I have seen outside of England, yet
we aren't even talking about the green

swimming beyond the windshield, we are
talking of Italy, our love affair
with the Tuscan hills, brown and gold
hills with their spiralling vines,

grapes, and swallows over the olives
shading the red dirt as we sweep
across these green spring hills where
you live with your wife and babies,

you I would have loved if life
had just twisted in another direction,
the way the alley off the main piazza
in Pisa, where you lived the first

year you were married, turned a certain
way, so you learned to find the market
with the open stalls where they sold
the lemon yellow peppers you loved,

the sweet lemon peppers you ate
that year you lived in Pisa. How
you relished them plain, sliced,
whole, steamed, raw, in salads.

The car twists and we crest over
another hill different from the one
back a way and yet the same green.
I loved you once. But never did.

All those years commuting together
and we never touched. Until the night
before I was to move away, with friends
around us in the restaurant, you pressed

your mouth on mine so the shape of
my mouth after that was never the same.
And I love my long-time husband,
and your wife now is, I know, much

better for you than I could have been,
than you would have been for me.
These hills, so many, almost alike,
green after green. Maybe one summer

we'll meet in Italy, maybe we'll rent
a farmhouse with room for our children.
When I go home to my husband, how
can I fit these greens into our car?

I left a winter overcast sky, gray mud.
But now, after flying back, and
driving home, everything here too
as far as I can see has turned green—

lime, moth, juniper, cypress, mesquite
foaming lace over the grasses so soft,
moist, I want to lie down in the field.
And as we talk of the mail that came

while I've been gone, the native sweet
acacia, *huisachillo,* blooms a sudden
start by the road, gold as the little
Tuscan peppers, sweet, crunch, home.

INHERITANCE

After my father died, my mother talked of a tree
she had seen at the edge of a field in fall:
a great tree as if on fire, she said, and she wanted
the rest of her life to be like that, one blaze
before the leaves fell, before it all was gone.
Now in the entry near her front door hangs a print
of a winter tree, rounded, heavy, white with snow.

Late winter, you and I have walked this way so often.
I thought I knew what to expect, oaks dropping
their brittle leaves, pushed off by their own buds.
Juniper, scrub. Grasses bent, shadowed with mold.

There is never a way to describe the things that rise
before you. A flush of white straight ahead, a breath
lifting. We turn from the path we'd been following,
into the mud of an abandoned road, to face this scent
of blossom, these circling bees, this bursting:
an old pear, gone back to its wild, original rootstock,
blooming over its intricate branches, a perfect oval.

PICNIC MAKINGS

Fourth grade cafeteria lunches. If you
brought your own you sat on the floor.
A sea of crowded children. I'd look inside
my paper bag for the cookies and sandwich:
cheese, or baloney, or peanut butter and
jelly on a good day. Sucking the last
bit of milk at the bottom of the carton.

~

When we dated, I would ask him, could we
stop to eat, and he would always say "Sure,
how about here," swing his bright white Healey
into the nearest drive-in. He'd always be ready
to eat, or cook, and even baked the first time
I stayed with him in his trailer. Made me
oatmeal raisin cookies, a double recipe.

~

In Guadalajara my uncle showed us around.
He knew just where to eat, knew the owners.
In the streets he cried, *Look, people*
are eating wherever they like, they simply
sit down on a curb with their lunch, eat
together right here in the square,
in Guadalajara it is always a picnic!

~

On the train we ate on the pull-down table,
I trimmed green onions with an army knife,
we shared a quiche we had bought in Chartres.
Cherries. We gathered the pits into a kleenex.
The train swayed from side to side, rocking,
we had the whole compartment to ourselves,
and finished two bottles of wine, easy.

~

South Padre Island, the end of August.
On the sand you hold a spoon to my mouth,

soft white ice cream on the spoon. I take
the cold in my mouth, hold it on my tongue
before I swallow. You put your spoon back
into the cup, offer again, Would you like
some more? Here. Have some more.

EATING SAN GIMIGNANO

Towers of gift-wrapped cakes rise
over the counters of the pasticceria
across the street from Hotel Bel Soggiorno
where three of us share a room.

Powdered in white sugar, packed
with blanched almonds, hazelnuts,
and honey, these torte sell whole.
The old woman whose cheeks

gleam red as roof tiles
will slice them if you like, serve you
a piece of *panforte, mandorlata,*
golden, brown as the towers

that cluster near the center of town.
We have climbed two. We imagine
life in the thirteen hundreds,
what it must have been like

to be a Guelph, building a higher
tower than anyone else, soaring
over the Joneses, the Ghibellines.
From the tallest tower we can peer

down streets that twist
into threads of dark caramel.
Our dinners are included
in the price of our room.

We order à la carte: *tagliarini arrabbiata,*
devil's chicken flaming, sprigged with rosemary,
a bottle of *vernaccia,* and, for a *dolce,*
tiramisù, slices of soft cake, layers, white

cheese, whipped cream—"lift me up," it means.
As if eating this much this well
were not adding to luggage
already too heavy

for a fast change of trains. As if
we are filling only with lightness,
our bellies and buttocks spreading
like summer clouds

billowing over the Tuscan hills
where swallows float
above vineyards, hazy, and dust
sifts like loose sugar

from dry soil, from cracks
between bricks of towers, old
heavy walls, as the evening bells begin
to lift, lift and fill.

WALKING WITH YOU

down to the dark lake, lights
clear at last on the other side.

Just enough to see
each other's faces, half a moon.

Something invisible is blooming
into the balm of this spring

darkness. Jasmine?
I haven't seen any.

In the morning, I might find
star jasmine twining

around a palm,
buds bursting in clusters

that open, tonight, our breath.
Or is this perfume roses?

White roses lining the hill, gone
to sogged tissue from the rain,

browned outer layers. Inner
petals still white, so lush,

scented, they cause all thought
to stop, even as they fall to the path,

almost over now, except for
the swelling hip. Or perhaps

this sweetness comes from the familiar
shrub by the back door

that has turned to a froth
of cream petals

surrounding a budding seed.
The leaves, strong fingers,

radiate from the blossoming.
I don't know why I am trying to decide

where the scent comes from.
You have taken my hand.
We are walking in the same direction.

WAY OF WHITENESS

> . . . until the whole field is a
> white desire, empty, a single stem,
> a cluster, flower by flower,
> a pious wish to whiteness gone over. . . .
>
> —W. C. WILLIAMS

All month the moths hovered,
bits and slaps of white pricking
the green mist: yarrow
at Fountains Abbey, dotted blossoms
clustered among leaves and branches, the white
rumps of lazing goats on the hills,
two white horses, muscles
grazing moorland above the Haworth parsonage.

This summer I have been tracking whiteness.
Clusters like doilies, caps, crowns,
but away from our own country
we aren't sure of the names.

You said elderberry, it could have been Queen Anne's Lace.
And on the train the row after row of windows,
one after the other, rhythm of lines
of trees bordering fields, furrows.
The colors friends wore changed daily,
jackets of jade and pink, yellow, green, brilliant
as the crème de menthe at one time
I had thought a fancy drink.

Until this trip I had never had time to walk
behind Chartres, to stop and face the row
of white blooming trees, hawthorns, I finally decided,
masses of white clustering sweet flowers.
Tree after tree, each one almost
as tall as the cathedral.

In Strasbourg on the river blackening one night
someone spotted a swan and suddenly

there were dozens gathered in a cove
of the river, a progression of white neck after
white sliding into the dark.

Miracle of sweet milk in coffee.
Dissolving.
Until, finally at Canterbury, there was only this: white
clouds sweeping behind a spire, the spire
easing into the white
sky filling vision.

And this was even before the music
filled the interior spaces
of the choir at Evensong.

From POEMS' PROGRESS

(2002)

PRACTICE

Honing   I'm
Sharpening   my
Knives   for
Cutting   cleaving through
Greenpeppers   opening their
Halves   crackle moist
Dark   white feathers tiny
Seeds   clinging.

This green
meat   will make
good eating   I
will swallow   the seeds
and grow   wings.

ONE LEMON

Still house after rain in the night,
small sun drops over the floor.

On the wood table
one lemon, fine-grained,

two daffodils, still dripping
from the garden, still too wet

for the water to pearl.
Stems green-lined like thin veneer.

One lemon. Daffodils, the yellow
that's been missing

all winter. Even the chickens
had stopped laying, we had

to use market eggs, pale yolks.
The smell of these flowers

is from another earth.
Cut open the lemon, squeeze

and stir in honey,
maybe heal a sore throat.

EXORCISM OF A NIGHTMARE

I sit on the bed, warm under blankets, and
there you are
on the chair facing me, probing,

"Why no poems these days?
Actually none of them are any good,
just more fifth-rate clutter

robbing the woods of their bones again.
Why not let the child use the paper
for his charming drawings?

Why not his father? The paper would help
start the fire, cold mornings."
But I'm eating my words.

One day my mouth will open and the words
will roll out, thousands of miles
of scrolls with red lettering

and the air will fill
with words like Chinese kites
surging and dipping in the air,

dances even a child can read,
and we, lightened, will quite simply
walk across the street to King Tsin,

sit at the windows, order squid and ginger beef,
laughing at the leaping of the kites,
at the scrolls of silver flying in blue air.

THE DOGS OF SOFIA

A woman's head from a basement window,
a restaurant, behind her a table of olives, peppers,
onions and oil, but she is feeding the dog
with treats sweeping the leaves on the sidewalk,
its tail wagging, not leaving.

~

Grizzled, head lowered, eyes forward,
the brown dog on San Stefano is barking, insistent,
repeated, unstopping. A car is trying
to park on the spot of the sidewalk where
the dog will not give ground.

~

Little white-eared black dog curled in a crumpled
pile of leaves and plastic bags by the curb
across from the front door to 28 Marin Drinov
where one of the tenants when she leaves in the morning
hands it a heel of bread. Even a sausage.
Odd hours the dog watches, an eye closing,
an eye opening.

~

In Doctor's Garden the leaves on the paths
are of no use to anyone. A Rottweiler pup tugs
at an old tire. Bites it, snaps, snarls, backs off, leaps,
and scoots it through the leaves,
turns it upright and rolls.

STRAYS

Thousands. Unattached
to leashes, arms, or human

voices. Although the bitch
with swollen teats swaying

to the sidewalk feeds at noon
from a hand reaching

through a basement window
and the black dog who curls

at night in the hole
between a building's stones

waits daily for the slight
woman who swings

the door and hands the dog
half a loaf, a cube of beef.

Not all the dogs are lost.
Not all of us are found.

OATMEAL AND MORNING SILENCE

(for my mother)

Maybe it was the one meal
you didn't mind.
At least the house
was silent,

only the sounds of your spoon
in the oatmeal pan,
the clink
of a plate for the toast.

It would have been six
in the morning some years,
seventh and eighth grades
were double sessions,

the bus left at six-thirty,
often before the light.
You knew I could swallow
oatmeal, maybe a soft-

boiled egg, quiet food
with none of the tension
of the ground beef and mashed
potatoes at dinner

when we argued and hissed,
dropped our invectives
like forks on a tile floor,
and made the littlest sister

pick everything up.
Breakfast was liquid
as a pond, alone
with you in the white kitchen,

the mulberry trees outside
still part of the darkness
while I tried to eat
enough cereal

so I wouldn't ache
for my bologna sandwich
by eleven, in Mr. Stutts'
social studies class, memorizing

the exports of Argentina.
You'd already eaten.
Or had you? You didn't talk,
kept our silence on the stove

like a kettle
steadily steaming
before the sun burst through,
my sisters woke,

the day came
to a rolling boil.

WHAT CEILINGS

O, reason not the need!
—*King Lear*

Descending from the cool
ceiling of an antique shop on Royal Street:
chandeliers—hundreds, crystal
petals, gardens, waterfalls, concentric
galaxies, light exploding
over dark wood, carved
jade, inlaid pearl, old
man asleep in a velvet chair.

On the street the wail of a lone
sax winds out of itself
until it seems we could leave
our constraining
joints, freed from sharp
angles, weight of the concrete,
and lift, cluster, dazzle,
like all this glass.

I remember my room as a child,
its single ceiling fixture
a plain glass square
barely covering two light bulbs,
their hard glare. From the window
I could see only empty sky, no trees
grown high enough to move
beyond that pane.

In Nova Scotia, authorities have condemned
the home of a man who keeps
pigeons, hundreds, in his garret.
He has long ago lost count,
has never minded the mess.
He leaves the windows open.
Four generations under his roof.
Family, he says, all he's got.

The sound of those wings
overhead, among the rafters, fluttering
his ceiling. The years of droppings
whitening the dark floor. Soft fiber
of nesting, soft rustling of wings.
Sounds from beyond the ceiling that could be
water bubbling, wine glasses
clinking, people murmuring of love.

POEMS FROM PARADISE

(2005)

I DON'T KNOW

where you came from.
Always, you were there.

Our steps, easy, even
on the narrowest

paths. Your back, hip,
moving, mine.

THE FIFTH DAY

I found fruit, red, and
freckled, small

under their pleated
leaves. I almost missed them.

Wanted to show you.
The pleasure of watching

you eat them too—
little sweetnesses.

LEMON, OAK, CYPRESS

But there were so many others,
leaves like new lace,
fine crochet, and so many
kinds of seeds—round, like bells,
butterflies, or birds' wings.
And the trees with the big leaves,
the leaves, like your hands.

THE THIRD WEEK

I noticed the orchids,
petals, calyx, and called,
and you said yes, yes,
but it was the water you saw,
streams, both sides of the path.

What you loved—and what
we looked at for a long
time—was the dark water
beside the pale orchids,
the steady, even flow of it.

OH, YOU SAID, YOUR

fingers and half-open
mouth pressing bits of me

I had thought were ordinary,
separate pieces of my body,

till they began to swim
together with your hands.

OUR SMALL

touching. Breezes. I turned
my palm. You stroked

a leaf, cup, widening
lake, the shuddering tree.

AT FIRST YOU INSISTED

it wasn't passion
the way we fell
silent, alongside

silences deepening
the spaces among
damp leaves

till there was no
space anywhere
between us, light and

air my breasts, your hands,
our breath, our breath, our
unbroken breathing.

AT LAST

we swam in the lake
of each other. All night
the current washed

rocks from shore, eased
the jagged edges, dissolved
stones into silt

reaching under
the highest of tides,
entire body of water.

BUTTERFLY

After, we lay still, our backs
in touch as if we had

become one body.
Our heads, knees resting

on the ground, leaned
to either side, wings readying

for the flight ahead.
We did not think in halves.

WE SAID

we wanted to cross the lake.
For something we could not

name. To push from the sway
of water. I don't remember

how we found ourselves, rocking
the stones on the other side.

IF I WAS THE ONE

who took another
path I couldn't say.

Cries in the wind.
Blanks among trees.

THE DIVIDE

Where was that spot on the slope
we were both so silent, when

high over water, transparent,
the air wrapped us?

NOW YOU ARE

nowhere. I can't even
remember our

mouths, tongues:
petals, one full

rose opening
after light rain

and not yet
yanked from the plant.

I HAD WANTED TO SAY

let it be a gentle leaving.
From the trees, a little shade,

dappling to shape our
walk—until we cleared

a path through brush,
thickets tangling in on me.

AT THE GATE

the steps
drop steep,
hard, force
the knee
to bend.
Again.
Narrow
for human
feet, easy
to fall.
The long
cold rain.

SURROUNDED

by snow. And black lines
of trees, limbs, stumps.
Unsteady footing.
Whichever way I set out
to find you I will sink

THE SNOW

You could not follow me.
Bare spots among rocks.

I have left the sloping
hills with their lilies

and lakesides, your body
a living stem. I am

winding through mountains.
Sleet as I leave.

THIS FENCE

goes on forever. Stones,
markers, set as if
on graves, but graves
placed close, touching.

AWAY

Wind shifts, grasses
bend to each other, away
from each other. You are so
far from me, even the trees blur.

I HAVE BECOME

imperceptible
as dry seed scattered,
cast from familiar
ground, wisp in air.

BARE

stretches of earth worked over,
fought over. Crops of rapeseed.
Stones in the walls are missing.
I have forgotten
the language of the field.

THE ROCKS

of this house fit
one into one, bones

with no cartilage.
Weary of motion.

Months could pass until
I let the door swing.

MAYBE I LISTENED

to your namings till
my body ached, hollowed.

Did you think me
a kind of drum

to announce your presence?
You wouldn't have known

me as a bell, tongue
swollen in silence.

TOO BUSY

for all that. Laying out lines.
Grids across the flattened dirt.
Separate plants for each square.

They must not meet across
these borders I will be sure
to maintain. High expectations.

Yields. I have no time for you.
Even if you walked right up
to the edge of my boundaries.

I THINK

you never existed. I named
you into my life. Or you
named me till I was nothing

but a rib torn from your lungs.
And still this ache to slip back
into your body, breathe you.

Or I could give you one of
the bones lining my long chest.
More: come live in my marrow.

TO RECONSTRUCT

those paths would take more
than we may ever

learn to do. A dove
calls from a branch

I can't see. To rebuild
what we had. Softness of

mosses. Your turning
to me, offering. Silken

air, streams trembling.
The way the moon filled.

THE SNAKE

uncoiled until
I reached for you.

A braid of us
pulled tight. That rope

swing we played on.
To save our lives.

Spiral. Hang by
a single thread.

BUT I COULDN'T

leave this field to find you.
I know where the rocks lie.

Working around them
takes no thinking, familiar

granite angles.
Past any further step

earth may crumble
to a labyrinth of caves,

or worse, stretch so vast
beyond me, I'll vanish.

WHETHER

one of us breathed
the sky or skimmed

lake shimmer, we didn't
ask of light that wove us,

keel and pool, air
and water. We never

asked if one of us
was an illusion.

We lived as the calla
lily's tongue lies

embedded in the creamy
bloom, full sail.

THE POOL

Small fish break the surface
but always I am waiting
for the deep-rooted lily
to bloom again, planted
so down in my silt.

YOU LOOKED

me to life. What you saw.
Apricot, cream, and blue
of the pool. Lavender.

I am not of those things
you do not see here
moving among leaves

and twigs, but if I were
to learn to cultivate
the vines in rows, I could

move into the open
furrows between, and from
a distance, you would find me.

YOU

missing, bone
hard the trees
seep their white
bloom through stem,
tendril, leaf.

And your beard:
light curling
through the sweet,
dark hair, all
blossoming.

How far do
these white clouds
reach, from here
to that place
you are now?

I WANT

all the poppies to bloom
a carpet, bright bed where

you could lie down. And if
I knew where you traveled,

I would cross the river,
climb unraveled banks,

ravines thick with brambles,
and pick their fruit. You might

not know these tangled
arms, but I would bring you

berries, plums, if I knew
your thirst sunk deep as mine.

IF I COULD SHAKE

you like a mat from my floor,
pick you up and throw your dirt
out to a long wind, away.

But you have brushed each room of
my house with your scent, have touched
these walls with more than color.

Winds that flatten even boldest
trees could strike all this, right
to the foundation. And still

you would thrive underground,
a firm root, food I would need.
Even if all that were gone,

you would be here: every
one of the tunnels of my
body spills with your fruit.

ONCE

the scent of jasmine sifted
air, there was no moving

back, no turning from the sway
of stem, petal, trunk,

till neither of us could
stay upright. Leaning, dropping

to the softest grasses,
how strange that afterward

we simply rose. Was it
jasmine that blended us

into these intricate twinings?
And such a tiny blossom.

SOMETIMES

when I am whispering
to myself about you

as I go, leaves begin
to sound like your voice

as if that song could
settle into me, now.

COLORING

of the pond has turned reed brown,
yellow, red, orange, purple,
lavender where those ripples

slant under the indigo
of the shadows, clouds
pooling lilies in the cove

but already everything
has changed, sun shift, wind
clearing even memory.

YOU STANDING

in a field of fallen
green apples. I am dreaming

this I believe. You are
upright above a sea of

dropped unripe fruit, looking
off as green mist lifts to

branches, twigs of the scarred
trees around you, as green air

opens, uncurls fronds, leaves
through the whole wood. You

have not yet moved among
these buds, this whispering.

THROUGH

layers of rock the softer
dirt collects, fountains with moist
leaves of mint, scilla, purple
hyacinth, and primula.

❧

Boundaries, margins, hedgerows.
Maintaining separate fields.
But the leaves, branches, white hair
of roots press beyond fences.

❧

The clouds have woven countries.
Rain falls here and somewhere else
you might be moving, your feet
touching the same earth as mine.

GIFT

The stone you handed me.
Oval as your face, palm

of your hand. How long
I have carried it with me.

That something so heavy
could help me rise.

SO THIS

is what you saw. By
leaning down over
smooth stones around

the calm of the pond
I have seen my face.
And to think I was

worrying about
the flowers I would
wear when you find me.

IN THIS RAIN

it all comes back. Gentle
now. Your face, a mirror

of small rain drops. Blossoms
of these two dark trees by

the path, bursting petals.
Pink, white, and the darkness

of the inner flower
barely perceptible.

EVEN ROSE PETALS

fan out, away, yet still
touching till they drift

like blown rain to the ground
that drinks them in.

Maybe you have been closer
than I had thought,

across a crest
of another hill, just ripening.

EVENING

lake's blue burnished, a long
quieting of ripples.
Entire gleam a mirror,
bronze gong, a deep bell
declaring. Is this you
beside me or a bough
almost brushing the dark?

PINE

needles yield to my feet, surface
crisp, soft underneath. From
somewhere

I believe I can hear you come
this way, quiet, no announcement

other than the earth quivering,
the air filling clean with your scent.

THE RETURN

will come when I least
expect it. Moon rise
into my field. Your
face, your brisk step on
my small estate. Calmed.
Bright body. Shadows
dissolved. The clearing.

WE ARE

no more outside the garden, or
inside fences, walls. Surfaces

dissolving. When I—or is it
you—look up, countless butterflies,

yellow flecks, little lights that pierce
the veil of what we thought was air,

dart, flutter, in, out of this
unlimited space we enter.

IF A GOD

comes to you
a small
fish in the night,
simply
become water.

~

If a dove drifts
under your sheets
let him stay,
tuck his head
in a soft place,
rest, until
you are feathers.

~

He may come
as a lizard, a slip
of a green
slither across
your wall, crevices
left from past
freezes and thaws,
as he turns
translucent, persimmon,
ablaze.

~

Or a monkey,
who leaps
your crenelations.
Weightless
motion of silver-
brown fur, uncurling
tail, and keen
eyes focused
in, beyond.

~

When a god comes
to you as a man,
you will have no need
for questions, blossoms,
or bracelets.
Even a name.

BETWEEN FRAMES

(2006)

MORNING SCREENING WITH THE FILM CRITICS

Semi-dark. Empty seats, except for me and the four film critics. 9 a.m. The film hasn't arrived. Due any moment—hand-carried. Supposed to be an Oscar contender, though one of the critics, the one whose wife will be late, says he's not so sure. Hates anything too serious. Life's bad enough, he says. I haven't had my coffee. Smell of carpet cleaner. Rows of tiny lights lining the steps like markings for miniature runways. The movie still hasn't arrived. I stand up, say I'll be back, walk through the entire multiplex, in, around, and out of every one of the empty theaters, the screens all blank.

OLD ANNIVERSARY

A year and fifteen days since
we were officially
divorced and yet he is calling
this morning, a voice like a cup
of coffee I no longer drink, though

I still miss the hit of caffeine,
that kick in the pants. He tells me
his mother is probably good for
only a couple of months, late eighties
and failing fast, my ex-mother-in-law.

Last week, our son's twenty-fourth
birthday, and today, we would have been
married thirty-seven years. My neck aches
from holding the phone at a bad angle.
I don't want the recipe for corn bread

he recites to me: "Got that?"
All those cups of lukewarm coffee.
The effort to struggle free from
comfortable poisons in the blood.
Weight of the old talking, round and

round, every day, as if there were nothing
in life but nuances of corn kernels
(frozen, fresh, canned) in corn bread.
His mother is dying. We are divorced.
I can hang up at any time.

TRASH

"Trash," he said, as we walked the line
between our almost-country properties.
Again I pointed, trees and shrubs
whose names I didn't know, but "trash,"
he said again. Anything not oak.

That neighbor knew three kinds of trees:
live, pin, and Spanish oak. The rest should go.
And now I've lived here twenty years
I know how chainsaws take out everything
that isn't oak, not just the junipers

that choke the other plants nearby, but also
Texas buckeyes, magenta blooming in
the spring, redbuds, *huisachillo,* sweet acacia.
Mexican persimmon's bark blends velvet
grays and silky browns, its rounded leaves

bright yellow-green before the purple fruit
draws birds that nest on into June—
buntings and the wrens above the grasses,
gramas and the bluestems. November,
the seed heads in waves of burgundy, of red.

Our city council said they'd leave the trees
when clearing for the city hall. But like
that neighbor years ago, they meant
the oaks. Now they've called a meeting.
Oak wilt has hit the neighborhood, and

oaks are what we're left with. Too much
construction, trimming of the trees, their
wounds not treated. The virus travels
through the maze of connecting roots.
And once a tree's infected, it's trash.

WAS IT WHEN

the rock band next door
finally stopped, the first day
in months not bound to someone
else's pitch, volume, starts,
stops, rises, decibels?

Even slicing lemons took
a mustering of resistance
against what pulsed, what
permeated membranes of our
walls, windows, double-paned,

and useless. Was it then,
when the boys stopped, that
the birds returned? Chickadees,
their quick darts—and the jays,
jostling the feeder.

Territories. Whose? This morning
the cardinal, in the sun's first
silence, his chirr, chirr, chirr, chirr.
Music. Announcement of turf:
I am filling this space, I am a feathered

pebble in a pool, I am rippling
circles and circles of waves,
I occupy more space
than you can imagine,
and as for you, you stay put.

THE WORLD IS DIVIDED

Even on a green patio, some will lounge
alert to rustlings under leaves
that never quiet the sorrows of their bones.
As if the breeze carried echoes
of sudden boots slicing the stair, axes
crashing the precision of clocks, a grandfather's
spectacles ground under, a mother's skirt
ripped from her thighs, upside down.

Others will look past the shadows
cast by grassy blades with only vague
uneasiness. They'll focus on the proper
placement of forks, angles of picture frames.
Traveling, they pack knick-knacks into luggage,
arrange them on the mantle. Figures
from the villages, carved by hand from
indigenous trees. Folk art with a signature.

The way leaf shapes are brushed onto
the parchment of a hand-painted shade.
How a lamp can add a fine touch
to an unremarkable room, diffusing
light that issues from the incandescent
center of white heat, the burning globe.

AT THE END OF AUGUST

An hour of pattering
rain and though the soil's
cracks still gape, on the roof

two fluffed woodpecker
nestlings flutter off.
The stray tabby is lapping

goat milk from the bowl.
We have emptied our luggage.
The clouds have moved

from currents beyond us,
their moisture might have
lifted from fields in Tibet.

How far will we travel
to arrive at a moment
we call home?

THIS IS NOT

even your own face
in a copper bowl,

hammered, tarnished,
above the stove.

Dented, with no surface
for reflection,

only the curved line of
light on the rim.

The small indentations,
the half-spheres

repeat in rows of
concentric circles, uneven.

The crumpled spot
at the apex of

the dome is a rose.
Take it from its nail

on the wall.
The crumpled spot is a base.

Set it down. Stare into
the space it holds.

BANNED

The side door unlocked. The manager's key loosening the metal grid, sliding up in its grooves. An empty theater. Only the rows of vacancy, a sprinkling of critics, the quiet air of the dark, and then, color, focus, the film.

China. A city. A small home. The subtitles are missing. A girl is bathed by her mother, her sister, rubbed, and rinsed. The water is warm, liquid down the current of her spine.

The movie is banned in China. The director can't go back. The girl is sent away to the plains, to army camp, it is required. Then she is sent further, to the distant hills, to herd horses. With a man whose penis has been sliced off.

She is a drought of loneliness. He builds her a bathing pool on the side of a hill. Looks the other way. If he touched her he would burst into flame. He does not touch her, even to pull the cover up to her chin. I want him to touch her.

The first of the men to arrive is cheerful, young. He has connections, will get her back to the city. Her pupils widen. She lets him in. The men who come again are never him. Sometimes they walk right into the tent, and then drive off.

We don't talk until the car. I can't believe, you say, she was that naïve. Those men were yahoos. When you're that lonely, I say, you do anything. For a while. Until you give up.

DE NADA

Yellowing in the park, these leaves
beyond the window, on the balcony, in the cold
remind me of nothing, not even graves.

Not the glimmering bird on your Chinese vase
or the smooth lengths of our bedroom sheets, their folds
unlike the barrage of these loosened leaves

that bear no resemblance to the fleece
of your hooded jacket that staves off cold,
or the cornmeal muffins I bake that you rave

over and we butter above the gold-
green cloth spread across the mahogany leaves
of our oval dining room table; these

remind me of nothing, sweeping past eaves
and into the gutter, this torrent of yellowed waves
as the veined leaves loosen their hold.

MONDAY

Light bores in. The news. Earthquake in Turkey.
A four-year-old with a gun. Clinton's traveling.
They're blasting a mile away, at the quarry.
Wake up. Get going. The trees behind the post office
were bulldozed last week. For a final care facility.
At the supermarket they bus them in, the seniors,
riding the carts. Independent. Another ozone day.
I'm on the interstate, too late to go back.
The carry-out girl tells me she won a trophy
for best costume on Halloween. Shows me a snapshot
of a 5′7″ Bugs Bunny facing the camera, holding
a plastic carrot, no one else in the picture.
I want to get home, walk before dark.
Sometimes the brown hare that lives under the gardenia
is there munching on grass, watching.

PAIN: MUTTERING

You do realize, it's saying, if he's shut the door
and all you hear are the keys of his laptop, a hint
of violins on NPR, Listener's Choice, it means
he's sick of you, lazy, slattern, sleeping till noon,
your mouth open and snoring. You can't even
finish a poem. You beg friends to read drafts.
And can't you do laundry without making noise?
Talk on the phone without shrieking? Cut garlic
without the thump of a knife? Brush your teeth
without spitting? For all you accomplish, there is
no reason to reach for your robe, even get up.

PAIN: SECOND THOUGHTS

It's hovering above my eyebrows. This guy you've
hooked up with, it's saying, not even tall enough to lean on.
What if you fell, what then? He couldn't pick you up.
You should never have left your husband, big enough
for a sofa, a stove, a refrigerator. So what if this one
makes you laugh, gasp at night. I'm going to sit on you,
remind you how good it felt, all that weight of your husband
hanging on your shoulders, telling you the right way
to cut a potato, dial long distance, put on your shoes.
I'm going to push on you, push down, you've been missing
all that weight, haven't you, all that old upholstery puffing up
around your neck, that couch you could fall into, all that
furniture you put on MasterCard you could just collapse in.

PAIN: MANAGEMENT

It moves from my right shoulder toward
the spine. A fist. It digs in. I'll walk,
take a long walk. How far, it asks.
It's almost dark, it says. I say I'll read.
What year, who wrote it. Not you, it says.
I open the back door, step onto the grass.
A leaf gleams. No matter, says the pain,
it'll all be drowned, the rain, and then, the cold.
I move inside. What have you done today,
it says, almost over, out of time, time's up.
Come morning, it's still asleep, I try not to wake it.
I'm loading the washer. The easy things.
Laundry, I tell it, go back to sleep. Why bother,
it says, nobody looks at you. Its fingers open,
reach up to my neck and pull.

PAIN: INHALATION

It's taking a cigarette break. I'm allergic.
Too sensitive. My father's smoke, four packs
a day. It's back already. Don't breathe
too deeply, it says, take in as little as possible.
Who do you think you are. Try this, it says,
breathe into a paper bag. Better yet, plastic.
Careful, we're dealing with limited resources.

UNTITLED, AT THE MOVIES

There is a woman on the screen with eyes like mine, and hair. The movie is about rejection. The woman ends up alone, on a bridge. The camera cranes higher, travels. She is a smaller and smaller shape, a speck on a long line across water. The camera lifts to a moon. Before the credits, thick clouds roll over it, cover it. I have reached for my Kleenex. The story is not my life. The woman on the screen is composed of flecks of light. I hook my purse over my shoulder and walk out of the dark rows of seats into the lobby, out the glass doors, into the parking lot, my car key ready.

REFLECTION

Massacre in Kosovo, but I
am folding blankets on our bed,
nap of the wool, weave over weave

neat and ready for sleep after
the ten o'clock news: homes blazing
raw-boned to blackened skies, smoke

mingling with cloud—or is it
fog? Nothing blurs these
dislocated faces. Last summer

in the flood friends lost their home
of thirty years, everything downhill.
I've started folding the towels.

Lengthwise, in half, and again.
Outside in this morning light
the male cardinal cheeps in pyracantha

at the window. Flitting, as if ready to nest,
but we haven't spotted his mate.
All last year we woke to her beak

attacking the bedroom window. Over
and over, the glass rattling our heads.
She began at daylight, broke our dreams.

I've heard they die
that way, not knowing it's only
a mirror, a reflection of themselves.

AFTER TEACHING *THE WASTE LAND*

Rosie emails she's delivered
a month early, Caesarian,
can she make up the midterm?

The wet cave of a mother's body.
The damp curls of her newborn.
Clusters of hyacinths in rain.

Rosie, with a furrow in her belly
that this year has bloomed
as mine did once and only once,

though after, I kept on reading
through the night, dreaming
of mountains where I might feel free

without a husband whose unburied
memories and desires kept him
from meeting my eyes

as I held on tight, knowing
nothing, seeing nothing
in a closed house, the coffee at ten,

while our son struggled to sprout
above the weight of a past
tangled by unspeakable nerves.

Even now that he's grown
and the years have flowed on
softly, the arid plain now behind us,

dust will leak under the shadows
of our roofs and porches
as I huddle silent

over brittle pages, dried laundry,
and the coils of electric burners.
What is that murmuring

under the door? The wind?
Or Rosie, rocking her baby.

SERIAL MONOGAMY, ON THE HELP LINE

Tim is the fourth, the most compatible.
I've spent less time with him than with
Brian or Travis, even John, but we click.
It's the serial number he's asking for,
at the back of my printer that won't work,
that smears, no longer clear, like marriage
gone muddy, clouds around words, fog
and spilled ink, permanent.

The back of my printer is gray, blank,
featureless, but Tim's voice is crisp.
It was John last night between 11 and 1
who said while I was upside down hunting
for the little sponge behind the ON switch
that I sounded like a very attractive woman.
It was with Travis, though, that I found
the sponge, and cleaned it according

to his patient drawl, cleaned it with Q-tips
sopping up the blackness that has oozed
over my printer's innards since my divorce.
After Brian, who stuttered like the sound
the printer makes before it starts spitting
ink and the paper rolls through,
I almost went looking for another.
When a friend helped me set this one up,

my belongings were strewn through
the house I had just left, the one I live in
now, the apartment I'd leave
in six months, a storage unit, and my car.
Tim's back on the line. The company
has agreed, 7–10 days, they'll send
a replacement, identical. Exactly
what I'd thought I wanted.

AT A PERFORMANCE OF JOYCE'S *THE DEAD*

Here they are in white stage light:
the mother, son, husband, and wife,
even the elderly aunts. Family.
Gathered in the dining room,
arena of the dead, the dying.

You and I have little history.
Hardly ever entertain.
But our round wooden table
is laden with the dead I brought
with me into your house.

A drunken grandpa, father, husband.
Shoutings over the darkened grain.
And the house already crowded
with people I've never met, gifts
from women each hoping to be

the one you'd invite to stay.
A carved stallion, vanilla candles,
embroidered cushions for the sofa.
You say nothing of them.
We live in a cemetery of unmarked

graves, where someone could pop up
from underground, enter the scene
stage left, bringing a covered dish,
a bowl of spiked punch, spill
everything about you I don't know.

FLOOD

The garage gone under.
Boxes of letters, the ink
smeared, typescript bleary
as a bad morning after.

We'd said we wanted
the past cleaned out,
but not like this, the years'
pages so compressed

that Claudia's script merges
with Cynthia's, Sandra's,
Rudy's with Dan's, and
even as we struggle

to separate the sodden
bricks of envelopes stuck
solid as if the paper is
pupating back into wood,

even as we work to free
the few limp pages we can
pull from the water's weight,
the fiber shreds in our fingers,

our past lovers' words
scattered on the porch,
damp as new moth wings,
not quite ready to fly off.

THIS GARDEN

was here all along, but behind
the main road I drove
without pausing to take

the back way through slow
streets of overgrown
shrubs, your windows open

behind the house where
calm rests like sun on a pond,
like the quiet born from talk

that has sprouted between us,
words that have opened
and followed words slipped

one after one the way jasmine
blooms along tendrils,
words bending and dipping

branches strong enough to sway
the two of us in a hammock,
branches filled with easy

shade, a ceiling under which
we rest and repeat
the phrases that seed, burst

into grasses that murmur
air the way water rushes
onto the banks and swells

blueberries, tender, held
in the mouth, and swallowed.

WAKING

Mornings in bed, lace
of new sheets a veil
like the wool fluff

of the blanket's loose
threads that resemble
flarings on the sun.

The red coverlet's fringe.
We play with the flames.
Wake them, tease, flashes,

sparks, higher and higher
till they leap at the window.
You and I missed the comet

that blazed through last year,
but miss nothing now.
Every night catches fire

until the skies open clean
rain and we lie, one fallen
onto the other, unscathed.

FULL

Light splotches on the bed,
mesmerizing the morning.
Why rise from this dazzle?

But outside the kitchen door,
for the first time, flickering
in the pittosporum's froth, a dozen

dozen monarch butterflies ignite
the green, their freckled patches
shifting, rapid as a blink, and gone.

Not so the evening primroses
that open as the light is leaving
and remain even as the moon lifts

from the trees, even as you sit
steady above your book, until
you rise, and bring me your hands.

WEDDING CRASHERS

In the film they pop up in pews and country clubs like floppy silk flowers on a hat. Salt in the stew, sugar in the tea, hops in the beer. Swing dance with the toddlers, yarn swap with the uncles, wrestle with the boys. Icing on the cake. Even found out, bawled out, kicked out, these guys get women, what they want.

You feared we'd have crashers, as we planned for June, seven years after my divorce. But only a swarm of sisters, graying friends, and my grown son. And these new lightsome selves of ours, laughing, dancing like strangers who've waltzed in unannounced and taken over. They won't leave, already home.

THINGS OF THE WEATHER

(2009)

SUNSPOTS

Perfect, this orb, unblemished,
constant, pure—unlike its fickle,
pallid sister sphere that crooned,
feckless, to love-starved cats, that
pulled the tides of women's wombs
until they bled, flooding our sheets.
No shadow-shapes of rabbits,
vague contours of human faces.
Clear and fat, an egg yolk
clean of any slime, a gleaming
round, Apollo's lyre, logos—
the lofty eye of God.
No splotches on this realm.
Yet ancient Chinese sages,
medieval English monks,
and later, Galileo saw
what in the nineteenth century
Schwabe and Carrington confirmed:
a cyclic rage of solar flares, titanic
tongues whose mass ejections
hurl a billion tons of TNT
our way, paralyzing satellites,
slicing into messages, our cells.

CONDENSATION NUCLEI

Sea salt, pollen, and smoke.
Particles the air
needs to form a cloud.
A pebble in the palm.
Phrase dropped on a plate.
Your words I've collected
and lined up like bowls
of ash, or sand,
stared at, and wept.
Or like our lidded glass
containers: oats, wheat,
and opalescent grains
we use to knead
our bread, yeasty
loaves with raisins.
Rain, relief, the irritants
washed back to loam.
Saliva, the body's
juices that digest
grit between our teeth.

AURORAS, BOREALIS AND AUSTRALIS

The Vikings saw the Valkyries.
Tiberius thought the port of Ostia
on fire, while Ezekiel's heavens
opened to an amber, sapphire,
ruby wheel, the word of God.
Antarctic midnight, 1998,
surveyors on the ice could read
labels on their gloves, minuscule
markings with no hint
of the magnitude of tongues,
the particles of plasma burst
from inside the sun, electrons
hurled down to us from space,
colliding with oxygen, nitrogen
molecules awhirl and causing
pagers of detectives, pharmacists,
even lovers to go dead.

CONTRAILS

Lines that reverberate
beyond the actor's exit.
A bite embedded,
burr in a Bermuda lawn.
An enemy's position
can be calculated
from a plane's traces.
The exhalations freeze
as they leave the tail,
it's ice crystals we see
as a trail of tissue,
nail clippings, a snake skin
the plane has moved beyond.
But sometimes the lines
retain their sharp edges
and criss-cross above
like blades slashing
the last word.

NEAR-EARTH OBJECT

They said a second moon,
a bright new sphere
orbiting our planet, another
presence we can count on.
Have you seen the moons tonight,
we'll say, they both are full!
And suddenly our small
circumference has swollen
to the size of Saturn's—first
one moon, then two, in time
we might have rings, a crown
of moons all following
the wisps of our transparencies,
the clouds, the drifts of all our storms.
But no—they're saying now
it's the last stage
of an Apollo rocket launched
thirty years ago, returned from
decades revolving round the sun.
A boomerang's ellipsis:
a word we uttered once,
flung back to us.

SOLAR SYSTEM

Most stars in other nebulae
occur in pairs,
triplets, quadruplets,
sex-. Not like our own
sultan to this harem
of planetary wives and countless
asteroids, concubines.
We nine (or eight?) revolve, trailing
and unveiling our emerald, our topaz
atmospheres, our eunuch-moons.
But not so much polygamy
as a case of astronomic
solitude. A star alone
without another of its kind.
No one near who can reciprocate
with equal flaring tongues
while we, vague miasmic Venus
and sweet malleable Earth,
are constantly presenting
the rounded colors of our curves,
faces turned from the seraglio
toward all this gaseous heat
that spews atomic particles
at whim, in which we bask
and, agitated, spin.

LUNAR ECLIPSE, ALTO-STRATUS

Can't see what we've heard
we should be able to see,
which is, after all, only
invisibility, though they
say that what is visible
will slip by stages till
what we often can't see
will be erased and we'll be
amazed as if someone has
died who we never knew
but thought we did, a glimpse
of a shadowed surface once
in a while, a faint gleam
through a misted window,
half-latched door—no hearty
invitation, hand extended,
no name, no curling smile.

STRATUS OPACUS NEBULOSUS

Not a verb in sight,
the train blocking
miles of traffic, no end
to these errands, piles
of provisions, necessary
comestibles, heavy sacks,
a vegetable persistence.

BROCKENSPECTRE

Can't shake it
on this flight, a bad penny,
an albatross, persistent,
ought to get lost
like an old suitcase
of clothes we wouldn't
be caught dead in, faces
that should have stayed
at the gate, a voice
from the ground
we don't claim: shadow
of our plane on the cloud bank
below, a reflection of
ourselves blocking the sun.

THUNDER

To Descartes, one cloud falling
onto another. To the Greeks,
Zeus's shield shaking, a forerunner
of Hopkins' shook foil, that grandeur,
gathered and charged. For the native
tribes of the plains, Thunderbird's
wings beating. Such magnified
oscillations are beyond us, yet
the very air we breathe is grumbling,
a succession of compressions,
negative and positive ions colliding,
as someone in the next room
is about to explode.

CUMULONIMBUS INCUS

Build-up of white
turret upon white, *but wait—*
half-way, dark, *there:*
a wedge, break, em-dash—
pause in the tumult as
warm air cools, takes
a breath, forms a second-
story floor, shift in the plot,
new base for the chapter's
finale, moist hot risings
to hammer the storm.

HALO

The moon gone blowsy
beyond itself, a blown
fullness, a rose almost
over. Reflected,
this light shimmering
the evening. You reach
for me, places I cannot go.
Dust from your sleeve
slips to mine, to the ground.
Our mutual orbits—
as one glance lightens
another, sifting focus.
To bring the far near.
Cloud wisps, ice crystals
in air. Never nothing
between us and a stone.

FULL MOON, CIRROCUMULUS, LIGHT BREEZE, AND IRIDESCENCE

Ocean and crater, iris, wide pupil,
until a thread, a clump
of cloud startling
the way a car door
thumps closed, the face
turned to the wheel,
down the drive,
gone. And silence
as a canoe slides
past the dock at dusk,
the plash of the paddle,
ripple of water, tip
of the prow drifting
beyond a branch,
the planks under us
even now rocking.

THERMOKARST

> Over thousands of miles in Alaska's interior, patches of forest sink into thermokarsts and die as swamp water floods them. It is a frequent sight on the roadside: a stand of tamarack, gray, spidery, dead, rising from muskeg water.
>
> —WILLIAM K. STEVENS, *The Change in the Weather*

Tamarack in old habits—
firmness of permafrost's
hard layers beneath—
till underground ice pockets
thaw, and earth falls in,
diagonal. The sky
no longer up, and roots
awash in bog. Melting
causes spring, and health,
and sex, we think, liquidities
like mother's milk,
kindnesses that would be
kindest if dependable.
When sudden flood
befuddles us, how to find
the bottom, or the stars.

WANING GIBBOUS MOON

Froth of the full-opened
wild carrot, folding its cup.
Shimmer of rain fallen
on the street, our need
to say *goodnight, goodnight,*
friends we may not see again.
A second of silence after
the aria's crescendo.
The moment you slip
outside of me
and we begin the drift
to separate sides
of the wide bed
before one of us rises
to let down the blind,
feel our way in the dark.

CUMULUS AND CIRRUS

About such majesty
they were dead on, those Old
Masters of the page-long
paragraph with parentheticals,
semi-colons, punctuation
marks as spirals, curlicues,
and always, the light
behind the foaming flesh
of turbulence, perhaps
even a god in the air.

ALTOCUMULUS, MACKEREL SKY

Freckled, a dappled thing,
it hasn't yet decided whether
white or blue, fair or foul, coming
or going, riffles, puff balls, dandelion
shreds, a breath, another
river, the current, brimming, gone over.

CUMULUS HUMILIS

Articles, separate,
unattached to any
nouns (far below, those
heavinesses: barn, road,
tree, bicycle). Rather
not commit, these breathy
the's, puffs of *a*'s,
drifting, afloat, gone.

FULL MOON, ZENITH

You have opened your door
and answered my questions.
Even at midnight, leaves
of the oaks, persimmons.
Seven deer on the lawn.
We could read in this light.

SINGLE CIRRUS

The flotilla out of sight,
just a smidgen, a dash,
a skiff, canoe, isolate
kayak skimming the open
lake on a whiff, a breeze,
aspiration of the *h* in *hello,*
a hand extended, fingers
unfolded, lips pursed for
a shy kiss, more to come.

SUNSET, CIRRUS, CUMULUS DECLINING

A woman's widening
mouth around
melon slices, fuchsia
bloom above
the plum silk of her loosened
blouse, lips
opening as she slips another
slice between
the flush of her cheeks
as the juices
fall, pool in the dimming
shell of her plate
where the blackness glistens
with dropped seeds.

SUNSET, CRESCENT, WITH VENUS AT GREATEST EASTERN ELONGATION

A whisper touch,
your lips across my wrist,
and there, up there, surrounding us,
a violet calm, a gauze
contentment, and a sliver of light—slim
canoe—suspended on the float
of lavender, mauve, pastel
haze through which this single
disk of light off to the side
gleams down to the fading—almost
colorless—green of the lawn
where rain lilies lift their petaled
whiteness, as many lilies
nibbling at the coming dark
down here as stars.

WAXING GIBBOUS MOON

This humped asymmetry,
as if the scissors slipped,
a segment missing in the arc.
We're waiting for the song's
last notes to be resolved.
Yet here beside me,
your face in profile
is still your face,
the whole of it, which
I can never grasp, even
between my hands, all at once.

HIGH SKY

The sky has slipped its stitches,
the feathered cirrus, wool of cumulus,
gauze shreds of layered stratus
gone with the unexpected guests
who left this morning
after a night of pelted rain.
Now the sun flashes and shears
the few seams left
till bare skin bursts through
and we're down to ourselves,
two loose threads, the knot undone.

NOTHING BETWEEN US:
THE BERKELEY YEARS

(2009)

TEACHING *UNCLE TOM'S CHILDREN*

He was the only other honky in the room. But wasn't. Blond natural. Was his mother or his dad white or black? Kid played the best sax in town and only fourteen. Sax so sweet and cool the moon rose cream over the hills and stars broke the fog. He didn't talk much. Neither did I, that first Black Lit class any of us taught. I didn't know what to put on the board. Erased everything I'd written before, but the erasers were full of dust from the chalk. The blackboard turned powdery, a blur, clouded. We moved on through *Nigger, Black Boy, Native Son.* Not a kid caused trouble. Small sounds, fingers flipping the white pages of the paperbacks I collected and stacked in the corner cupboard after class. Slap of gum stretching in and out of a mouth, hard sole of a shoe on the floor, scraping the surface, an emery board. And the train, track barely a block away, the train running the whole length of the San Francisco Bay, cry moving ahead of it, toward us, that wail.

EUGENE THOMPSON, THE HALL MONITOR

Old enough he'd sung "Old Man River" in most East Bay productions, but not so old he didn't still do it. I'd never seen a performance. And wondered if he took his glasses off—so thick they ringed watery circles round his eyes. Glaucoma, he told me, and he'd probably go blind. He'd never seen his wife naked. Over thirty years and she always had to be covered somewhere, wore a little flannel vest to bed, only time he'd seen her breasts was when she nursed their first baby. They'd even gone to the doctor because their sex had been so bad. Found out her clitoris was a long way from where it's supposed to be, and that explained it. But his little white lover over in Richmond knew what he wanted, always opened her door to him without a stitch on, even cooked him dinner like that. All the time he talked he'd be standing in my classroom door. I'd never thought about anybody going to bed with more than one person. You got picked for your role in life. You sang it. You didn't cross town to try out for a different play.

HOME ROOM

A full period, fifty minutes, right before lunch. I had a traveling schedule. Came all the way from the other wing, the third floor, and my favorite class. Those kids would even stick around after the bell, keep on talking about *A Tale of Two Cities,* but I had four minutes to pack up my books, lesson plans, my purse, and run down two flights of stairs to make it on time. Thirty-eight kids in the typing room. The J's, all the Johnsons and Joneses in the school. No Asians. Seven whites. The typing teacher Lillian Hillis didn't mind if I used the desk. I'd prop a book next to the flowers she kept in a little jar. A long room. Dozens of Royals and Underwoods covered up. Six of the Johnsons spent the period leaning over the floor. I knew they were throwing dice. At least they weren't fiddling with the typewriter keys, no little bell sounds of the carriage return coming from their direction. On the board behind me was the chart for finger positions. Right before lunch. Forty minutes. The announcements took five. Attendance two or three. Handing out forms maybe ten, but not every day. A window faced the courtyard. One small tree grew out of the cement.

FOLKS

I didn't know what I'd been doing wrong in the Track 2 class. Till one of the counselors told me to stop saying *folks.* Not a friendly word, especially since the assassinations, Martin Luther King and Malcolm. Almost as bad as *coloreds, nigras.* Didn't even realize I'd been saying it—okay folks, time to get out your pencils. Thought of it as a neighborly word, an offering, sort of like a covered dish at a pot luck. A long way from my own folks in Phoenix. Family. During that first semester James Carmichael would stay after second period and help straighten the desks. Don't you worry Miss, he'd say, they'll most of them be fine. Just take them a little time to get used to you.

One Friday around the middle of October, Calvin Jones cussed so much in class I led him out to the hall and leaned into his face: look at me, look me in the eyes when I'm talking to you. At lunch the other teachers told me he was just being polite—you looked down, showed respect, never looked straight into the eyes of your teacher, especially your white teacher, especially your white woman teacher.

It was later in the year that James Carmichael joined the Black Muslims. New black slacks and tie, stiff white shirt. He'd been right, most everybody, even Calvin, had come around. But James had stopped smiling, his eyes gone somewhere else. He still turned in his work on time, still made B's. But there was nothing between us, never had been.

RELATIVE

My husband's Aunt Mary couldn't stop saying what a beautiful place we'd moved to. All year long, something blooming. And the houses, some excellent properties in the hills. She sold real estate in Tucson. What a climate on this coast, she said. And neither of us had to drive even ten minutes to our jobs. She'd taken Greg and me out for dinner at the Claremont. 180-degree view of the Bay, all three bridges. Butter molded into rosebuds. Tomorrow we'd cross one of the bridges into San Francisco, maybe go the long way round to Marin, and take the Golden Gate back home. Maybe the fog would lift. She wanted to take me shopping, buy me new clothes. Start with Macy's, find me some things that would hold up. A good idea to stock up on high-quality, well-made, tailored clothes, discreet, tasteful, the kind that never went out of style. Some things were just classic.

REHEARSALS

I liked the high school's theater. Walls painted black, black curtains, no proscenium. I could sit up close, watch Greg as he led the orchestra in the pit, change seats whenever I wanted. The black walls worked really well for a play like *The Good Woman of Szechuan.* The drama teacher Paul did a Brecht play at least once a year, wanted the kids to experience politically and philosophically significant works. Musicals were harder to find. *West Side Story, The Fantasticks* were naturals for these kids, but shows like *Oklahoma!* or *Carousel* had been done to death, and besides, they were tear-jerkers, crowd-pleasers.

The back of Greg's neck. His hands, lifting to the violins, shifting over to the cellos. He'd bought a tux for the performances. This fall they were doing *Gypsy.* Little Nora Kaplan, a junior, her lilting mezzo, her reluctant strut down the ramp specially built to jut out into the house. Her precise and ladylike strip. Let me entertain you. Long black gloves, unbuttoning, inching down from Nora's slender upper arms, elbows, wrists, one finger at a time. A clarinet entering before the flutes. Paul's yells to everybody they'd have to redo the scene. Greg on his high stool, leaning over to the second violinist as they chuckled over something I couldn't hear. I'd grade papers, get some work done, and between scenes, a couple of the kids would keep me company, offer a sip of Pepsi.

WHAT YOU GOT

The way they brushed my seat when I walked down the hall for a drink of water between classes. The little folds of the skirt, the red one, knit, so it kind of clung and then swept around me when I walked. I knew how I looked. Once one of the big black girls hollered at me as I was coming back from lunch, striding out between the cafeteria and my building, hollered out so anybody could hear, *Why you wear your skirts so short, you already got a man.* So loud, it rang and rang even after the bell.

Seven classes a day. Two remedial. A hundred and sixty-three students. Four preparations, one of them Poetry of Pop Music. At home the guy who lived downstairs slammed open the door, clomped across the wood floor in his nailed boots at three a.m. before he'd play his Chinese funeral horn.

I was learning to serve in tennis, one of the P.E. teachers was helping. I'd bought a white tennis dress, its own panties sewn in. I could lift up, bend down as far as I needed, wherever the next ball came. When I got home, my husband was inside the headphones. Sometimes he came out to refill his glass, and sometimes he stayed inside for a long time.

SHOP TALK

We were having a drink at Harry's Bar across the street. Julie had been saying come on, how about Friday? After the halls and classrooms, the cafeteria, Harry's was like being inside an underwater cave. We were talking, whispering really, about the boys' P.E. teachers. Daniel was a sweetie, the football coach. Espinosa was married, with kids. Nice wife.

The tallest one? Ty? He means business. Julie's voice dropped further. I wouldn't encourage him unless—you mean business too. Our eyes held for a second. So many changes, we went on to say. So exciting with the new principal from Oakland, planning the alternative schools. So good to be starting with the mentally gifted, such great kids. Had to make sure we got the best faculty for them, that team had to be really strong. Another drink, Johnny Walker on the rocks, just a little water. Really, you know, I like what comes before the—actual real sex part best, do you? Julie tilted her head.

I guess I do too, I said, still not sure what to do with the little plastic straw they gave you. Finally I put it on the napkin that said *Harry's, A Berkeley Tradition.* Should I not talk to him at all?

That's up to you, Julie said. But be sure you know what you want. I fiddled with the peanuts, finally picked one out of the dish, sucked off the salt before I chewed, and asked Julie: What will happen to the teachers who don't want the alternative schools, don't want to team teach, even with all the federal money? Julie brought the rim of her glass close to her mouth and held it. She smiled, a big one. The teachers who get in our way? We'll run right over them.

FRIDAY NIGHT WITH THE ENGLISH TEACHERS

Hilda had gone to check on the lentils. Phil sat in a half lotus on the wood floor. The first step, he said, was to stop talking so much. Listen to the silence. Even his sixth-period kids were mellowing, meditating ten minutes at least now in class. He'd moved out the desks. The kids had brought in old pillows and Hilda was sewing covers. Sitting at a desk was not a natural act. Besides, he'd all but quit giving writing assignments. They wasted resources, and he knew their grades anyway. English was not limited to the word. You had to stop talking to open the inner silences, like right this minute, he said, we should all stop talking, open ourselves. I started to close my eyes. But just then Hilda swung through the kitchen door and asked Phil if it was okay, sorry to interrupt, but could she put dinner on.

SUNDAY MORNING, GO FOR A DRIVE

Up the coast. Or down. Bring the binoculars. Get out of town. Breathe. Always hungry before we got where we were going, Stinson Beach, Bolinas, Point Reyes. Greg would want a big meal—two cheeseburgers, double order of fries, a full pitcher of Bud. I'd want a tuna sandwich, banana, orange juice. No matter how I'd try to focus the binos, no matter what rock I scrambled up on, I could never spot the bird I wanted to see up close. Feathers confused among branches and twigs. The wind off the water roughing my hair. And Greg's voice, breath smelling of tannic acid, saying hurry it up, time to go.

EXERCISE

All the lights coming on, evening. A kitchen window, someone moving across the room. The trees darkening. The next house, kids around a table, a man pulling out a chair. I was jogging, trying to avoid the swollen places, cracked, in the squares of the sidewalk. Hills so steep up and down, my shins got a workout for a while and then my calves.

Greg had been talking about sod houses. Insulating with straw, you could even build partly underground. They did that in the Midwest. He'd begun ordering things from *The Whole Earth Catalog.* Maybe he'd make his own beer. On one page there was a picture of plaster molds made from four penises of different sizes and shapes lined up in a row. One was Jimi Hendrix's. They were numbered and named except for one that said, "A Friend."

Three kids burst out from the bright opening of a front door, branches framing it. A porch light snapped on. Then four dark houses in a row. Then the gap, view of the flats, all the little lights, the red and white moving ones that were cars, and then the wide black opening of the water, the bay. But some of the places on land weren't lighted, and in the middle of the bay were buoys with beams flashing. Hard to tell where the ground ended.

AFTER SCHOOL

The way the halls loosened, softened. You couldn't call what the coaches did walking. Even the metal lockers seemed to move. Those jogging suits with zippers down their chests and straight up the sides of their calves. Colors of candy, lollipops, suckers, lime, cherry, orange. Didn't make a sound with their feet, the way they walked as if they were running but in slow motion, all the parts of their bodies moving together. Mmmm. You new here? Where you from? What do you teach? Voices like insides of M&M's. Halls cleared of kids, they moved through like syrup through a snow cone.

Seven periods of trying to keep ninth-graders from shrieking, tearing at each other. Somebody thrown into a locker, Pepsi and sudden ice over the floor, slippery. All day I'd picked up trash, books, ragged spiral papers.

The tallest coach would hang back from the others, stand at my door, basketball nestled in the crook of his arm, talk direct as a shot clean through the net. When the Home Ec teacher had a party where the air hung thick and milky from the great dope somebody'd gotten out of Nam, I went ahead and close-danced in the corner to Roberta Flack until four. Seven periods a day, five days a week, telling the kids to calm down, sit still, keep their hands to themselves, and I didn't move his hand away when his fingers found my nipple and began to pull as if it were soft, sweet taffy.

STITCHERY

In one package you got the yarn, cloth for the pillow cover, and directions with a picture—a knight and his spear on a white horse clip-clopping along a green road lined with pink daisies toward a gray castle. I piled the papers that needed grading on the dining room table. French knots for the horse's eye and the flowers. Chain stitch for the leaves. I bought a half yard of linen, a book on American embroidery, made a sampler of stitches: stem, feather, star, cross, herringbone, running, and New England laid. Fewer weeks when the table was cleared. I began to work a remnant of burlap with thick wool. Stretched uneven petals zigzag across the weave. I'd been having the students do free-writing. Anything they wanted to say, the way they'd talk to a friend. Centers of flowers like eggs, spirals, like cocoons, leaves like wings. The flowers exploded in colors that shouldn't have mixed. Harder and harder to spot spelling errors, comma faults. The strands hurled across to each other. I stopped embroidering. Tired of prickings, the little stabs.

WORLD'S FINEST

I helped him carry in the cartons to the front hall closet. Just selling chocolate, Greg's orchestra kids could raise enough for their concert tour. I told him I'd find another place for the sheets and towels. He tossed the pillowcases on the hall floor before he lifted in the cartons. Couldn't keep them at the high school, they'd have been ripped off. They filled the space to the ceiling. White slick paper over silver foil, the high school's name on the outside, semisweet. He asked if I could go around the neighborhood when I came home from the ninth-grade campus and sell a few bars to the neighbors. He wouldn't have time, not with the extra rehearsals for the music festival coming up, not to mention his workshops out of town. I said I'd try. All that sweetness, wrapped up, inside.

SLOW DANCING

Ty didn't move much. At least his feet. But his legs, long thighs. And his cheek and mouth against my ear. His fingers holding mine to his chest. And that unmistakable cylinder rising against my belly. All for you, he whispered. Come to my place. Come tomorrow. He didn't bother stopping between songs. Most everybody gone when (and I couldn't believe I was doing this) I took my hand from his shoulder and reached down. For you, he said, again, so quiet. On the way home, fog billowed across the road, the white stripes, the dividing line.

DESSERT

A planning meeting at seven, I told Greg. I'd have to leave right after the dishes. No need to rush through dinner. After six years we were down to the basics, meat and a vegetable, maybe a salad. But no soup. Or pie.

I'd pressed the bell for the third time when Ty strolled up from the sidewalk. You like wine? I got us cream sherry. The man at the store said it'll be sweet. He keyed me in. The light from a single lamp. Two clear glasses.

We barely touched them. But it was sweet. And easy. Easy as the time when I was a little girl and my mother's friend said, go ahead, honey, it's just custard—milk, eggs, cream, they're all good for you.

Ten thirty by the time he turned the light back on. I said I'd come back, after school, Wednesday. He'd have a little snack for us, some cookies, or maybe ice cream. If I didn't mind eating on the couch. He didn't have a kitchen table.

REMEDIAL READING

The smallest classroom in the ninth-grade school. Yellow walls, and the ceiling seemed too high. Boxes lined up in bright colors on the tables, each a different level. This class for retards? This a toony class? The kids swaggered and straggled through the door, unwilling. To be seen here. Laminated cards, one at a time. Second-, third-grade skills for fourteen-year-olds. Mostly boys. I'd been assigned to help the reading teacher, her thick gray hair bunched and slipping along with hairpins and combs. Ruth organized field trips, took her own beat-up station wagon. Once she drove us up the coast to the great blue herons' nesting grounds. We walked up and up until we could look straight down into the tops of the big trees. She showed us how to spot the saucers of nests resting in the branches.

I never got the kids to move beyond a level or two. Nobody stayed on task. Once I was pronouncing vowels with Lester Sims, light-skinned, freckled, a skinny little dude. *O: okra, Oakland, Coke. And o: butter, supper, dove.* His eyes shone. He was standing beside me. Doves, he said. We can talk about birds? Sure, I said, and told him about the finches I was raising at home in as big a cage as I could afford. Man, why didn't you say you wanted us to talk about birds? And he was out the door. Before the bell rang for the next class he was back. I was putting cards away in their boxes, red tipped ones in the red box, brown in brown, folding the lids closed. You like pigeons? he grinned. I do, I do, I said. He unzipped his jacket. I don't know how many wings flapped out from him, ruffled my hair and fluttered all through that yellow room, a sound only feathers can make, as Lester told me every one of their names.

INTEGRATION

Almost lost in his mouth. He'd told me I didn't know how to kiss, I was trying too hard, and showed me, so our mouths ripened to plush opening peonies, ruffling, even a bit messy at the edges. More than a mother's mouth, nipple, these kisses. Shape to shape, unforming and reshaping, play of inner cheek and tongue. My consonants: so crisp, he said. Every one of my syllables clear, enunciated. But this now was a time for vowels, color, the fibrous textures of slow diphthongs, blurred edges letting *i*s blend into *u*s, long *e*s open into *ah, o, oh, oh, oh.*

ON THE BAY

It was the art teacher Norm who had the doctor friend who was leasing the twenty-seven-foot sailboat we took out onto the bay that Saturday before Margie the history teacher's party and we smoked dope all day on the water. There for a while we drifted out beyond the Golden Gate into the open sea before we knew what we were doing so it took about three hours just to get back under the bridge, everybody laughing except the one guy who'd had the six sailing lessons so he knew what was maybe about to happen. Norm was getting it on with Nini on the foam mattress under the prow and everybody else was sopping from the spray that was everywhere over us. That whole day no fog at all, even after we docked back at the Marina and stopped at the Safeway to pick up some Cribari red for the party where Margie had put out candles on the tables, all sizes and shapes burning down puddles of different colors of hot wax around their flames like the lights of the city we'd just spent the whole day sailing past, turned on.

HAIR

Not yet thirty and he was already bald but just on top. So his caramel-colored head rose over him, soft and glistening. But plenty of hair around the rest of his head, nappy, close. Mine was short, a pixie cut. Not even a few fringes drifting below my collar, or across my pierced ears. We'd done it in the kitchen, an ice cube behind each ear lobe. And my sister was right, it didn't hurt. So far I hadn't decided what kind of earrings to buy, so I stayed with the small gold studs, 24 karat.

The first time I'd gone to his second floor apartment—he'd been asking me for months—he said it was like a cherry. I hadn't known I could come on my own, before he did. He kept going and going, over me, he was staring out the window above the bed—later he explained he had to keep his mind off it or he'd finish too fast—and asked me, said, you haven't come yet, go ahead. When he turned on the light there were little black coils of hair all over the sheets. It wasn't long after that I decided to let mine grow, see what it did by itself.

SWORD

When I started weaving, Ruth gave me one. Funny to call it a sword. Hand-rubbed, dark grain of the wood smooth as a camellia leaf. So beautiful I could just hold it. But I learned how to separate the warp threads with the silky tip—lifting one thread up, keeping the next one down, up, down, again and again, all across the vertical strands. To turn the sword so it held the top threads out from the rest, make space to let the weft threads through. It worked as a comb, or beater, too, another funny word for working with so many kinds of softness, pushing the thread you've pulled across the loom's width down into the forming cloth. Strange how the sword parted the threads away from each other, lifted them and then pressed them down, firm, together. Soft thuds on wool on wool, and after a while, regular as your heartbeat.

FREED UP

He said I had nice ones, even though I'd always thought they were so little, but why did I bind them up? One day I left my bra in the drawer. All day could feel the feel of them. Couldn't forget they were there. Felt good just leaning down to throw a wad of paper in the trash. And standing up, nipples like third and fourth eyes, looking straight out at whoever was coming toward me in the long hall. Looking clear inside. Into secrets, hiding places. Until they were out for good, out of the muffled fiber-filled shells, elastic tightenings, hard-wire frames. Like bare green leaves unfolding in April, swelling as they opened. Leisurely, soft, brushing into a hand.

STICK SHIFT

One of the counselors offered to teach me. Disaster to let my husband coach me on anything having to do with driving. If I could shift for myself, I'd have more control. After a while I practiced alone in a parking lot. Neutral, first, second. The timing with the clutch. And then, slowly, on the side streets off Marin. I kept away from the hills. But no matter how gradually I raised my left foot, the car always died at a stop sign. The honking behind me. I'd get so nervous I'd just stall and stall. When after a few weeks I'd managed okay on San Pedro, Shattuck, and even down University, I decided to try the freeway. At the entrance onto the Nimitz I could see across into the wetlands of the bay, a great blue heron along with the usual gulls. A car right behind me. Riding me, flashing its lights. Refused to pass. I let the clutch out, shifted, floored it, and eased over to the far left lane.

EGGPLANT

I'd never heard of it. A plant like an egg? Hilda's casserole at Ellie's party, mixed up with tomatoes and onions and olives. The eggplant didn't have much color, but it tasted good. Ellie said the French called it *aubergine.* A pretty word, sounded like jewelry, something shiny, an expensive watch—Longines. I couldn't find any at the Coop. Finally I asked the guy spraying radishes. Sure, right here, he said, and pointed to a pile of purple globes next to the carrots. But how could those pale cubes in Hilda's dish come from one of these? Oh yeah, he said, they're good, these are the kind called Black Beauty, grow right here in California. He helped me choose a firm one with no bruises. It shimmered in my grocery cart, dark as midnight, purple as a royal orb. He said he couldn't tell me how to cook it, but he'd heard that in Turkey, there were over a thousand recipes. I didn't know even one.

TEACHERS' LOUNGE

Ken always sat in the pink high-backed chair. He'd started selling real estate on the side, just residential, he didn't want to get into apartment buildings, not with all the riffraff moving in these days. The whole place had changed so much he felt he was living on Mars. The trash on the streets now, and he meant human. Why the hair. He wanted me to know, because, he said, he could tell I was a nice person, not one of these wandering bums the school district was hiring, and he wanted me to understand this city had been the Athens of the West until the hippies started running it. Even just a couple of years ago the kids had manners. He thumped his pipe into the ashtray already filled with butts, cellophane strips from cigarette packs, paper clips and razor blades for correcting dittos.

I should have been grading papers. Or preparing. Compound sentences. Conjunctions. And, but, or. I was pouring water over a two-day-old tea bag when Ardis Baine the Latin teacher walked in, black eyes snapping, and slid her ditto master into the machine. Ardis had three degrees from Howard University. She glanced into my cup. What on earth are you drinking, honey, she said. After she left with the fresh damp stack of purplish paper in her hands, the room turned silent. My tea tasted like polluted water. The next day I brought in a jar of instant coffee. Made it strong and drank it black. That was before I stopped coming to the lounge at all, unless I had to use the machine to run something off.

SLIPPING IN

The first time I'd left Ty's place late, really late, the streets black-wet, quiet. Straight through a red light at Shattuck. Had to have my phrasing down pat, rehearsed—the meeting ran over, I couldn't leave, too racially sensitive, and Julie talked me into going out after. Even as I unlocked the front door I heard the snoring. Shoes and socks, tapes and LP's, the headphones, orchestra scores over the living room rug, the empty green gallon jug on its side. Dishes on the kitchen counters, the stove. Greg still dressed lying in bed, belt unbuckled, pants unzipped, wine glass on the floor. An orchestra, I told him the next morning, of snores—triple forte. But he only wanted to talk about the new score. After last night he was ready to put it into rehearsal. He showed me the conducting pattern he'd worked out, his arms driving tracks through the air. I was trying to get dressed, had to leave for school in ten minutes. Oh, he said, I forgot, how was your meeting? Okay, I said, okay, buttoning my blouse. Good, he said, but tonight I want to take you measure by measure through the whole score. Show you where the oboe slips in, before the violins take over from the cellos and bassoons. How the crescendos begin to build.

FLAVOR

Ty had to explain what it meant when he'd tell me, *I got a nose job behind you.* They said it back in Georgia—you couldn't stop thinking about somebody, you followed them around, you'd fallen for them, you were hooked. And he couldn't believe it, what with all that new pussy at school, all the new teachers. The Swedish one with the accent, her thick white-blond hair piled up on top of her head, stiff white blouses and high-neck collars, lace, maybe, but underneath, those great big soft boobs. And the German one—kind of like Marilyn Monroe but fatter, nice sloppy behind, and laughing, real friendly. And he still liked to check out the little sister from Kansas, the math teacher Roberta Gibson, those legs—sweet as cinnamon, those huge black eyes, close little natural.

Last year after school he'd always be going over to Ortman's for a double scoop, maybe triple. They kept getting in more and more new flavors, some of them better than Chocolate Mint Chip. Maple Swirl was a good one. Chocolate Marshmallow. And the kind they got in last June just before school was out, Coconut Almond Peach.

But this was different, he said. He was rubbing his nose into my neck. He'd brought the donuts into bed the way he did now when I stayed all night if Greg was out of town. Sunday morning, he'd get two of each: jelly, chocolate, and plain glazed. He was playing my nipples between his fingers, pulling them. Only woman who could take all of him, he said. And the way we talked. About anything, anytime, nighttime, daytime, like straight up noon when he'd bring his sandwich into my classroom and tell me about the morning, about still trying to teach that math genius kid named Gerald how to do setups, how to learn to cut through the others and aim at that one place where you really wanted it, and score.

HALF AND HALF

I'd eaten less and less, no carbohydrates, mainly protein, hard-boiled eggs. At first I thought the school I'd been assigned to was ninety percent black. Naturals swirled black halos around me till even at home at night I thought I would disappear. By Halloween I knew it was more like half and half. That was around the time I heard the whispering outside my classroom door after everyone else had gone home, felt afraid as I had during the riots in South Side Chicago. The whisperings grew louder, what they would do to me. I stood up from my desk and walked right past them and down the hall to the principal's office before I started to cry.

All this was before Ty was there. Nobody knew, and we made sure we kept it that way, but I could think about him all day and at night, about the way his darkness slid right into me, how he filled me with himself until I felt I'd split open.

One Saturday night when I didn't go home, I stared for a long time at his one poster hanging on the wall. A little black boy dressed in white and sitting in a white chair in a room with white walls, white ceiling, and a white floor. Sometime in the night I started to shiver, cold without a nightgown. I was half asleep when he went to the closet, pulled down a brown wool blanket. From his mother, he said, when he left Georgia to play for Colorado. And he'd needed all the warm blankets he could get in Boulder, those high white mountains. He made sure I was covered up before he lay down again next to me. Sweet smell of his hair. In the morning I didn't want to leave. He brought the donuts into bed, the kind with the soft cream filling. That was when he told me where the scars on his shoulders came from. If you ever have a son, he said, don't let him play football. You can get torn up, bad, before your time.

CLAY

Some lunch hours Karen sat on top of my desk in her Levi's and tie-dye, swinging her legs while she bit into a ripe avocado. Solid vitamins, she told me as she swallowed. I'd be eating a ham sandwich. Salt, she said, too much. Meat. Her father taught philosophy at Cal, her mother did clay. When we had Arts Day for the Mentally Gifted, Karen brought two buckets. I got my hands down in it. Karen said, Don't waste your time, whatever you make, there's no place we can dry it, there's no kiln. I mushed in and down till my hands were wet to the bone, and cold. Why don't you ever go up to the Avenue and march with us? Karen would ask. The sixth-period remedial kids were finally coming to school, most days. Hated hippies, wouldn't listen to any white woman who wasn't tidy-looking. I kept squeezing the clay, arms brown to the elbow, a second skin, thickening. I wasn't thinking of what could be made with the stuff.

MACRAMÉ

I never got into it. Too many knots. Rope or string, mostly white, or that pale yellowy color, twisted in on itself, maybe a few beads. All that work just to hold a house plant off the floor. I was weaving. Different yarns. Crinkly silk, like hair from an unraveled braid. Silver. A fat wool, furry, the shade of lichen under a pine. And blue, a deep teal, turquoise, the way you remember an inland high sky in winter. Purple, fuchsia, orange, sunsets. Dawn. Sometimes I thought of the students I liked while I worked. Frances, her low voice, her cello. Jennifer's little giggles. Charles, his wide smile, giant Afro. Andrew, trying to get me to read *Dune*. The warp strands sturdy, brown. Backstrap loom tied to the window latch. I pushed the weft threads down, a soft thud. Over and under. One color showing more now, another the next time. I gathered eucalyptus bells that fell under the tall trees in the hills. Clean-smelling, a good medicine. I liked working the dark seeds into the pattern. I wanted to make something big, fill a space, soften a wall.

"HEY, MR. TAMBOURINE MAN"

The gravel of Dylan's voice rising from the floor below, *Play a song for me.* Cold morning, the fog. I didn't want to grade papers. Didn't want to read. At least I had Ellie's party to look forward to that night. I'd wear the new striped dress I'd bought last weekend at Julie's parents' store, and the big dangling metal earrings from the Renaissance Fair. Greg wasn't going—didn't like Ellie's parties. The record downstairs wasn't all that loud, but I was tired of Dylan's whine. Sometimes I wished he'd just open up the back of his throat. There it was, though, my favorite part, *Dance beneath the diamond sky with one hand waving free.* I hadn't slept well, not much the last week or so. Somebody in the park had been playing a flute all night. Those pure high sounds piercing the air, over and over. Clear breath. Like a wide-open moon swimming through fog, full, into focus.

TENNIS

Ty didn't learn to play in Georgia. Not till he got to Colorado, the second year of his scholarship. One of the rich white girls took him out on the court. Little balls the color of vanilla ice cream, the new ones fuzzy as those soft bears the sorority girls kept on their day beds. Sound of the strings against the ball—after the first whack, one long vibration. Kind of like a Charlie Parker riff, he was saying. Or a cool trumpet. Miles, Miles Davis. Your turn, my turn, now you take it. Not like football, everybody coming at you. And those old white men pawing you at the half, give it to them boy, keep it up, doing great. Pawing you. All that dust, smoke, hollering. A tennis court's clean. Grass, clay, even cement, they're clean. You got your side to yourself. Doubles, only you and your partner. You got room to pull way up and way back to serve. That little ball just moves on out from your racquet like a guitar singing a song—you hear this one? Now sing it back to me.

MAKING A BED

He liked the way I did it, asked me to show him. Not that he hadn't been doing fine himself. But my corners stayed. Think of geometry, I said. A sheet's just a big square, all the threads are straight lines intersecting at right angles, so start with them lined up on the mattress. Even. Flat. My hands slid across the surface of the bed. I slowed, leaned down to make the triangular fold at the corner. Ty bent down too, and the rest of the clean sheets, pillow cases, stayed on the chair, along with the blanket, the spread, and the crocheted afghan with orange nubs rising up like little buds, or stars—the browns and tans, blues and whites all curled into each other.

ALARM

I never got used to it. No warning, and it wouldn't let up, not like a shout, or a car backfiring, or gunshot. The tide of teachers and kids to the double glass doors, the gray light at the end of the locker-lined hall. Not every day, more like eight, ten times a month, some weeks worse than others. The questions. Fire drill? Another bomb? A real fire? Everybody trying to find their friends in the crowd of naturals, the typing teacher's tidy curls, Shirley Jensen's fly-away pony tail, Phil Friedman's brown waves to his shoulders, and the white girls' hair floating around them like scarves. Buffalo sandals, boots, Adidas, moccasins, clogs. At the doors, no way at first to move through.

As soon as I could I'd spot Ty. On the other side of the cement courtyard, he'd be cradling a basketball and joking with the boys around him. I knew exactly what he'd be saying: stay cool now my man, stay cool. And he'd catch my eye, hold it so I'd stay calm, be able to talk to the kids around me, distract them. It could take an hour. The speculations. His eyes touched me every once in a while, but not so anybody'd notice. At opposite ends of the grounds behind the ninth-grade school, we stood so we never lost sight of each other, until the all-clear bell, when we crowded back into our separate buildings, and carried on.

GRANOLA

Ruth brought some in a cellophane bag. All natural, she said, good things in it. I needed to be fattened up. She knew I'd been drinking too much coffee since I'd bought the Melita pot with the filter. This stuff was brand new at the Coop. Raisins, dates, oats, almonds, I could snack on it, didn't even need milk, although that's what it was of course, cereal. I needed to feed myself better. Not to hurt my feelings, but did I know some of those bad-mannered kids called me Twiggy? She had to go now, get back to her husband who'd be wanting his supper, and then she had worksheets to grade tonight. A shame my husband was so busy, gone so much. I should come to dinner sometime. The fringe of her shawl brushed the wall by the front door. Her necklaces were made of wooden beads and seed pods. Every summer she went to Oaxaca. They wove every color you could imagine into their cloth, Ruth said. The new cereal wasn't like Cheerios. The closer I looked, the more ingredients I could see, even sesame seeds, tiny little ovals of white.

ADVANCED TECHNIQUES

Different ways of wrapping the warp. You could pull a few threads together, tie them, make little bundles. At our new alternative school teachers' meetings at lunch time, the twelve of us were dividing into groups. First into twos. After we'd decided what bird each of us wanted to be, we joined another pair. Then we all four drew our birds, showed them, and next we'd think of what character in a novel we were. Weaving I did alone, at home. I liked the bundles, bringing the threads so close they almost seemed like one. At lunch Fred said I always made him think of Catherine in *Wuthering Heights.* How she poured tea in the drawing room but her real self was racing the moors, calling for Heathcliff. I hadn't read it since high school. We didn't use that novel, even with the gifted students. I finished the tapestry with the bundles. Got an idea for the next one. The entire warp pulled into clusters, each one wrapped so long, so close, the entire fabric would open.

LUMINOUS

Luminous was the word he used. Repeated it. Yeah, he said, that's it, that's what you are. Luminousness. Each syllable a slow mouthful. Luminescence. His tongue and lips made full contact with every consonant, as if he were walking deliberately through a dark, vacant room, turning on all the lamps. But I never told him how even before he opened the door to my classroom, I would know. A quiet grew behind the clanging of lockers, the hollered motherfuckers. A soft silence that had nothing to do with speechlessness. The volume just turned itself down. Even in the middle of the hall's screeching at second lunch (*where you think you be walking to, honky bitch*) he brought with him a thick-carpeted room of sleek and steady upholstery, padded back and arms of a good chair. No fear of a lamp's being toppled, or the cord yanked.

NOTE CARDS

Stacks of them all across the bed. Where a fold of the blanket made a little hill, they slipped like shallow steps dropping down a slope. White with faint blue lines, 3 × 5. Ty's penciled writing. A big paper coming up for his graduate class, "Motor Skills in the Secondary Schools." One whole pile of cards on approaching the serve. Most people didn't understand—a good serve begins a long time before the racket and ball ever meet. The backswing. Preparation. You have to let the racket drop completely down your back before you bring it up over yourself and forward. Supposed to write it like a chapter in a textbook for teachers. Make it easy to understand. Hey, here's a good quote in this book, see, this lady, she teaches at UCLA, she's talking about building confidence in kids, says to divide all the skills into little parts. You let the kids get real good at one thing before you show them how to move on to the next. Yeah. I think I know what to do. The stance. The grip. See how you helped me already. His head turned to mine, that sideways smile. Let's get this mess off the bed.

SWEET

You know those cups you had growing up, he said, those paper cups with the wooden spoon that was sort of rough on your tongue. Half vanilla, other half orange sherbert. The Home Ec teacher had just told him about vanilla ice cream, how the taste of it came from a skinny brown bean. Funny, he said, you never thought about something like that, where the taste came from. And funny how I made him think of that kind of ice cream. All sweaty and out of breath from running bases as a kid, and some nice church ladies off to the side of home plate handing them out to everybody on the team. Take your time dipping into that stuff, nice and cold—good in your mouth. Some kids ate all of one kind first, saved the vanilla or the orange for last. Not him. He took some of each, every mouthful. Orange and white. When he pulled off the lid there they'd be, shaped kind of like those black and white designs they sold in the hippie stores, those Chinese things, black dot in the white part, white dot in the black. Sometimes when he'd peel an orange, the white fibers stuck to the fruit. He'd eat them too, had heard those stringy things were good for you. And he sure did love that new nightgown of mine, color of peaches, a little bit of lace, just like cream.

COURT

He liked our walks in the hills, especially afterward, when we'd dressed again, brushed the leaves and dirt off our clothes. At first he hadn't understood what my sport was, most people had at least one, volleyball, softball, tennis. Sometimes he'd lead, sometimes I would. Once when we drove down the coast we climbed up over the road and up an embankment, slipping together in the mud, laughing, holding on to each other. Little pebbles, bits of roots. That night in the motel I said look, and he did. In the mirrors on the sliding closet doors like the two halves of a tennis court, net down, there we were. Stretched out across the whole length, his legs around my light ones, my arms over his back. Layers of us. Little movements. My hair, his neck. Leaves brushing. Murmurs, currents. When we'd climbed to the top of the embankment, we had to get our breath. The whole Pacific spread out.

SAX

Cool slow riff, under, over, around and around one central note that took a long time to find. The sheets ruffled across the bed and down, spread like a fan, a loose shawl. Wet spot dry now. Sprawled pages of the paper. Fog breezing into the window over the bed. His arms. Warm. As if I were wrapped in my own little girlhood, cradled for Vespers in my granddad's boat, oars shipped, stilled in the shallows of the evening lake as the singing began on shore, *carry me home, coming for to carry me.* All the notes of those voices. Ripples of the water, colors of pearl in the darkening, boat rocking. The wide water. Then back across, oars dripping, across the lake to sleep, in the long quiet of the night. Until waked by a cry coming from the center of silence, loon call, tremolo rising across the brush-tops of the pines in the blackness. Joined, by another, and another, by another.

CROSS WEAVE

Taffeta, for example. Our instructor Liz was explaining at the Wednesday night adult extension class. Warp and woof threads of two different colors. Plain weave, equally spaced. Both sides of the fabric identical. Usually contrasting colors, say for instance, burgundy, navy blue. From one direction you'd see more of one color. Turn a little, you saw more of the other. And the moment the cloth moved, whether gathered, folded, swinging out from you if you wore it—or even just rumpled, the colors shifted. Liz handed out samples. I shook mine, gently, watched it shimmer. The cloth turned fluid. Waves of shades, changing. It was a green, a blue green, iridescent. Mesmerizing, like the ocean. For a moment I could float in it, almost dive right in, and at the same time, never leave the air.

COUPLE

I didn't know why he said he'd never get married. He just said never. I believed him. One weekend we drove up to Marin. Poked into shops, and I bought a candle. Everybody strolling, families, couples, mostly white. First time we'd done anything right out in public. But nobody stared.

I couldn't imagine not being married to somebody. The every-morningness. The regular breathing beside you through the night. The shoes lined up, left beside right, heels, flats, tennies, boots, wing tips, sandals. Pairs. The same cups filled, sipped from, washed, put away with the chips facing the back of the cupboard.

Ty licked his double scoop till the ice cream lay flat in the cone, and then dug in with his teeth. I nibbled mine around the edges. He'd finished his cone, a little bit of his tongue slid over his upper lip. Good, he said again. I was going to spend the night. He'd picked up eggs and English muffins, didn't I like those, and the kind of coffee I drank now. Sunday morning, Greg away on a concert tour, I could stay as long as I liked.

CHOPSTICKS

We walked for blocks before we decided where to go inside to eat. Past plucked chickens and ducks, cucumbers, postcards, pale jade. Neither of us knew quite what to order. But we knew to ask for chopsticks. More fun that way, without the metallic scrape of the fork, the hard grate of a knife. Two slim prongs. Light wood. Each moving toward the other, each coming from another direction to grasp the same kernel, pod, grain, cube, sliver of carrot, ginger. We'd never been here before. Never to Chinatown together, even to San Francisco. Summertime. We had our sweaters with us. Took a long time to finish. I've had better, he said, but he ate everything I didn't have room for. Before we got back onto the Bay Bridge, we stopped for ice cream. I asked for lemon custard and coconut almond. His was rocky road and chocolate mint chip. We each licked and nibbled at our own cones, and then held them out so the other could taste, held them steadily, carefully, so none of the sweetness would topple over, fall.

WARM-UP SUITS

He couldn't wait to show me. Now that Joanie his old girl friend had quit teaching in the Mission and was flying for American, she could bring them back from Frankfurt, Munich, places like that. New kind of knit material. Soft, stretchy, and not just white. Colors. Blue, and gold, and red, bright red like those flowers the stores put out at Christmastime. All the coaches wanted one. He was keeping the black and tan for himself. Only had to sell two more and he'd break even. After that, pure profit.

He didn't know why his main man Arthur Ashe only wore those boring old Munsingwear waffle knit white shirts with the little black penguin. Those wings sort of half down and half up like he was standing still all polite while somebody's saying, *little bird, no way you can fly.* Like he wouldn't know how to hold a racquet if somebody handed him a brand new stainless steel Wilson. Like still hanging on to that old wood. Those little penguins—their days are past. Pretty soon there'll only be color, both sides of the net.

BREATH

Ellie was telling me over our tuna sandwiches in the teachers' cafeteria how to make a soufflé. The secret was in the egg whites, you had to whip as much air into them as you could. The word *soufflé* was like the French word for breath: *souffle.* I'd never made a soufflé, but *souffle* sounded like "poof," a little bit of breath, a soft blow on a fluffy dandelion seed head, all the tiny arrows flying off. Like picking petals from a daisy. *He loves me, he loves me not.* Ellie began describing her date for Friday night. He had nice hands and eyes, she whispered, and she wanted to touch him. They'd gone to a couple of movies, that was all so far. School had started again. I was tired of talking. Was picturing a soufflé rising in the oven. Wondered how you'd serve it onto your plate so it wouldn't collapse.

AUDIO VISUAL

One of the boys would help if the film broke. Some of them even knew how to fix the oldest projector, the one that sputtered and cluttered and moaned to a stop in the middle of the story. Like when Ulysses had himself bound up, so he could sail past the sirens, or when he was barely making it through between Scylla and Charybdis. A couple of the girls would stay and talk over their sandwiches at lunchtime about Mr. Taylor who always asked for help in the auditorium's projection booth whenever they showed movies for all the history classes at once. He'd accidentally brush against them in the dark, then take his time feeling them up. They laughed about it. Everybody thought he was pretty cute. The administrators had their eye on him to get his credential, be a principal in a year or two. Movie days were a relief. The sound drowned out the traffic on University Avenue, and even late in the afternoon, with the blinds down the pimps didn't bother to hassle their girls through the windows, hollering in, *Inetta, you get your black ass out on this street, Yvonne, you hear me girl.* Even with the volume turned up high, the sound track distorted, everything seemed just that much quieter.

CLASSICAL

Seventh period Track 3, the unit on myth. I started with Zeus, the big daddy, king of the gods. He liked to buzz on down to earth and dress up like a swan or a white bull, and kind of get involved, play around on earth. Like with Io, I said, or Leda, and every time, his wife Queen Hera got angry at those girls and sometimes even their children had to pay. I'd never seen them so wide awake after lunch. Mouths stopped sucking on Jujubes, stopped mid-chew. They just listened. Nobody fidgeted, scuffed the floor. I know what you talking about, hollered out Loretta. I gotta uncle just like him, got his hands busy over everybody, first my sister, then this Thanksgiving he mess with me. And my auntie, she don't do nothing. But she be mad. Christmas Day, she don't give me one present. And that old man, he won't show his face.

2001

The way the dark rectangle shot up—slid—graphite slick, towering. Opaque. The Track 1 boys told me to read the book. Just one thing different, and everything changed. After the first time two of the pimps climbed through my windows to get their girls working the street by four o'clock, I never walked through my classroom door in the morning the same. Candy wrappers, dandelions, on the grass outside. And in the spring, the way the tanks snaked along University Avenue right outside my windows—all day a metal river, sludge flowing up the street my class looked out on—when Reagan called in the National Guard. Only the white students cared about People's Park. I hadn't had time to go up there much. But after Reagan declared the city an occupied zone, I knew the helicopters. Just outside on Saturday hanging clothes on the line, their whir and clatter, sudden, right overhead, giant insects. The cockpits like eyes of huge flies. I'd be pruning roses, and there they'd be. Swooped right down, cruised, hovered. You could see the guys' faces, sun glasses, looking.

THE GRADUATE

Jeff would ring our door bell anytime, even at midnight. There he'd be on the front step, springing up and down on his legs, jerky, like a battery-operated toy not yet run down. First chair horn in the high school jazz band, he'd helped Greg out in the orchestra till he graduated. In the neighborhood, he'd say. Gotta take a leak. Wouldn't even shut the bathroom door. Strip off his T-shirt, soap his pits. We wouldn't always hear his bike roaring up the street. He'd park on the lawn. His old man was on his case all the time and he wasn't even dealing any more. We'd watch TV, Greg in the threadbare armchair, gallon of red half empty on the floor. Jeff would plop down on the paisley-covered mattress we used for a couch, sprawl out next to me. You got a fox here in the missus, he'd say to Greg while blowing smoke rings, but you know that, don'cha, a stone fox, right here, and he'd raise his bare arms to cradle his head, his cigarette the highest point of light in the room. The hair of his armpits was dark and fine. Good thing I know you're taking care of business, he'd say to Greg, and take another drag. The TV screen flickered. You two are better than parents to me, I mean that. He'd turn on his side, look me in the eyes, face maybe six inches from mine. His long legs. Don't know what I'd do without you, he'd say. And then he'd jump up, slam the front door, out of there, not even saying goodbye.

LIBRARIAN

A crashing out of sleep. Jangling, glass breaking. Thuds, from downstairs. Somebody screaming. Lois. Three a.m.

The relief when she'd moved into the flat downstairs. Weekends, afternoons, the tea kettle. Evenings, typewriter keys, the little bell. Once in a while, an LP, Judy Collins, or Vivaldi. A librarian, she'd said, in Albany, but she wrote on the side, and one of her stories had come out in *Playboy*. When I'd walk down the drive that sloped past her window, I could see she'd repainted the orange and purple walls a pale cream.

4 a.m. by the time the police got there and we were drinking coffee with Polly and Ben next door. At least 6′6″ this guy was, Ben said, telling us blow by blow how he'd grabbed his granddad's pistol out of the drawer, pulled on his pajama bottoms and run down the drive, jumped into Lois's kitchen window through the broken place, landed flat on his feet, held out the gun, and found he was pointing it higher and higher at the dude holding Lois in a stranglehold. You just put that thing down, man, the guy said. But Ben wouldn't leave till he knew Lois was okay. She was bleeding, he said, from her head and her arm, and crying.

Lois told us afterward she'd had to move every few months to get away from him. She didn't want to have to move again. They hadn't been lovers for three years. But he always found her. She hadn't been able to work him into a story.

ASPARAGUS

Ty liked the tips. Especially on that new style of pizza with everything on it. I did too. One night when we made dinner, we steamed asparagus, and ended up throwing out the stalks. Tough, Ty said, stringy. At home I'd put the tips in a soufflé, and the next day, Greg would eat the leftover stalks. He said he preferred them. Closer to the ground, thicker. Ty didn't like to cook, would rather order out, or fill up on ice cream. I loved the feel of shining bowls, spoons. My new wire whisks spilled out of a ceramic pot like metal flowers. Greg would come in while I was beating egg whites and pat my bottom so it jiggled, crack jokes about my big butt, little tits. When you grew your own asparagus, you couldn't harvest the spears for at least a year. Greg had started spending most of the weekends digging in the garden, the dirt solid clay. When I'd go down to help, my shoes would get so heavy, so caked with mud, I could barely make it back to the house.

HOT TUB

An hour after dinner at Barney's, people would start leaving the living room. As if something pulled them. Funny little half smiles. One or two at a time. After the first couple of evenings, Greg would go too. I'd stay with the wives left in the living room, talk about relatives, or movies or books, all of us perched on the half-dozen not-yet-refinished chairs. The people who'd left had grabbed their can of beer or glass of wine—or bourbon or Scotch, brandy or Cointreau—from the floor or the credenza. They had their clothes on when they came back out. I never went farther than the kitchen. Greg always told me, though, about the sizes and shapes of all the tits, whose he liked best, which nipples. Once, around two, as we were leaving, right by the coat rack near the front door, he grabbed Jeanette's through her caftan, rubbed them slowly around and around under his cupped hands, grinning, and she just stood there, grinning back.

CAKE

I always bought the applesauce cake they sold in the teachers' lunchroom. The ladies with the hairnets behind the metal folding window sold it for forty-five cents. Raisins, and lemony icing, the brown cake just a bit spicy. But I tried not to give in. I had to get rid of the little bulge you could see at the top of my thighs when I wore my shortest minis. One day Fred told me—in kind of a whisper—that my skirt was so short my cheeks, that was the word he used, showed, and I probably shouldn't wear that dress. But he smiled—they're delicious, he said. I knew I turned red, even though I'd heard he liked men. And I didn't wear that dress again. I did pick up the pace of my Royal Canadian Air Force exercises. Maybe it wasn't only the dress. Maybe my buns just hung too low. Julie had shown me a good exercise—you walked across the room on your bottom. Really worked those muscles.

SYNANON

We were still in bed, a half hour left before I had to go home, when I asked him outright. Did you ever—with Diane Eisenberg? Yeah, he said, the year before you came. Just one time. Yeah, it was good, but not that good. I thought it would be, you know, those huge boobs, but she wants it all done for her, she just kind of lay there. I don't think she thought I was great either. I asked her, and she said, oh, about a C+, and laughed. We're friendly, though, I like Diane. The kids do too. The administrators always give her what she asks for, she gets the best schedules. She talks so quiet, that nice soft voice, her little smile that looks kind of sad—even the worst kids calm down around her.

He still liked remembering those rich ladies in the tennis clubs down in places like San Jose, or back in Boulder. They knew they'd been missing it. Doctor husbands, lawyers, too busy and important. Those women appreciated every little thing he did. He'd give them an hour lesson for their money, and then spend the rest of the afternoon dipping into their honey pot. Some of them were good tennis players. Three or four, he said, still write letters. See that picture over there? That's from one of them, she painted it. She went back to college, got her degree, teaches second grade now in Palo Alto. We'd been talking about Diane's decision to join Synanon, give over her salary and her car. She was marrying the director. No possessions. No wedding presents. A small ceremony, nobody from outside. But that wasn't the worst. She'd confided to Ty that her fiancé barely touched her, couldn't even keep it up long enough to come. It was all right, she said, and laughed her sad little laugh. She'd had enough hard dicks to last a lifetime. She admired his principles. She'd get used to it.

THE FEMININE MYSTIQUE

No, I hadn't heard of it. Ty was telling me everybody was talking about it, this Friedan woman. He had to read it for his class at Cal. Maybe I should read it. Yeah, why didn't I read it, and then he wouldn't have to, and I could write his paper for him. Easy for me. I said I didn't mind. Okay. When I finished reading the whole book he wanted to know what I thought. I wasn't sure. But I didn't have a hard time writing his paper. I just said things the way he'd say them, organized it all into paragraphs, made sure everything was correct. Did I like the book? I didn't know. Maybe my mother had been like the women Friedan wrote about—the problem that had no name. I didn't really want to talk about it, as long as the paper was good enough for him to turn in. And tonight—if I could stay with him, not have to go home.

SHOWERING

He liked to shower two, three, even four times a day. He never jumped right out of bed after, but within a half hour he'd be under the spray, running his hands over his hair, scouring his chest, cleaning all of himself. I would lie a long time with that liquid bit of him still inside. I'd never met his family. His mama would like me, he said. But he'd never have kids, he told me plenty of times. Too much weight hanging on a man, teaching was enough for him. He'd come back to the bedroom rubbing the nap of the towel across his long back, sit down beside me, and talk, tell me again about his aunties back in Georgia, his cousins, his uncle, his sister. I'd never been to the South, never to Georgia. Didn't know what grew there. Pecan trees maybe. Peaches. The shapes and shades of the leaves, the sizes and patterns of the branches—the way the fruit ripened on them—I had only a vague idea.

BULLSHIT

You shouldn't listen to that bullshit, he said. I was lotioning my legs. All those guys are full of bullshit, they're just trying it out on you, see how far they can get. You shouldn't listen to me either. I pulled on my pantyhose, up to my waist. Is it bullshit, then, everything you've said to me? Ty looked down at the bed, top sheet mostly on the floor. No. But it was at the first. You shouldn't have listened. You should stay with your husband. I zipped up the back of my dress. He moved away from the jungle sheets, brown, yellow, black and white tigers, giraffes, panthers, and stood over me, his head bent down to my eyes. His index finger brushed my chin. I didn't expect to be feeling this way about you. Get it? I didn't expect. You just looked like some good pussy. You hear me? You should stay with your husband, have some nice white babies. I turned to the mirror, put in one earring. Tiny ivory flowers. Bullshit, I said. I put in the other earring and turned around. Tell me something. What do you mean when you ask if it's your pussy? His arms were around me, stroking me, and he rested his cheek on the top of my head. Fingered my left earring, swaying it back and forth. Stroked my cheek. You be here. That's what it means. Doesn't sound like bullshit, I said. Doesn't sound all that hard, either. His mouth was moving my name through my hair. I don't know, he said. I don't think you know how hard it could get.

BEETLE

Little, and gray. Unobtrusive, I could blend in. A shell curving around me above the wheel. Secondhand, one of my Danish friends had needed to sell it, fast. Hundreds just like it. Anonymous. Nearly invisible in fog, at least two or three parked on his block. I knew his old girlfriend Joanie, who'd moved with him from Colorado, drove a blue one. They'd had their own lives for a couple of years now, dated other people. Still helped each other with car troubles, rent agreements, things like that. Sometimes on the Nimitz I'd see one of them off to the side, all crumpled in. They didn't do so well at high speeds, weren't really built for distances.

ENCOUNTER GROUP

Ty faced me across the circle. My lip was trembling. Can't some white people understand, aren't some of them okay, I had asked. He almost sneered back, leaning toward Roberta Gibson's shoulder, tell her, Robbie, tell her, tell them what's happened to you, tell them how it's no better than it used to be. He was looking across the blank space of stained carpet in Martin Luther King Junior High's library with the smell of burned coffee in the air, looking straight at me. The stain at my feet began to separate from the carpet's threads. It was a face. It was a head with a huge Afro, it was a cloud. A storm. I fixed my eyes on it as Robbie's voice began, listing the things whites had said, had done. The stain began to take over my sight, blurred through tears, but I couldn't, not here, not here, let them fall.

KIND OF BLUE

That's how people usually are, Ty was saying, slipping a Miles Davis record from its sleeve. It's a common pattern. I'd been telling him just how furious I was. Why did he have to be so negative in our encounter group Saturday? And yes, I answered, when he asked, I had gone home and had a really good time with my husband. We even took a drive up the coast on Sunday. Fog never lifted, but we had a real nice lunch in a restaurant. And yes, I had liked being with my husband, he'd never do anything like that in a group.

He was standing next to me pouring 7-Up. All the tiny bubbles, countless, a quiet hissing as they burst. He took his glass over to the couch. You're following the classic expected behavior pattern, he said, that's what the psychologists call it. His glass on the table. Coltrane now on the LP. Drizzle outside, January. People in a triangle—one of their partners does something they don't like, the other one all of a sudden looks real good. The faint sibilance of the turntable's needle following the groove. And Miles, taking over.

FEDERAL FUNDING

Three dozen of them, Ty said. And he could have ordered more. So he went ahead and got one for himself. The English racing kind with the skinny tires. Nobody seemed to care, he just turned in the order. Didn't know if he felt right about it, but then he'd be taking the kids on field trips, that was the great thing about the alternative schools, you didn't have to worry about schedules, he could order a bus for a whole day, they could leave early, get up to Marin, bike around Muir Woods. Why not? Kids would learn biking, nature, how to follow a trail. And nobody'd miss $350 when they were spending twelve thousand on bikes and a hundred grand for the whole department. Yeah, it didn't feel right. But the money didn't really belong to anybody. Might as well use it for a good cause.

GREAT DANE

He was only taking care of Lady till Joanie found a bigger place. A brindle, taller than the tops of his thighs, and calm, happy padding around his carpet. He ran her every day. Was keeping a few things for Joanie for awhile. A chair, some records, a couple of blouses in the closet, a leather coat. There was a framed photo of her on the dresser.

He liked to bring Lady along when we met in the hills. Lady never bothered us, just sniffed around under dry leaves until we put our clothes on again and were ready to start walking. Inside his house, Lady left us alone. Only when we sat on his low sofa to watch tennis on TV, or listen to an LP, did Lady back herself up and lean her full weight against our legs.

One Saturday, I was taking my VW to the service place he'd told me about on San Pedro, when all of a sudden Lady came bounding up. I turned away just in time, but before I slid into my front seat and closed the door, I managed a quick sideways look at Joanie—thinner than in the photo, sharper, less makeup, facing a mechanic bent over the car. Not as new as mine, and darker. But the same model.

SATURDAY ALL-DAY EXTENSION CLASS

I decided to take it with Margie. We needed the credits to qualify for teaching the gifted kids. It sounded fun, a day in Golden Gate Park. He was there greeting seventeen of us, brown lion beard and buffalo sandals. Pete, his name was, but today we should call him Rambling Man, because that's what we were going to do, learn to ramble, take it slow. Nobody ever saw what they saw, he boomed, but today we were going to look, really look at everything around us, see what we saw. The fog had cleared already, ten in the morning, and the leaves of the shrubs were gleaming. We started off, Pete in the lead. Almost right away he stopped. Here's a fallen leaf, he said. One leaf, something we trample with our shoes and don't even notice. Let's examine this leaf. Veins, bruises, see here? Now each one of you stop, stop right where you are and reach down and pick up something, anything, by your feet. Okay? Got it in your hand? Now look at it. Stare right into it. His voice had stopped booming. Margie and I were trying not to laugh, couldn't meet each other's eyes. He was thick as a redwood trunk. Now, he said. Find a place to sit down and draw what you're holding in your hand. We found a place we could sit together on the sloped grass in the sun. Margie's M.A. was from Cal. She'd wanted to go on for a Ph.D. but she and her husband decided he should get his first, in history of the Far East, so that's why she was teaching ninth grade. I began to draw. Pete was lying under a tree a few yards away, his eyes closed. The sun brightened even more and everything became very quiet. I'd found a clump of petals. A whole bloom fallen from the tree, petals still curved in close to each other, not yet decomposed.

IMPROV AT ASILOMAR

The sand cold under the seat of my Levi's with the fire hot on my nose and cheeks, everybody shadowy against the flames. All day in the workshop. Drama Skills for the English Class. Warm-ups, pantomime, role playing—new ways to build self-esteem, lead to positive behavior, increase awareness of physical expressions. Amazing how much we'd done in a day. We'd brought a couple of jugs of Cribari to the beach and were passing around a joint. On my right was the woman who'd worn a low-cut blouse all day and kept bending over in front of Barney—Angie, her name was, the one who'd pushed her way into his car, and then kept telling him all the way to the beach what a great workshop leader he was. Charisma. Now she was lying on her side and her sounds were slurred. Frank had just announced *The Atlantic* had taken his first poem. Angie was sort of wriggling on the sand. I sipped my wine. Barney and I were talking about one of the warm-ups, how to use it in class. And then Frank stood up. Time to perform a public service, he said to nobody in particular, and walked over to Angie. The two of them moved a couple of yards off down the beach, away from the light of the fire. I could see him unbuckle his pants before they lay down. Everybody kept on talking. When Barney rolled another joint, I took a long drag before handing it back. We didn't start giggling until later.

PORTER

I was crying again. Loved him. Didn't he love me too. Why couldn't we get married. I wanted a baby with him. I reached for more Kleenex. Said through the sobs I just wanted him to love me like I loved him. I don't think you know what you really want, he said. And you don't act real lovable right now. But he kissed my neck, and held me for a while. You know I told you I couldn't do marriage, he said. Not this man. Not me. No way. Couldn't do it. But I'm here now, aren't I? I was calming down. Wiped my nose. Wadded the Kleenex into a hard wet ball.

Later that afternoon he told me about his first job on the trains. How much he liked it, especially the first class sleepers. Lots of ladies on those trains. The first time it happened he answered the bell the way he always did, knocked on the door of the compartment. There was this naked white lady on top of the bed with her legs all spread out, just there for him. Some of those ladies were rich, gave him presents sometimes. Most of them were real lonely. Rode his car a couple of times a month, made sure they knew his schedule.

"MONDAY, MONDAY"

Telling him what I'd give up for him. It wouldn't work, he said. I was frying the bacon, he was stirring eggs. Instant coffee, Tang. He'd bought a kitchen table, big enough for two people to sit down to a meal. Green formica, matching chairs. The fog had lifted, a peek-through view of the Bay from the window over the sink. He didn't want to live with somebody all the time. I wanted to zip open his chest and climb inside. But didn't I realize, he was saying, dropping the bread in the toaster, I wouldn't like it. He'd always be playing tennis, or basketball with the coaches. Yeah he liked movies, and sure we liked to talk about people and the kids and school and even books sometimes, but I'd get frustrated, he knew I would, and I needed to accept that. And besides, he'd told me over and over, no marriage for him, no big commitments. Enough of this kind of talk, let's eat breakfast, he said, and we did, watching the sunlight play on the rose bushes outside. After the dishes, he stroked my hair before he helped me get ready to go.

HATCHED

I liked Ty's place better, mine had too many windows to the street, too easy to see in. I liked driving over to his place, parking, waiting a few minutes to make sure no one I knew was going by, and then striding out, as if I belonged right there, to the sidewalk leading up to his door. And his opening it, his little smile. The brush past his tall body to go on in—or, the door closing and the two of us staying put, my purse dropping to the floor. At his place, he took care of things. Only his mail, dishes, his laundry.

But Greg was still away and my zebra finches' eggs had hatched. Embarrassed for Ty to come so close to the mess of the cage—newsprint at the bottom musty with droppings, scattered with millet—but I wanted him to see. I led him to the back room, to the big cage on the far wall, and pointed him to the round opening of the wooden box hanging inside. Tiny, the hatchlings, littler than your thumbnail. Scrawny, bald, their swollen and still-blind eyes. Dark inside the dark enclosure. He peered his head around the door. But he couldn't make them out.

BALLOONS

Even with Greg out of town, I worried. The neighbors might see. And Ty wasn't exactly an invisible man. Not that the neighborhood was all white any more, but his height, his baldness, his black and tan Mustang. I wasn't saying no, I just wasn't sure I wanted to right now. Wasn't sure. I was staring at my left knee, my legs crossed over the carpet. I just didn't feel safe anymore. So much strong feeling and no public place to smile it, sing it, shine it out. Like that musical we'd seen together, *Black Balloons,* the hundreds of balloons let loose in the theater and floating, floating higher and higher as if all our heads, hair, all those naturals were lifting, lifted up over the heavy rows of hard wooden chairs. And everybody carrying balloons, airy, shining, out into the San Francisco streets before they popped.

BASEMENT

The way to the garden behind the house. Damp smell of old things. Once Greg had found a World War Two shell case among the piled up *Reader's Digests, Saturday Evening Posts,* and *National Geographics.* I used it for a vase. That second summer Greg was away working on his doctorate, Ty brought over some stuff to store down there while he was closing on his house. Wool sweaters, cotton sweatshirts, Converse shoes, LP's. Cardboard losing its stiffness in the damp. His jackets, jeans, draped over the blades of Greg's tools, the base of the electric drill, the old metal trunk with the sharp corners. He'd hung on to a couple of sweaters, a windbreaker. July could be foggy, chilly. Especially on the coast, and we wanted to take a little trip or two the way we had last year. Always cold by the ocean, no matter how warm the sand felt. One Saturday Greg surprised me by driving home for the weekend. He'd missed me, he told me in the kitchen. And a whole month left before he could come home, start the new school year. He didn't even bring his dirty laundry, never once went near the door to the stairs leading the way down.

COLD

Ty didn't think I needed to spend so much time on how I looked. But I sure did look good in that new blue soft dress. And what was this talk about not driving over to his house afternoons. Nobody'd found out, had they. What was he going to do if I didn't come over and give him some at least sometimes. Maybe not the way we'd been doing, maybe only once a week. Or twice, twice'd be good. Why'd I have to be talking like this right now, when I knew he was thinking about cutting out ice cream because of his new little pot belly. Cramp his style if he had a big old belly hanging out. I knew he'd just decided to cut down to single scoops. And he knew I could handle two men, I'd been doing it all this time. He could see if maybe I'd decided to put the lid back on the honey pot once in a while. But to take it away—cold. He walked across the room to me. His chin dropped down to my forehead. Nuzzling. A whisper. Could I say no to this.

GIMME FIVE

Julie was always low-fiving somebody. With the principal, the coaches, the head counselor, even Willie Jones when he told her he hadn't missed one class in the last six weeks, no blue slip sent home to his mother this time. Anybody male, she held out her palm, her bright red nails facing the floor, and said *gimme five,* her San Francisco private girls' school speech dropping east, down, and south by half a dozen states. Even in a miniskirt, she did the lean forward, the dip down from the hips with the back straight and almost horizontal to the ground, one knee lifted up toward the chin, and finally, the laugh. I could never get it right. But you didn't see the other women teachers doing it, especially not the black women. And you never saw them in miniskirts. True, the girls' track coach Louise walked around in her gym suit all the time, but you never saw the Latin teacher Ardis Baine, or Roberta Gibson, with her groomed little Afro, in a skirt much above their knees. Julie was almost one of the guys—talked football, basketball, passes, tight ends, overtime with all of them. Only a few people knew about her mother, so bad an alcoholic she couldn't even look up to focus on whoever came through the door, let alone put an arm around her daughter's shoulder. Been that way off and on for years. And her father—I met him once at their clothing store. He gave me a discount. But I heard him complaining to Julie, he wished his daughter could help him out sometimes on the floor. He was sure she had some spare time once in a while, she didn't have to teach on weekends did she, couldn't she give him a few hours once a week or so?

INVITATION

Hand-written, on a card with roses on the cover and a gold script *Thank You.* Come for coffee, after school, next Thursday. Frances had been telling me for weeks her mother wanted to meet me. Could I come, please. She liked to stay after class, help straighten desks. Sometimes she'd come into my room over lunch and write in her journal, her tidy writing. She said she'd never raised her hand in class before this year. Her mother shook my hand hard, brought her other hand up over mine. I can't thank you enough for what you've done for this young lady, she said. Frances never had faith in herself till she was in your class. Doilies on the chairs, perked coffee in thin cups with saucers, cookies and slices of spice cake. Sun through white curtains. Frances swept her pleated skirt under her as she sat down. Her mother asked where I was from, how long I'd been married. I hate to see a good teacher like you quit, she said, handing me a refilled cup of coffee, but you're going to want babies, aren't you, same as I did. I don't know what I'd do without my Frances. My comfort and my joy. You need some babies, honey, she said again. Don't let those people at that school mess with you, don't let them mess with your head, you hear what I'm saying? You got your own life, your husband, don't you? I hear from Frances, how you be there for the kids, how some of them call you in your own home. She bit into a cookie. You can't be giving yourself to other people's kids all the time, she said. You need to save some of yourself for your own.

ORGANIC

Greg brought home a five-gallon stainless steel pot from a store he'd found in *The Whole Earth Catalog.* For canning things. And he'd picked up a case of glass jars, metal lids, and the rings that screwed down over them. Peaches, apricots. Boil them up. He found a recipe in the *Chronicle* for brandied cherries. Got out the copy of *Mastering the Art of French Cooking* that my mother had given us for our anniversary. *Boeuf bourguignon.* A slow simmer. Hardly any bubbles, you had to keep the heat down low, use plenty of wine. And maybe it was time for a family. His pile of compost was already feeding the tomatoes. The new books that had come in the mail from Rodale Press explained how we could be a self-sufficient unit, grow all our own food, even wheat, grind it ourselves, raise chickens for protein. The secret was compost. We could recycle our scraps.

ANSWERING MACHINE

We got one because Helen Cornwell wouldn't stop calling. Middle of the night, how this time she'd really do it. I'd pick up the phone breathless from running down the hall. Silence. Little gasps through the receiver and then, the slow intake of a breath, and sputtering. At school Helen would slink down the edge of the hall. Thick and slow, frizzy pale red hair around her slumped shoulders. Vague-eyed, till she spotted me. Her left hand had begun speaking to her in a language she was beginning to understand. Her right hand was interfering. She might cut it off. She was only safe in my classroom. She had written thirty new pages in her journal. I was the only one who understood. Couldn't I talk with her after school again, meet her somewhere. She dreamed I was her Angel, her Bright Savior. Little gifts appeared on my desk. A braided bookmark. A candle. At first the calls came in the evenings. Then after two weeks of being waked at three in the morning, I told Julie. The answering machine was her idea, she knew where to get one. Helen quit calling. But Julie was practically the only one who left a message. Relatives, friends—they just hung up.

BLOODSTONE

Over and over the same families of words. Lester was trying. Side by side in the brown chairs at the table. Battle, tattle, rattle, brother, another, click, flick, nick, fight, tight, night. Luck—no, keep him on track. Let's do some writing, I said. Head almost touching the table, he gripped the pen, pressed down hard. His small motions, impatience, there, that good enough? So, some reading. A story. Somebody doing something. On the street. Till I took my eyes off the page and saw my ring sliding off my finger. No. No, Lester. I had his attention. You like this ring? he asked. Yes, I like it, I said. But you couldn't get much for it. Please don't try that again. See, it belonged to my granny's mother in England, where my mother's from. I've never been there. A bloodstone, the green was almost black, the red veins and pools so tiny that, until now, they had been almost invisible.

OIL SPILL

Karen talked me into going over that night, said they'd been working around the clock, they needed everybody they could get. Thousands of birds. Cages. Mostly grebes. Feathers clotted in thick crude oil so they couldn't fly. The warehouse a hive, a make-do hospital, everybody working in twos and threes—pony tails, headbands, long sweeps of straight hair fanning down over pairs of hands. One to press the wings—with the thumbs—close to the body, keep the bones of the wings from spreading out, and, with the fingers, hold the cold webbed feet immobile. Another to hold the beak shut, everyone had been bitten. One moment of relaxing the pressure and—panic, flapping, out of control. Hundreds of lean backs bent together in small groups over birds, swabbing with detergent. The grebes' red eyes. No one knew the detergent removed the birds' natural oils. Nobody knew that when the birds were released, their feathers would absorb the water they had always surfaced on, to rest. It wouldn't take long for them to drown.

LAST

If it meant going dead I would rather. Better just not see him, or talk. I can't even come in and sit in one of the kid's desks next to you at lunch time? he said. Not even that. If the soil were packed down hard, solid clay like the earth around the old mildewed roses, no room for air, no sand or humus, maybe nothing more would grow through. Tamp it all down, not even room for a strand. The answer was no. Take the green pillow case I had kept and fold it into a box and seal it with tape. Same box for the photo of his big head in front of a redwood, smiling at me. Put it all away. Close down shop. Move back to the desert.

ALWAYS

In winter the rain. I was remembering Hemingway, wanting to teach *A Farewell*. Mr. Hewitt said he didn't think these kids were too young, whatever I thought would be relevant. I remembered how in the novel Catherine said she saw herself dead in it. January so damp and chilly my shoulders tensed from hunching under my umbrella. I didn't care whether it was good for the students. I wanted to reread Hemingway. And *The Sun Also Rises*. How they tried to learn to live after that war. I wanted to find the part in *Farewell* about the dog, toward the end, nosing the garbage cans. *There isn't anything, dog*—that line. Some of the kids didn't get it that the baby was already dead—or maybe they just didn't finish.

EMPTY LOT

Turning another corner onto the lot thigh-high with anise flowering. Pungent, airy yellow, a vague scent of childhood. Almost a vertical slope, barely room for a foothold down into the property. So overgrown you couldn't see the Bay.

We'd often walked there, summertime, afternoons. Sometimes we tried to imagine building. Slippery. We found the one place we could sit side by side, without fearing we might slide. Where I told him.

A complete severance. Long after I had moved away, I found myself walking there during a visit back to see friends. The anise gone to seed. No one had been able to build on that steepness.

TOOLS

I gave them all away. Frames, dowels, the hand-rubbed comb Ruth had given me. The sword. Even the yarns. Spools, coils, wound balls—boxes and baskets of textures, metallic, thin, angora, nubby, dozens of shades of colors. I'd had an idea for a tapestry. Two huge trees, the whole thing would be seven feet high. Partly woven, partly stitched. I wasn't sure how I'd do it. The bark would be mottled. Each tree different, one birch-like, silvery, maybe a eucalyptus, and the other like a pine, or redwood, darker, taller. But the leaves would intermingle, you would hardly be able to tell which tree they came from. I'd have needed an eight-harness loom. Would do the roots first. Reaching, lacing, interlocking, a base for the design, threads that would have followed.

DESSERTS

The year after I left him, I got into French cooking. Desserts. Best was the Charlotte Malakoff. Ladyfingers. Squeezed from the cloth bag with the silvery nipple. Fragile in their rising on the pan, flaky tongues, sifted over with powdered sugar. Whitest white, creamy white. Pale fingers upright in the mold, holding the dark mousse inside. The bitter chocolate and heavy cream, pulverized almonds, sugar beaten in butter, and a liqueur that cost so much we'd be down to the wire halfway to payday. The first time I made it, our friends around the table stood up and applauded. All the hands clapping, hands slapping against their own. Mine lay in my lap. But after they'd gone and my husband was sleeping, I'd run my fingers across the plate, scraping what was left.

MINISKIRTS

How short was short? Trying them on at Julie's mom and dad's dress shop in the Marina, I wanted them as high as I could get but not show the bottom curve of my buns. At least when I was standing up.

That was three years before Julie killed herself, Julie who knew without question her boobs were her best attribute, who wouldn't lose weight, carried a little extra because if she dropped even a couple of pounds, they shrank. One of the P.E. teachers, which one was it, said Julie had a big sloppy pussy, really liked to be gone down on, but in the end, after she'd been found dead with the principal's baby inside her—someone said he'd refused to divorce his wife in Oakland, and Julie had wanted to get married and have his baby no matter how black—in the end, it turned out it was the girls' track coach, Louise, who'd wanted her most, and Julie couldn't decide. By then I was long gone. Earth shoes, corduroys, no makeup. Hell with it. Just do what you gotta do, get on with it.

AFTER

Color, even in rain. Tie-dye, paisley, fringes. Afros, naturals. His hovering at my classroom door, racquet brushing his leg. A blanket in the hills under the redwoods, the eucalyptus, their brown seeds like bells. After school. His bedspread the colors of moss, of leaves. And month after month, on his sheets with the brown stripes, furrows across his bed, we laid our two selves down, while around us on the streets, in the parks, the halls of the ninth-grade school we taught in, the students swirled like uprooted flowers, seeds with no good dirt to drop down into. He asked me to write his graduate papers for him (and I did), and he always asked (and I always answered yes), if it was still his pussy. Summers, my husband gone, we'd spend nights, go out for ice cream late. 31 Flavors. Double cones rose from our hands, so many, so many possible combinations.

FROM THE MOON, EARTH IS BLUE

(2015)

ORDER

From where does it come, this desire
for the fitting niche, cradle for a flower,

shelf for a long boat, and hanging
hooks for the oars? To organize

handfuls of our lives, establish
the planets of our possessions in

cycles, predictable. A comet misses
earth by a million miles, almost

a collision. The green chair out of place:
a bruised shin, a ripped toenail.

Regular orbitings—dish drainer to top
drawer by the stove, cupboard to the right,

detergent to the left. From the east
the sun rises. Clear mornings you can see.

~

In the Museum of Modern Art, chaos
displays itself tidily. Even the viewers

know the dance: stroll, stop, gaze, whisper.
Stroll, stop. The cycle continues

until someone tires, moves into
the center of the room and sits

down on a bench, free to observe
more than one wall at once.

White of the paint between
frames, lines of the frames enclosing

angles, spheres of brightened
human flesh, dabs, splotches

of movement. Spirals of yellow
stars contained in a space

smaller than a clothes dryer. Within
a cylinder within a cube, repeated

identical revolutions tumble
the wrinkles out, our socks and

shirts grown lighter, loosed
of the clutter of lint, softer,

less abrasive, so close to
the irritable thinness of skin.

STERENFALL

(Anselm Kiefer, 1998, Mixed media on panel, Blanton Museum of Art)

Splattered gravel, burned-out forests, residue
from forklifts, excavators, back hoes
glued onto this panel and taking up
what seems the whole wall so you can't walk by,
you're sucked into a mammoth
3D sinkhole, staring at these clumped twigs
like abandoned camp fires, or what's left
of flattened or fire-gutted houses,
as if, with one spark, leaves, birds, lizards,
anything that wiggled or fluttered was gone,
leaving only crumbled stone and dried out
splinters, as if you're peering down from above the planet
at ridges, fault lines, escarpments, canyons
that resemble the land down your own street
gone to bulldozers, gutted, ripped
of root and vine, the rock bed under
the trees split into rubble
to be scraped away before foundations are poured,
as if the ground hadn't been foundation enough,
but this huge piece is about what's left after
everything's been ground
down, after we've exploded it all,
taken ourselves out, and the only thing left
will be faint tracings of the stories
of stars you used to look up to.

BLACK

Paintings began when
a woman plucked
a blackened chip from
the cave's fire and
outlined her lover's shadow.
He was leaving, upriver. Then she drew
her own shadow as
it overlapped with his.
According to Pliny.

~

"No black in nature,"
said the impressionists,
but other lore had it
that black paints were
made from carcasses.
Medieval ink: from
oak galls, swollen growths
around wasp nests.
T'ang Dynasty gentlemen
used black to portray
landscapes of the mind.

~

From our small
boat, over the surface
of the black lake
we fling petals—
coreopsis, lilac,
mallow—along with
our mother's ashes.
Pink, lavender,
yellow scattered on
the surface and then,
the lake closes over, black.

THE LOST BOOK

said something about memory,
the way it slips when

you remember, liquid
between covers, a spine, and drops

into place on the shelf, there, so
you can forget it.

ASSISTED LIVING

The Mill Basin Sunrise Facility's doors
open to galleries of soft-focused

reproductions: *The Rosy Wealth of June,*
The Painter's Daughters Chasing

a Butterfly: Gainsborough, Pissarro
framed in elaborate patterns of gilt.

Once through these doors, you have no choice
but cheer, the waterless vases fountaining

improbable clusters of manufactured
peonies, irises, sweet peas, chrysanthemums.

For breakfast it's whatever you want, as long as
you like sunny side, over-easy eggs, your fruit

canned—prunes, applesauce, peaches floating
like goldfish in a sugary juice.

What you can't have from now on out
are bare walls, spaces in which

to focus on the long and twisted
corridors of the years that carried you

here where the flowers need no water,
are designed so they won't fade

like the frail heads around you
bent like overblown roses

nodding into their shallow bowls.
No mirrors anywhere in sight,

no way in any of the public rooms to see
what it is you've begun to stare into.

CLOSETED INDIGO

It's the full moon we notice, not the night sky.
The white cat, not the shadowed grass.

Almost invisible, slipped between blue
and violet: Newton sensed it was there.

A color is only waves, motion we can't hear.
Veins near the skin run blue, bleed red.

We barely see the blueberries plucked in the night
silence when a loon cries on the lake.

There are ways of bludgeoning so the bruises
don't show, closets with walls no one can see.

It's the light glinting on leaf shapes
that dazzles us, the shimmers on the river.

What color is the wail of a horn uncoiled,
a saxophone's moan through the door?

THE SHADOW

(Jesús Escobedo, 1939, Lithograph, Philadelphia Museum of Art)

You're alone in an alley, a solitary street lamp behind you
half a block down as you turn to the chalky grid of the wall
on your left to fumble in your pocket for—glasses? a smoke?
the address you're trying to find?—but here they are, spilled

on the sidewalk like somebody's guts, someone who's just
been knifed open, still raw, but they're your own guts, these

twisting heads and bones jammed into the slit-open sack
you've carried through the years: the clinging hungry baby,
the gaunt-eyed mother, a set of disembodied fleshless ribs,
the curled-up children hugging their sagging bed, the gnarled

thick-jointed fingers wrapped into a fist, and the single
uplifted hand—what could it do? what could it ever do?—

and bulging at the bottom of the splayed-wide sack
mirroring your very shape is a heavy-lidded eye that
won't close, so even if you button up your jacket,
turn and walk back, facing right into the street light's

glare, you're still carrying all this weight flattening you
into blackness, a cardboard silhouette, impotent ghost.

SIN TÍTULO

(León Ferrari, 1964, ink on paper, Blanton Museum of Art)

Needles tangled in wisps of thread?
Five distinct rows, like a musical

stave. Eighth, sixteenth notes dropped
into nests of string. Or knives, these

jagged black marks on framed white
paper I can't move past? Daggers

blunted by intricate knots twisted
around them. And why this terror

facing a piece without a single human
face, with no mouths stretched

wide in pain or eyes confronting
some gargantuan specter. Could this

succession of black darts, or stabs,
be our cries when surfacing from

a nightmare, struggling to be heard
yet smothered by blankets? No,

this is code for wails, moans aimed
at webs of lies, spiralings to trap

the tongue. See how these
splutters begin in the first row,

minuscule, then lengthen into
lungfuls, shrieks? But by the final

line's end, only two barely
audible whispers, shrouded. Gagged.

APOLOGIA FOR BROWN

> A good picture, like a good fiddle, should be brown.
> —SIR GEORGE BEAUMONT (1753–1827)

Half light, candle light, window
to a street awash with slop.
Sienna, ochre, burnt umber,
Cassel earth derived from peat.
Bister: soot from birch bark.

Roof and mantel, fallow field and
pumpernickel (a word formed
from "pumpen," "fart"), roasted
beef, saddle and shoe, potato skin.
Pitchy murk they dug from soil.

Least glamorous of pigments.
The impressionists got rid of it.
Oozings of the lower gut,
a meaty sauce, a sobering glaze.
Caravaggio, Rembrandt, Van Dyck.

Eyes looking out like inner
rings within the cores of trees.
Hard maple, spruce, carved and
varnished till a violinist draws
a horsehair-fitted bow across

the belly of an instrument
that, strung in those days with
the dried intestines of a sheep,
might, even now, wrench us
beyond our fetid rooms,

the way a spotted moth will cling,
a dark stain, to the wall of the garage,
till it wafts its small
hand's width of weightlessness
through transparent air.

COMPOSITION IN GRAY

Dust to dust, but it's not that: dirt is yellow, brown, or red.
Ashes, not even that, for these are also chunks of bone.

Desaturated light, the volume turned below our vision.
Her pulse at twelve, then under seven beats a minute.

Throat-choking fog through night and noon, a pall that blurs
angles of walls, the street signs turned to fuzz, illegible.

Our senses can't discern the subtler shades
of avian plumage, the various grays on chickadees.

Not even that. As though her ashes in the jar had drifted out
and, lofted by the air, have sifted over everything.

And now the lake has died, the parasites, giardia, the scum
of algae multiplied, loons abandoning their nests.

Buried within the Munsell Color System's inner core,
achromatic, oxymoron, color of no color.

And still she stares at us from photographs.
A cinema in black and white, continuously reeling.

At the end, I stroked her toes, bare of their familiar polish.
Within the room, not even shadows, even shade.

TRANSPARENT

Even cooked, onions are never.
Slice after slice, half

moon after quarter moon.
Or a meeting's report, paper

thin sheets of an old bed.
Only at a certain angle, with

the light just right:
bottom of the lake, moss-

feathered stones.
But you, I can't see through.

RAPTOR

Was it his feathers, drift of beige on brown,
loose-woven tufts crowning his head?

The circular eyes, large-pupiled, topaz,
haze of sun on my hair, the heat beating.

Or the way his handler's arm held
the claws gripping a padded leather sleeve?

That beak: a single talon curled and hooked
for prey—an absence present in our midst.

And the crowd of us, our scattered reasons
for driving to our city's Greenfest in the park,

abandoning our cluttered piles of laundry,
mail, accumulations of upholstered dust,

chattering as we rummaged among pamphlets,
booths—cosmetics without cruelty, solar power.

Was it the heft, upright column of his body,
gaze that locked with mine, unwavering?

And was it rapture, this press of tears?
This inability to speak, caught, seized

by a clean ferocity—without a syllable
to swoop across a field, focus

eye and claw and beak, on
whatever it is that keeps us breathing.

APOLOGY FOR BLUE

Don't prate to me of divinity . . . but of blue.
—WILLIAM GASS (1924–)

A form of black, said the Greeks,
cousin of gray, species
of darkness, opposite of light,
not a mention in Homer
with his wine-dark seas.

Even the Bible doesn't note
the celestial vault is blue.
We've three times more synonyms
for red—cerulean lacks
the force of blood's vermilion.

And yet Cennini's quattrocento
brought back lapis lazuli
from Badakhshan, ground
the heavy, gray-veined stone
to paste, kneaded it like bread,

sieved, melted, strained the stuff
through linen, then mixed in lye
and slapped the lump with sticks
till the blue drained off, a powder
stored in a leather purse.

Reserved for the Virgin's lap.
Color of meekness and profound
piety, the heavenly spirit,
that woman's body cool,
unsullied by carnality, wrapped in

blue more dear than gold.
But nineteenth-century scientists
observed, in the Bunsen burner's
flame, the highest heat is blue.
The hottest stars are bluish white,

and objects hurtling near light speed
show bluer than the slower ones—
in physics, blue's the color
of collision, fire, the laser's beam
that centuries of artists showed

streaming to a mortal woman's lap:
fulcrum of our heated lives,
hinge and spring of our renewal.
Hard to see what's closest.
From the moon, earth is blue.

CATCH

Hovering, the word,
invisible,

a ball batted so high
the sun blots it

from sight, so far
there is no reaching

for the shape of the word,
letters scattered

till they all, a, c, h, t, c,
fall to earth, my open hand,

where I order them
onto a page, and breathe

the relief of one who
hasn't lost the game.

A CROWD, A HOST

(Brooklyn Botanical Gardens, May 2003)

The magnolias, narcissus, lobelia,
birches, hay-scented ferns, bayberry,

and now: an opening field—
bluebells under beeches and oaks,

forty thousand. Someone has counted,
printed the sign on the path,

forty thousand of a hazy sky-lit
blue as if a brush had dotted

each flower from the same tint
of paint, each cluster a staff,

blue note on blue note, a song
in unison, unaccompanied,

unlike the pruned garden of roses,
every labeled clump of stalks

struggling to produce
a single perfect bloom, for show.

Here is no question of hierarchy—
each blossom alone

adding a blue curl to the procession
we follow, held in our mind's eye

even on the pathway
to the street, to the subway

station a block away, the stained
stairs leading underground to the long

cars clanking through the dark
tunnels, rocking the faces within,

faces more various than
all the blossoms in the gardens,

even without the man in the royal
blue-brimmed hat, singing along

with his headphones, music
he alone can hear.

PROCESSION

Chickens are loose.
The fence won't stop them—

feathered rumps up,
bony beaks down,

claws askittering the leaves.
When the neighbor's guinea hens

march up the drive
early afternoons—pea head

follows pea head, a wobbling
line of black and white.

Zen mendicants after the bell,
yoked in meditation

before they return
to squawk an old mantra,

settle into stillness,
that fertile, resonant round.

LIGHT PINK OCTAGON

(Richard Tuttle, 1967, Canvas dyed with Tintex, Blanton Museum of Art)

Like nobody's skin. Or skirt, blouse.
Nobody's flounce, neither ruffled nor scalloped, nobody's ribboned

basket. Or bonnet, or roses. No carnations, no half-sliced roast
beside the wine glass, no ruddy

cheek of a maid shouldering wheat,
no dimpled buttocks of Venus or Bathsheba, no thundering

Jehovah-splintered sunset, no velvet-tasseled curtain, no fizzy drink.
Not like skin, no veins traversing

flesh, no one begging to be touched.
I could move into this unadorned, open, plain-woven canvas,

a pastel simplicity, an unclouded fabric billowing
rugged as a mainsail uncurled,

heading out to the wide ocean
with the wind, this aerial cotton swath, unsplashed by any paint,

uncluttered by any pen or brush, this unframed shape—arresting
as a full breath.

THE IRISES

lined by the pond
must have been planted
by a traveled eye

since the stripe of yellow
on the mud-brown bank
mirrored in rippled water

recalls a time in France
when canvases, wide
as the room, precipitated

an immersion of floating
petals and depths
of paint more ephemeral

and wet, more dazzling,
translucent and dark,
closer to stars

we can never see
than this tidy replica,
planted imitation,

a postcard I won't send
as I'm headed home
to you, sunning—I know—

this moment amid
the rampant and untended
grasses, the tangle

of our unpruned trees, unruly
hair on your forehead,
your undisturbed focus,

glance of your face,
its brown, and—flecked
with yellow—irises.

HIGH YELLOW

(Ellsworth Kelly, Oil on canvas, 1960, Blanton Museum of Art)

This is it. All you need. Though nothing
resembles anything you know. It's neither
star nor flower, this imperfect oval more
like a fat yellow cigar floating in blue so dark
and bright it couldn't be any sky that's ever
filled your breath. And the bottom third
of the canvas: pure green. You don't have
to do a thing. Can stop the churning of your
desire to turn this high-flying ovoid into an
ear of corn or a squashed halo. This is only
about color: yellow, blue, green. But your
mind is still recalling that the first two can
make the third. Like sun and sky make grass.
You keep trying to put names on these three
shapes, though they have nothing to do with
names. Yet you can't leave, for in the high
sky above this bright lawn, a widening sun is
about to drop the egg of itself into your lap.

ONE BLACKBIRD AT A TIME

(2015)

I HATE TELLING PEOPLE I TEACH ENGLISH

Like last August, after they'd finished my bone scan,
this combed-over mid-sixties guy starts chatting about the novel
he's written in his head, he only needs someone like me
to work it up, he never liked punctuation, parts of speech, all that junk
from junior high, and I couldn't get my print-out fast enough
to take to my GP, who likes to quote from his inspirational speeches
to local luncheon clubs. He's determined to collect them
in a book, though he'd need a good editor, do I know any, and meanwhile
I've been waiting fifty-seven minutes for help with recharging
my sluggish thyroid, and I haven't met any doctors who like giving
free advice about your daughter's milk allergy or your friend's
migraines or the thumb you slammed in the stairwell door, splitting it
open so badly your students interrupted your lecture on
pronoun agreement to note you were dripping blood from your hand
and wow, what happened? But it's mostly at parties I hate
admitting I teach English. I've never been quick enough to fudge,
the way a Methodist minister friend says he's in "support
services" so he doesn't get called to lead grace. I guess I could dub myself
a "communications facilitator," but since I'm in the business
of trying to obviate obfuscation, I own up, though I dread what I know
is coming: "Oh," they say, "I hated English, all that grammar,
you won't like the way I talk, you'll be correcting me," and suddenly
they need another Bud or merlot or they've got to check out
the meatballs or guacamole over on the table and I'm left facing
blank space, no one who can even think about correcting
my dangling participles. Once when the computer guy was at the house,
bent over my laptop trying to get us back online,
he asked what it was I wrote, and when I told him "poetry," said, "Ah—
fluffy stuff," and I wasn't sure whether he was kidding
or not, but I figured at least it was better than his saying he hated poetry
or that he had a manuscript right outside in his Camry and
could I take a look, no hurry, but he knew it would sell, could I tell him
how to get an agent for his novel about his uncle
moving to Arizona and running a thriving ostrich farm until the day
hot-air balloons took off a half mile away
and stampeded the birds, till all he was left with were feathers and bloody

tangled necks on fence posts, the dream of making two million
          from those birds a haunting sentence fragment—but then, I think:
I would never have wanted to miss the time a dentist,
          tapping my molars, asked if I'd like to hear him recite Chaucer's Prologue
to *The Canterbury Tales* in Middle English, which he did
          while I lay back in his chair, open-mouthed, pierced to the root.

TRUTH, BEAUTY, AND THE INTRO POETRY WORKSHOP

Still prickling from a neighbor's yelling "Shove it
up your ass" when all I'd done was ask if
he could stop his terriers
from yapping all night, I wasn't entirely patient when
the kid with the scarab tattoos effused about
beauty, said ever since Brit Lit
he's wanted to talk like Milton—"Yet once more, O ye
Laurels"—or Keats—"Those lips, O slippery
blisses, twinkling eyes," adding
he's in the class to "build the lofty rhyme." I reminded him
it's 2010, we don't wear cravats or corsets and
nobody waltzes anymore. He nodded,
so I asked what music he likes. "Deathcore—It Dies Today
and Suicide Silence," he said, and then,
"I'm a drummer." "Aha," I said,
"how about writing a poem the way you wield those sticks." Now
he's turned in a free-verse sequence leaded
with expletives about arguments
with his crack-dealing brother who never leaves the house without
his .38. His lines reverberate with the turbulence
of a 747 out of LAX. Yet I'm
lashing myself, worrying I did him wrong. I love Auden's
call to "Let the healing fountain start" from
"the deserts of the heart,"
but why not water this kid's land-mine-loaded sand
dunes with a little harmony? The human soul
needs beauty more
than bread, said Lawrence. Haven't I been yearning for a bit
of old-school beauty myself? Just last week
we watched a tennis princess
swear she'd take her fuckin' ball and slam it down the fuckin'
judge's throat. I know poetry's got to breathe
with the fumes of its time,
but I'd like to escape my own, forget about drugged-up
kids with guns. And it isn't even true nobody
waltzes anymore. How

could I have forgotten that night downtown a year ago
when, as the symphony in the outdoor pavilion
lilted into "The Blue Danube,"
a thousand people all joined in, arms lifting to arms,
lovers and uncles, grandmas and bikers, moms
and toddlers dancing
under the moon to soaring melodies barely heard these days,
till we became one rhapsodic, dactylic swirl.

EMILY IN THE CLASSROOM

Hovers at the ceiling's buzzing
fluorescent lights. The students crack
their paperbacks, pressing
the valves of her phrases, working them
like bellows, determined
to ignite a fire with compacted air, evade
the cold that could razor the tops
of our heads. They want to illuminate
the shadowy dashes, the slivered
chasms, seal them for safe-keeping
under glass. She hovers
at the ceiling like an unfamiliar freckled
moth, like Jehovah—Yahweh—
a name we cannot speak aloud. She is
hovering like a breath taken
further and further until released,
a slip of thread lifted
by the wind. If only they could spread
their feathers, gain an arc,
know how neighborly, the invisible.

HIS EYELASHES ARE NOT TARANTULAS

But I've been bitten, stung, and I want to tell this guy, star pitcher
on the university team—bare
arms so muscular I'm amazed
any straight woman around this table can utter a word—I'd like to shred
his printout and toss the pieces into
the nearest recycle bin. His poem
begins with a guy who's salivating for a "she" who's lolling her curves
on his kitchen counter, but when the "I"
licks and nibbles "her" moist flesh,
we learn "she" is only an apple. How do I count the ways I could sneer
his poem's fouled out? The students
are chuckling, "great humor," Adrian's
saying, but I'm struggling to calm down, behave like the mature workshop
leader I'm supposed to be while my mind
races like a runner stealing
third. I'm hurled back fifty-some years to my first steady boyfriend,
the one I even thought about marrying,
record-breaking pitcher on
our high school team, black lashes, eyes dark as Medjool dates. This kid
looks just like that boy. Something very sexy
about a pitcher—I'd sit behind
home plate—the ball coming right at me after the long wind up, intense
crouch over the mound. He made it
to the majors, the Braves, and once
I saw him pitch against Willie McCovey. I'd love to watch my student
in action. I saw the old boyfriend last
summer, after all these years, and
over lunch, without a smile, he reminded me I'd dumped him not once
but twice. He'd never forgiven me, his back
rigid as a Louisville Slugger while
he insisted on paying the bill. Or was he bored and eager to leave? When
was it students began to see me as old enough
to be their mother? That September
afternoon Marissa said in my office, "Oh Dr. Barker, your shoes are
adorable, they're just like the ones my mom
wears!" Now the apple arcs from

another direction—Belinda says maybe the poem's about sadness over
a woman's desertion, so all the man's left with
is one apple on the countertop. But—
I'll admit it—though this kid could be my grandson, he's so damned cute
I'm smitten and all too aware I've been
dropped from the team. Where is
that smooth-skinned girl my boyfriend loved? Forget the snide remarks
I'd wanted to make, the rant about
Rossetti's *Goblin Market* with
those leering men offering fruit so tongue-luscious you grew addicted,
sickened, died. Forget my desire to snipe
that women are not grapes, plums
waiting for hornets, yellow-jackets, to sting them dry. So I tell him
to read Shakespeare, write a new poem
showing a lover as nothing like
a piece of fruit—and add that he'd throw a three-pitch strike-out
if he just described an apple
so we'd hanker for its tang.

WAKING OVER *CALL IT SLEEP*

I'm the closest thing to Jewish in the class even though
at best I'm only one-eighth, according
to my English mother, who insisted the shadowy figure
of her granny was a Jew since nobody knew
her origins and everybody talked as if something had been
hushed up, shameful, and of course
everything about her hawk-nosed face was unusually dark,
especially the ringlets of her unruly hair,
or I suppose you could count the fact that I'm married
to a man whose grandparents arrived
at Ellis Island from what is now Ukraine only three years
after Henry Roth, yet none of these
students has the *seykhl* to know their teacher is a *shiksa*
and our group is as goyish as pork chops
but they've all been children, and they love this novel,
they know what it's like to be
speechless, powerless, afraid. Nobody needs me to explain
the terror of what lies beyond
the front door and what lies within, and the paralysis
that comes from never knowing
when to dash outside or stand by the window behind
the blinds. One year, while we were reading
Ginsberg, I knew I'd have to describe Kaddish
though I'd never even heard it
recited, but I gave it a go, saying in passing that only
1% of our city's population is Jewish
which was when Heather quipped: "Of course, they're all
in Hollywood making millions from
trashy movies." I put down my book and didn't move—
you could hear the whirr
of the elevator down the hall. When I spoke, I said, "That
was a *very* offensive comment"—and
I realized I was shaking, after decades of holding forth
in linoleum-floored classrooms. It wasn't
like the times I've heard someone saying *wet* meaning
wetback which are both despicable
terms and I argue those too, but this time it was as if

I'd been slapped full in the face, called
sheeny, kike, and I swear that tears came to my eyes though
I couldn't cry out "*Gevalt,* help,
take that back, you ignorant little bitch." The tension lasted
beyond the ten-minute break, which
I loosened to twenty, and not just for the smokers. Now
I've handed out maps that highlight
Galicia, Brooklyn, Tysmenicz, the Lower East Side,
Avenue D, and 9th Street, and a list with
explanations of terms: Passover, Ashkenazi, knish, shul,
and pogrom. We talk about Friday night
and the candles, and everyone is right there in the room
with Roth and with me and with my husband
who joins us after the break to tell about the author's
life with his duck farm and his goyish wife
and his writer's block, and I begin to wonder if any of these
students with family from Monterrey or
Laredo will some day learn—as a friend of mine did last year—
that a great-great-great-and-beyond
grandfather came over from Spain to escape the Inquisition,
and if it will happen—as my friend Raul
told me it did—that in the lighting of candles with relatives
gathered for a first Shabbat, an elderly aunt
in the corner will begin to sigh and to weep, and when they
press her, ask her what's wrong,
she'll tell them she's suddenly remembering an abuela
who covered her face with her hands
every Friday night to greet the Divine, the Shekhinah,
and who every week sent one grandchild
to buy candles. A child, I'm thinking, who wore a silver
cross around her neck and had never
heard *judía de mierda* hurled in her face with the auto-pilot
contempt of the six girls who chanted
at me in the bathroom once during second grade, as they
pointed at the color of my striped
dress: "Blue, blue, you're a Jew," but I didn't get it—
I thought they were saying *jewel.*

I'D SAID IT WOULD BE

Depressing, and in fact I dreaded it, hadn't even requested it,
an entire course on 19th Century literature by women. We'll feel
corseted, starved for breath, I warned on the first day,
and sure enough, after *Jane Eyre, Goblin Market, Uncle Tom's Cabin,*
and *Incidents in the Life of a Slave Girl,* when we come to Alcott's
Little Women, the whole class sighs in relief to read about Jo,
loping like an unfettered colt down the road, chomping apples
in the attic with a rat. Claudia says she liked the way Winona Ryder
wore Converse high-tops to create an authentic
athletic bounce in the film with Susan Sarandon who—everyone
agrees—was not our idea of Marmee, the mother we all wish had been
ours, who never lost it, never flew off the handle
and screamed at a daughter for spilling a glass of milk. But then
Holly reminds us that Marmee confessed to Jo she'd been angry
every single day of her life. She'd kept it inside,
pushed it in, just as those corsets pressed hard on a woman's ribs,
constricted the lungs, the intestines. Liveliest discussion of the whole
semester. Though am I the only one who never
identified with Jo, but with Meg, fretting about clothes? All this
week I've been poring over catalogs, pondering whether I could risk
one of those gauzy, swirly skirts everybody's wearing now. Yesterday,
shopping for new bras, I grew dizzy wandering through racks
of styles and almost all of them gel-filled or molded so that,
trying them on, I felt like two Wagnerian breastplates
had been glued to my chest, and I couldn't get out of there
fast enough, once again lamenting the passing of the 60s, when
we happily flopped around under our blouses, free
at last. How is it, then, that while every woman in this room
proclaims her sisterhood with Jo, I'm facing a barrage of breasts
bulging from lacey camisoles and push-up bras in this
roomful of moussed, streaked and unstreaked, upswept and
downswept spiral-curled locks of hair? Here we are, in
the twenty-first century, and we're still obsessing,
jittery, even frantic about judgments from the telescopic
lenses of the world beyond our closet door. The Academy

Awards focus less on the arts of acting and
cinematography than on Penelope Cruz's "white embellished
strapless gown" with its "luscious satin folds." I won't ask
how long Claudia takes to do her hair so it lifts a hillock
over her head and then drops like a waterfall, an auburn-
streaked cascade. As long, I'd think, as it took to arrange
Marianne Dashwood's looped-up ringlets in *Sense
and Sensibility.* I know the 90s ushered in the era of Girl Power,
and I'm not the sort of second-wave feminist who'll be
buried in her Birkenstocks, but I doubt we've made
that much progress when our guys slouch around all comfy
in tee-shirts and baggy jeans. I guess one of those swirly skirts
might look okay on me, as long as I wore opaque
stockings, hid my varicose shins. How I wish we could break
out of this whale-boned century and move on, at least
to the twentieth. Fast forward to Harjo, gallop
like horses of "fur and teeth," horses that burn like stars. Strip
down to hard, unadorned muscle and flesh, wade into Lucille
Clifton's poems, shake ungirdled hips with "space
to move around in." But we're laced tight to the syllabus, and
the only way out is for Jane Eyre to marry her Rochester,
for Jo March to wed Professor Bhaer, her "bear,"
after learning to bite her "abominable tongue." How long
before someone, anyone in this room, will begin to growl?

IN THE SEMINAR, TRYING TO LAUNCH *PASSAGE TO INDIA*

I've got to lecture on Forster and the Raj, the partition of Bengal,
but I can't focus, and it's not only
that I'm remembering my own months
in India, the smells of cardamom, turmeric mingling with charcoal
smoke amid rickshaws, water
buffalo, bicycles, camels, and eighteen
wheelers. It's that I'm still twitchy about the Englishness I inherited
from my mother, who sailed
to New York from Southampton
on the Queen Mary. So when Lisa complains the novel is confusing,
she can't keep track of the weird
names, I push my notes aside. "Okay,"
I say, "Let's make a list, start with the Brits." "Hopeless," spouts Richard,
"they're racists, all of them, imperialist
capitalists using their hegemonic power
to oppress the indigenous people. Detestable, disgusting, especially
Miss Quested," he grumbles. I've been
dealing with my Anglophobia
for years, ashamed of the way my mother and her snobbish brother
would blithely butcher names
of places, saying "Urnuhk*oo*lum"
instead of "Ern*ä*kulam," with the emphasis on the wrong syll*a*ble. But
before I can ask if everyone in the class
found *all* the Brits in the novel
despicable, Lupita asks why they have to live off by themselves
on the hill. "Because they like
playing royalty," sneers Richard,
adding, "They're recreating their own little England with their canned
peas and their stupid plays." He's
right. Yet I can't forget my third day
in Delhi, when Manjit led me into the sudden calm of the Hyatt
and fed me a lemon lassi, saying
she could see I'd been about to
go under from too much India too fast. And I'd thought myself
the consummate traveler—a dozen
stamps on my passport. I won't
mention the time on the beach south of Chennai when a horde

of kids followed me, clutching
at my kameez till I broke free
and stumbled into an Anglican church with its pews lined up
in rows. If it had been
1920, with a pink-cheeked British
officer nearby, I could have blubbered about those hateful boys
taunting and poking, could have
created as big a crisis as Adela Quested
when she accuses Aziz of accosting her in the cave. Now Marcy
is asking what the British were
doing in India anyway, and I've
got to backtrack to Elizabeth I, tea, opium, and indigo. But I hear
the fluting voice of my English
granny, a governess in the Punjab
who regretted the return to London, where she missed the neem
trees, the banyans, the spices,
the Bhatnagar family, and the bulbul's
song. "So what happened in the Malabar Caves," Annie is asking,
and Cathy answers: "Before Adela
entered the cavern, she was
Ronny Heaslop's fiancée, but inside the cave, she heard the voice
of her real self, so when she
came out, she'd changed,
just like India changed him, he's not the same guy she knew
in England, he's turned into
a bureaucratic jerk." And Michael
adds that, "After Adela left the cave, she heard an echo in her ear till
she finally confesses Aziz had
never bothered her at all." I didn't
know, when I arrived at JFK's Gate B31 for my first flight to Delhi,
my eyes the only blue ones among
hundreds slouched in plastic
chairs, waiting to board, that when I returned home I'd be headed
for a divorce. And I didn't
know, in towns like Ludhiana,
some men knew American women only from TV, believed us
all to be sluts, so I was half
embarrassed and half flattered
at the dinner party where the guy kept snuggling up, calling me

Marilyn Monroe, me with my
breasts no bigger than dollops of dal,
with my gray-blond hair, while my horrified elegant hosts
pried him away. But now
I'm telling the students how
I learned to say "atcha" in Punjabi, the one word I was sure I could
master, trying over and over until,
furious at my inability even to pronounce
the word for "okay," I lost it, blew up, hissed, snorted "uh-*chah*"
as loud as I could, and the whole
room shouted, I'd done it, I'd gotten it,
I could almost pass for Punjabi. Now even Richard is laughing. Yet
I don't mention how angry
I really was, how exhausted, frustrated,
and, unlike Adela Quested, up to my neck in "the real India,"
even though people were
oh, so kind, exclaiming how well
I was managing for my first time. The fluorescent lights begin
their erratic, crackling hum,
and Lisa catches my eye,
plunges in: "Mrs. Moore got it, didn't she, she liked sitting with Aziz
in the temple, he even
praised her by saying she was
'Oriental,' but why did she freak out in the caves?" Cathy explains
that "Mrs. Moore had trusted
people's goodness, but
inside the cave, all her old beliefs are erased. And see how on page 223
Forster says Mrs. Moore wasn't
the 'dear old lady' everyone
thought, India 'brought her into the open.'" Michael, José, and
Annie are nodding. Marcy is
jotting notes. I give it a minute,
take a long breath. "You know," I say, "we're all tired. What if
we quit for now. I'll see you
next week." But before I let them go—
I can't stop myself—I tell them about the first night I ever spent
in India, when the lock
to my room at the Delhi
YWCA wouldn't open from the inside, and my friends kept calling,

but the phone didn't work
and I couldn't figure out
how to let them know I was trapped until the clerk at the desk
agreed to break the rules
and allow my frantic
university hosts to climb the stairs and bang on my door, holler
at me, *"Are you there? Are you there?"*
like a blinding echo, and
I wasn't even sure if I was, or when I got out, who I would be.

ABOUT THAT "ONE ART"

It's a perfect poem, I say, and though no one
in the class is over twenty-five, everybody
nods. They've all lost: the Madame
Alexander doll fallen into the toilet, silky
hair never the same, the friend who
moved away to Dallas, a brother once again
in juvie. So many schools—thirteen in
a dozen years—I lost each friend I made
till grad school. And every move since,
something always missing—this last time,
the box that held my photo albums
of the sixties, that elastic, unveined life I'd
love to visit just once more. And now
the husbands of so many have diminished—
the cancerous prostates, the double
bypasses, the radiation, the chemo. One died
while napping. And how many women friends
have lost a breast? Or two? Now I wonder,
who'll be leaving first: me, or you? Just how
will that be mastered? And how is it even time
begins to lose itself? In class I ask why Bishop
wrote the poem as a villanelle, and so we
parse the form, say how such echoing
slows us, keeps us focused on each single
disappearance, so at first we hear lightheartedness,
a witty irony—but then the sounds grow
vaster, catch us off guard. And quicken.

TEACHING *MRS. DALLOWAY* I'M THINKING

How I'd like to buy flowers, how I'd like to place a sterling
silver bowl of peonies or cut-glass vase of tulips and irises
on the laminate seminar table in this windowless room,
and I'm thinking how I'd like to arrive before the one student
always a half-hour early, how I'd like to greet each of them
at the door, inquire after their sisters and cousins, their tíos
and abuelitas, and comfort the one who's been fired
from his job. Every Tuesday another novel about the modern
condition, those catchy phrases we use: "alienation
and fragmentation"—while for the past three weeks Jill,
the debate team captain on two scholarships, hasn't said
a word because, she told me sobbing at the break, her boyfriend
was found bloody in his apartment, shot by her brother
off his meds, and Angie, dispatching for Pleasure U Hot Line,
her shift moved to graveyard, slumps dozing
in her chair. Now Jeffrey is saying, "She's snobbish, Clarissa,
I don't like her, who cares about her maids and
her flowers, but she's right, I mean, she gets it, nothing like
a great party." It's the dinner hour, though no bells chime
on this campus, and only two of us have actually heard Big Ben,
have ever strolled through Regent's Park, ridden on
a red double-decker. But nobody around this table wonders
why Septimus hurls himself out the window, nobody
needs PTSD explained, and when Marita asks, "Wasn't it Woolf
who filled her pockets with stones and walked into
a river?" nobody says "weird," their two dozen heads bent over
pages littered with post-its. I'm thinking how I want
to say something, mend this rent in the air the way Clarissa
gathers the raveled threads of her ripped dress with a needle,
the way she draws everyone into her party, but already it's time
to pack up our pens, our notebooks, head out on the crowded
interstate, past all the newly constructed buildings with no
balconies, no wrought iron railings, these multiple stories
of steel and glass, mirrored so no one can see into them.

ALONE IN THE MUSEUM'S GREEK COLLECTION

Of course I'm reminded of "Ode on a Grecian
Urn," and wonder if, next fall when I teach Keats again,
I could bring the class to peer through all this glass
at the dozens of amphorae on their crisp laminate
stands. Amphora: from the Greek "to bear." And
how these urns bear up, carry sketches of a life we can
barely conjure, the pregnant middles of these glossy
vessels displaying such slender, muscular boys, heroes,
goddesses—and the Furies. But I fear I'd ignore
the students—I'd be mesmerized—as I am now—by an urn
labeled "Attic Red-Figure Column-Krater." Here's Orestes
kneeling on a pile of rocks, head bowed to the winged
Fury on his left, snakes writhing round
her arms. He's just killed his mother and her lover,
revenge for their slaying his father. His body is contorted,
knees and feet turned toward Apollo and Artemis, who
stand opposite, as if to offer solace. He seems
almost ripped in half. The way judges might absolve us,
saying "rightful cause," or a minister, reminding us we're
only human, and yet we're chased for years, threatened
with all the Furies' snakes. I think of the words
I muttered in the doorway of the room where
my mother lay dying, hurtful words she may have heard,
and of the words I couldn't say during the days before
my father died. There was the time I shook
and shook my colicky infant son and screamed
into his tiny face when he'd been crying for hours
and nothing I'd done could soothe him—his shrieks
shifted then to terror. Those Furies still
know where to find me, hurling their hissing vipers
around my shoulders. Though Aeschylus tells us Orestes
will be absolved, there's no release shown on this jar,
his body twisting at the core. Families—
the wars within that shape the wars without. How
can our deeds be laid to rest? Ripples in perpetuity.

ON TEACHING TOO MANY VICTORIAN NOVELS IN TOO SHORT A SPACE OF TIME DURING WHICH I BECOME

Stuffed, like a twenty-pound turkey crammed to the crust-slithery maw
not with croutons and giblets, but ribbons, pendants, waistcoats, ruffles, and plumes
till I'm dazed, logy, needing a nap trying to keep track during eight hundred
pages of Bulstrodes, Cadwalladers, Featherstones, Chicheleys, Plymdales, Hackbutts,
and Minchins, when those English villages didn't hold as many people as I pass
on the interstate in fifteen minutes or dodge at the mall the day after Thanksgiving
or slump down with at the gate waiting for the delayed flight or stare at on CNN
or MSNBC in an hour, surfing through head after talking head, each expounding
to me lounging on my couch as though we were all seated around a mahogany table
loaded with glistening plate and leaded goblets, embossed napkins, and candelabras.
But the sixteen of us at five metal-legged tables jigsawed together in our department's
closet of a seminar room with no possibility of pushing back chairs, leaning into pillows,
gazing into a fire, and holding to the light a snifter of cognac the color of autumn
leaves somewhere in an English village, are chatting away as though we are neighbors,
as if the characters in *Middlemarch* lived next door, and we've become vicar, solicitor,
seamstress, and a cousin all rolled into one, as we analyze Dorothea's encumbered vistas,
Lydgate's tightening financial noose—how lonely, how restricted, we say, grateful
for the roominess, the promise of our lives, though none of us mentions our MasterCard
or Chevy Avalanche payments, just as we ignore the fact that few of us have met
our own neighbors, since nobody ever asks anybody over for tea or drinks or Scrabble,
and if somebody is burgled or shot, we might hear about it on the car radio
driving home after Monday's six o'clock class, another night without dinner.

REREADING *THE GOLDEN BOWL*

I'd rather carry my grandmother's iridescent
Tiffany vase across six rutted parking lots while rolling
my briefcase and gripping my lunch than teach this
book. When it comes to the Master, I want to keep him
to myself, thread my own way through
polished drawing rooms and twisting garden paths. I'd
rather feel that if I'm hanging fire, speechless
in the middle of class, musing over Maggie's ruminations
to Fanny—all those suspicions about her
husband and her father's wife—I can pause as long as
I'd like. When Grandma's vase crashed
from the table, I was never sure whether the neighbor's
elbow had jostled it or my German shepherd's
tail. Two months after I'd rescued it from my cousin's
garage sale, potter friends explained
what the etched *L.C.T.* on the bottom meant, and then,
the next day, it shattered. We live our
lives through objects, I've heard an artist say. I glued
the fragments, a crude joining, but
the best I could do. All the flaws, visible and invisible,
within marriages. Friends of a woman I love
keep urging her to dump her imperious husband of forty
years. But once, when I dropped her off after
a Woody Allen film, before I pulled out of the drive,
I saw her through the front door's oval glass
with that potbellied man, an embrace so tender, so rapt,
I wanted to stay right there in my car in the dark,
absorb some of that closeness. How do we ever know
what goes on between any couple? Why
people stay, or wriggle free, or bolt? Maggie's husband
seems every inch a prince, though we begin
to wonder. Then we question our wondering. I'm finally
having Grandma's vase restored, by a woman
who understands glass. She says when she's finished
we'll barely see the gaps missing their
minuscule shards. Favrile—its color shifts as you turn it
in the light, violet to green to blue and

rose. A technique Tiffany patented in 1894, ten years
before the novel. It's not that
Maggie really lied, but that her subtle phrasings mended
her marriage—in the end, everyone was
"magnificent." For Henry James, broadcasting naked
truths would rip the webbing that holds
the world in place. I'll never teach *The Golden Bowl*—
even grad students might insist on finding
a single culprit, or demand an outburst, somewhere
in those labyrinthine paragraphs,
of uncorseted, unchaperoned emotion. Despite my
awkward gluing job, the fluted edges
of that vase lifted for all those years like petals, satiny
as the hems fluttering around
Grandma's nylon-stockinged legs that tottered under
the weight of far too many whiskeys
while she held my hand, stroked my hair, and called me
precious. Melting together various colors
of glass causes the opalescence of favrile. There's an
exercise I like to give in writing
workshops: Imagine you're holding an heirloom vase
in your hands. Turn it around, feel its shape,
its smooth or grainy, pebbly texture. Now look down
into it, where at the bottom you'll see
a wisp of thread or a hairline crack. Which is it? What
happens next? Maybe in time
one student will find a tattered copy of the book, will
open it with a careful hand, so
the pages won't crumble, the spine doesn't break.

WANG WEI IN THE WORKSHOP

Twelve hundred years
since the eighth century.
Of nineteen translations,
we've looked at five.
Lily is crying after
reading her poem
about her home city
of Hong Kong, where,
in a building designed
for ten dozen stories,
six men hauling waste
died when the elevator
shaft collapsed and
plunged twenty floors.
From that roof, no one
sees the house
of a small family
eating from porcelain
bowls on a wooden
table balanced
on level ground.
How can a moon
slip so far down
those concrete walls?

LANGSTON HUGHES' "WEARY BLUES"

Needs no explaining in this class. No one needs a gloss
on "Suicide's Note," that river so calm, asking a kiss,
yet none of us around this table
has ever been kept out of a KFC or a multiplex
because of our skin. "Nobody knows the trouble
I've seen," sang Lena Horne, who couldn't stay
at the Savoy-Plaza after she'd
made the crowd swing. Enough trouble right here
in this room. Ann's just driven from the hospice,
her gay dad's body shriveling into the sheets,
her mother and brothers refusing
to visit. Last week Robert's cousins were found
mangled by the train tracks in Sabinas for the Los Zetas
dope they were running, only way to pay for beans
and rice. This morning in my office
Christina soaked through the six tissues I offered
as she told how the fucked-up ex-marine raped her
in the ass over and over, his loaded .45 beside
the pillow. No wonder Hughes'
pianist "stopped playing and went to bed," where
he "slept like a rock or a man that's dead." I need
to focus on the poem, call and response, structure
of the blues. Nathan might help,
he's a musician. But already he's talking: "Hey, after
class, how many of y'all want to drive over to JJ's, awesome
piano, sax, bass." And all I say is, "Count me in."

WHY I DREAD TEACHING *THE SUN ALSO RISES*

When I used to picture the whole class, all fifty-six of us, lounging
around a bar, sprawled under a fly-ridden
fan creaking overhead with a bartender listening like a burnt-out priest
and a throaty half-lidded alto crooning to a mike,
I'd forget that always, even after I deliver my riff about World War One
and life in the trenches where the guys
watched their buddies' brains explode into bloody pulp after wading
for months in mud up to their knees,
one of the students, maybe Tiffany, will begin to whine, "This book
is disgusting, why should we care about no-good
drunks wandering around destroying their God-given bodies,
and as for Brett, she's a total slut, the fact
that Jake loves her tells you how sick he is, and anyway, why do we
have to read such depressing novels?"
Then Bryan will say, "Yeah, she's right, and how come these dudes
can afford to eat in all these pricey restaurants,"
and even after William chimes in to counter that Jake actually has a job,
Bryan will sneer, "Sure, he works maybe five minutes
between drinks"—and it's uphill work to steer the class back on track,
ask them if they've ever been hurt so badly
all they want to do is forget, but if I'm lucky it'll be William who pipes up
again to say, "Haven't y'all done Fiesta, come on,
you know how you party nonstop till you find out which of your friends
are the real jerks, the serious assholes, and
then you know the score, aren't fooled by anybody any more." Maybe
I used to remember the year when I traveled
with a cousin and his group of musicians, summer afternoons in Verona
over a three-hour lunch before the concert
when the notes of Vivaldi flew to the dome of the cathedral and lived
in my ears all the next day and the next as we ordered
Campari and soda before the evening's *passegiatta,* the long lounging
at a round table as we watched the women and men
saunter and the *ragazzi* jostle and the swallows lift above the piazza,
swirl and dip while the sun dropped and the sky
turned rose, before a few of us found a little *ristorante* and ordered trout
caught that morning from a stream in the Dolomites
where later we walked in meadows so far above the cars and smoke

we thought we'd been lofted to a snow-glazed heaven.
During those months I forgot everything but the sweet tang of the air.
But that's not the whole of it, not really the truth.
How I worked to forget the nights when that cousin was so drunk
he made Mike in the novel look like a hero,
made Frances's sniping at Robert Cohn look sweet and kind, the way
he'd yell at his girlfriend and call her "bitch,"
the way his hands would slide over the breasts and bottoms of women
before they even realized he'd crossed that boundary
right out in public, and why nobody slugged him I still don't know.
But then there was the semester when Guadalupe
perked up the class by saying that the novel reminded her of childhood
in Monterrey, when her father took the family
to the Plaza de Toros on Sundays and explained why the *torero* wears
a suit of lights decorated with gold and silver threads,
and how he uses the long skinny sword only for killing, how it's all a ritual,
and that—just like Jake tells Brett—you're supposed
to focus on the bull, on every little movement, so it's not so horrible,
it's like a ballet, a dance, though with death, and
so graceful it's kind of beautiful, but even so, she found it hard to see
all the blood, and hardest to watch the horses.
The students were lined up in rows of unmoveable desks, and
one of the fluorescent bulbs overhead
flickered on and off as the room grew quiet and nobody rustled a page.
It's not so easy to spot grace under pressure.
I always wanted to be one of the insiders—not a whiner,
sentimental, squeamish, like Robert Cohn.
When I taught *Lord of the Flies* to high school seniors, a couple of boys
brought in a bloody pig's head dripping
in a paper bag, and I only said, "Cool, where did you guys get that?"
These days I can't stomach anything stronger
than San Pellegrino after years as a Johnny Walker on the rocks
wannabe aficionado, and I've never been in a war.
But I know how it feels when someone in a group, even in a family,
goes berserk like a maddened bull, how it feels when
from out of nowhere, talk fired like a mortar shell explodes the head
sitting next to you, maybe your own, open
down to the bone, with no one who can bring together the viscous
edges of the wound, and you're so numb

all you can do is try to walk without stumbling, focus on the next step,
    the next drink, even if it's orange juice, because
this bull won't give up the ghost with a straight swoop of a blade.
    What you want is to go off alone and dive
into deep, clean water, start over with no carnage anywhere in sight,
    as if you could, and isn't it pretty to think so.

WHENEVER WE'VE DIPPED INTO *WALDEN*

Some sophomore will say "Sure, okay, I get Thoreau's
whole 'tonic of wildness' thing, but it's not so noble
to live off by yourself with the beavers,"
and I'll almost agree, till I remember sailing through
Norwegian fjords with a hankering to live out my days
gazing at larches and spruce, whirling
gulls and waterfalls. Those inlets more pristine than
Squam, the New Hampshire lake where I splashed
in the shallows before I could walk. But
living alone on a sub-arctic slope, I'd shrivel to a brittle
husk. Not only Squam's dappling birch leaves, expanse
of water beyond the pine needles
clustered in bundles snug as my sisters and me tucked in
our cots—we had those silvery nights and days together,
no alarms jangling us awake and
shoving us off to separate schools in buses crammed with
jostling kids. We didn't know then how often Grandpop
bellowed at Daddy after breakfast
or that Grandma drank herself dizzy before dinner,
didn't know why Mom ignored speed limits careening
into Plymouth for aspirin and
more sherry. Nightmares never infected our sleep
in the cottage where ancestors had dressed to be married,
no naggings interrupted our Nestlé's
cocoa in the high-raftered hall beside the field where our
great-uncles' horseshoes clanked before Vespers. Invisible,
our dead, like rings inside the white
pines. My sisters and I bestowed secret names on every
granite boulder we climbed. But over the years we drifted,
driven by calendars and deadlines,
by fears of Mom's sporadic rages, Daddy's withdrawals, hissed
breaths, the jangling ice in his highballs. And our jealousies:
which of us was prettiest, smartest,
nicest, which one Mom prized most. "We do not treat ourselves
nor one another thus tenderly," said Thoreau. Yet now after
funerals and weddings, divorces,
remarriages, after a son-in-law's suicide, a brother's multiple

myeloma, we've returned to the lake. During class, one
student will always remind us
that Henry David didn't exactly make it on his own
while squatting on Emerson's land, since friends stopped by
to talk about books, his mother
brought him fresh-baked blueberry pies, and he'd stroll
into the village for gossip and cornmeal. How could I
"suck out all the marrow of life" if
I were alone? By that New Hampshire lake, the past rests
underfoot like pine needles softening to silt. Last June,
after the semester's end, when my sisters
and I returned to Squam, while they were off with husbands
and kids, canoeing or napping on the porch or finishing
another 3000-piece puzzle, a familial quiet
pillowed the granite stone I leaned on, formed from the earth's
magma how many eons ago, those volcanic eruptions
that solidified into the rockbed
holding me to one small ridge, one ripple in a vast open
bowl, the lake where water is always leaving to become air.

PREPARING JEFFERS' "VULTURE" BEFORE CLASS

I'm already predicting the reaction: "Who cares 'how beautiful
he looked,' that bird gliding 'on those great sails,'
this guy is freaking weird
if he wants to be shredded like that." So I'm wondering if I should
mention what happened a year ago when
I turned from a booth on
wind power at our neighborhood's GreenFest to face a Eurasian
Eagle Owl on a man's gloved arm. Stared right
into me. I don't know
how long I froze, swept into that centered gaze. I guess tonight
I could propose that maybe death Jeffers' way
wouldn't be worse than
the doctors' slipping a gastric feeding tube into my father's
stomach, puncturing his lung, then jamming
a ventilating tube down
his throat, after which he never talked again. "Iatrogenic mishaps,"
such things are called, the complications, side
effects of common medical
procedures, like the euphemism "therapies" for the chiseling
through bone, the screws in my mother's knees,
the implanted defibrillator
that shocked her heart back to its familiar thud after it had
wrenched to a stop. Finally she gave up eating,
and then, even water. She'd
never read the Dylan Thomas poem, never raged against
the dying of the light. I know what Goethe
said, but is it really light
that leaves? I've read accounts of mystics who talk of luminosity,
radiance that beckons, leads them to die in
utter calm. That Eagle Owl,
its clean ferocity—a moment nothing short of rapture. No wonder
people say those birds connect us with
the universe. As if to scoff
at all our needles, tubes, the tinkerings, machinery we submit to,
hoping we'll delay what has to come. But
the vulture, Jeffers knew,
feeds only on flesh no longer living, and, even then, a social

bird, it calls to neighboring flocks to join
in cleaning up the land,
this bird that, for the Pueblo people, signaled purification. The Parsi
Zoroastrians exposed their dead on "towers
of silence," a final act
of charity, providing the birds with food that otherwise would
go to waste. *Cathartes Aura:* "Golden
Purifier"—in Buddhism,
compassion. Which is spacious, patient, allowing for existing
things to change. I remember reading
that once a toddler was
found on a mountain peak beside a vulture. He'd been missing
for three days, but was smiling, utterly
unhurt, though on his
grimy shirt were pierced two sets of talon marks, a rip
from a hooked beak. "What an
enskyment," says
Jeffers. What a way to begin a life, or, I'm thinking, end.

INNISFREE, THEY GET

These sophomores understand a lake—or the South
Texas shore, the Gulf. But they don't
know the birds. Or plants, or flowers. Today
with Williams' poem, Queen Anne's lace has never
been so remote a thing, and though
just north of town it takes the fields by force,
these kids have never noticed. I draw
an image on the board: the umbel
and its dozens of florets. My art work's
lame, but now the flower's in focus. I say
I know they've seen the grasses along
the interstate, the way in a breeze they dip
and sway, and just imagine a whole field
of these white blossoms trembling
like a single body that quivers from simply
being touched. Last month when reading
Yeats, everyone knew that primal
longing for water, if not an Irish lake,
then the pond at an opa's hill country ranch,
or the creek by an abuelo's house
near the border. Some even knew
that Yeats' bean rows referred to *Walden,*
and each one of them, I could tell
from their eyes, wanted peace to come
dropping slow. Laptops sat inert beside
that vision. But even I hadn't known
that Yeats' linnet was not some uniquely
Irish avian creature, but close cousin
to the same red house finch that flocks
to my own feeder, perches in our live oaks
and pittosporum every day, in the deep
core of my own life, where—and this
I won't tell the students—you are with me,
day and night, the fibers of that touch,
all a glimmer, and right here, at home.

I'M NOT SURE THE CHERRY IS THE "LOVELIEST OF TREES"

So from the first line of the poem I'm quibbling,
and I don't even teach this poem now
I'm pushing threescore and ten. All that counting
Housman has us busy doing, figuring
the speaker's age, and I know in class we'd end up
focusing on the stanzas with the math. Yet
students never had trouble getting hold
of the poem's carpe diem message: Inhale
the scent of roses while you can. I've never seen
a flowering cherry, have never known
spring in Washington D.C. or England or
been invited to a *hanami,* a party to view
the blooms in Tokyo. But I knew the dogwoods
lacing my first hesitant steps, have known
white pines' needles gleaming with
light reflected from a northern lake, and
I've known the palo verdes in the dusty Sonoran
desert where Rudy, my first boyfriend,
kissed me. And the olives I planted
with my former husband, shoveling down
into Phoenix hardpan. The eucalyptus lifting
their astringent scent in the Berkeley hills
where I lay in a carpet of fog-softened leaves, ecstatic
with a lover. The lemon tree by the front door
of the house where my son was born. I could say
"with rue my heart is laden" for these and all
the trees I may never see again: banyans and teak,
neem trees, cinnamon and coconut palms,
the bodhi tree—under which the Buddha
sat so still. And since I haven't many springs
left in me—a dozen? two?—maybe,
like the woman diagnosed with terminal
cancer who traveled seven continents
compiling a life list of eight thousand birds,
I could search out all the trees I've never seen,
including the blossoming cherry. In California

there's a bristlecone that's lived for almost
five thousand years, and in Sweden, a spruce
that's lived for close to ten. That woman's travels
kept her cancer in remission, her doctors
were amazed. But how can I leave our own
Mexican persimmon near the drive, its peeling
layers of coppery silver bark, its branching
trunk I can't begin to wrap my arms around?

COMING TO CATHER

I'm still afloat from last night's performance of Mahler's Fourth,
and the room is strangely silent till Michele
looks up and whispers,
"This is the best book of the semester." Everyone nods, but
their eyes are vague, unfocused, as if they're
surrounded by an earthen
sea of gramas and bluestems, wading through prairie
grasses that once stretched from Manitoba
down into Cather's Nebraska
and on into Texas. It's time to get the class going, but I can't
block out that theme from the third movement,
the violins. A relief
when Charlotte speaks up, says her family came from the same
Bohemia as Ántonia's, and that her great-grandfather
built violins, violas, and
cellos for his wife and kids, their own double string
quartet. She insists, "He'd never have committed
suicide like Ántonia's dad." But
Jason says, "It could zap anybody's spirit, plowing unbroken
sod," and Geoffrey adds that "Ántonia's father
was a really talented
musician, respected in the old country, so how could he
be a farmer, no surprise he shot himself, living
in a dugout hovel." I hear
the strings again, the violinists' bows lifting at the same
moment like the grasses in a breeze, stems
bending in one
direction. But I bring myself back to the book, and
we linger over lines describing the prairie grass
that "was the country,
as the water is the sea." Years ago, moving to Texas, I felt
adrift as if I'd entered Cather's novel, living
as we did on a parcel of land
out of town, no neighbors in sight. I tell the class about
the Polish word *tęsknota:* stronger than our
"nostalgia," meaning "pain

of distance." The sound of those cellos in the Mahler. My then
husband tried to grow all our own food. Wanted
goats, chickens, melons,
corn. Acres of land we couldn't afford, bugs, rabbits, deer,
hot wind biting at the garden, bad weather chewing
on the marriage. The dogs'
tails whisked through waves of the grasses like fins. How
that husband filled our narrow house with music,
sounds of his viola, silky
tenor lofting toward the trees. No human voice in Mahler's
Fourth till the last movement. A lone soprano
singing of a childlike heaven. It was
a long drive into town those years, as we tried to keep the pair of
ourselves afloat. Only five minutes left in the class
and I need to wrap things up,
explain next week's assignment. But I wish all twenty-two of us
could pile into our cars, caravan out to the hills
where now in November
the grasses are seeding. Mahler's work begins and ends
in a different key. I haven't wanted to return
to the place where the marriage
went under. Twelve, maybe fifteen years have passed
and finally, I hear the symphony, whole again.

THE MORNING AFTER OUR SECOND ECOPOETRY CLASS

I'm online reading that our infant universe rang
with reverberations of cosmic bells that rippled the primordial
darkness like a pond pounded by stones, and I'm still
thinking about Daniel's puzzlement last night
over the essay "Nature and Silence," in which Christopher Manes
argues we need to listen to the language of the world
beyond our human words. But even though Melanie
brought drawings showing how the Chinese ideogram for *bird*
developed from an image of an actual bird, and even
though I explained that *aleph* and the letter *A*
came from the Phoenician symbol for *ox,* Daniel was not alone
in wondering how rocks could speak. We talked
for half an hour about the way words can mask,
serve as distractions. Once, at Tortuguero, about to go zip-lining,
six of us chattered away on the platform a hundred
and fifty feet above the rain forest floor until
we let loose to zoom along the cable over the canopy, the kids
whooping like howlers, those raucous monkeys whose
cries I'd mistaken for rowdies at the hotel bar
the night before. We sped over trees so fast we couldn't have
seen a motmot or aracari if it had flitted right below
our ankles. On the ground, our guide pointed out
Jesus Christ lizards and spectacled caimans I might have mistaken
for logs. He knew the calls of manakins, oropendolas,
and toucans—he would stop and cock his head
to listen—but oh, how he would natter. Kayaking in the midst
of mangroves thick with the absence of human prattle,
he'd be rapid-firing details about the next
day's agenda. One midnight, four of us followed a local guy
onto the beach, the tide thrumming its mantra
beneath a spangling of stars. It wasn't long
before the green sea turtles dragged their four-hundred-pound
bodies onto the beach to dig their nests. We stood
beside one as she dropped a hundred eggs down
into the hollowed sand. Other than the rustle of surf, there was
no sound but the dry chuff, sigh, the gasp she gave

between each batch of half a dozen glistening eggs,
                the flesh within the carapace gathering strength for the next
        long push. These creatures have been around
for two hundred million years. Hindus say
                it's a giant turtle that holds up the world. Next Thursday
        I'll tell the class about that night, how none of us spoke,
even walking back up the beach and
                down the road. But how to describe a silence that echoes
        in the rocky crust, the mantle of my bones.

TEACHING "THE RED WHEELBARROW" THE 30TH TIME

I know I've explained how
Williams didn't like tapping
tired old symbols, but
these sophomores are
not convinced. They've
got that wheelbarrow hard
at work: it symbolizes life, since
it's red, like blood; they've
got it carrying feed, back and
forth from the coop to keep
those chickens alive so
they can be busy laying eggs,
though they're white, which
stands for death. Susanna
says the poem is about
her grandpa, up at four
and out to the barn. I'm tired
of chatter, of words dragged
around to mean what they
don't. I'm tired of stories,
of somebody always *doing* something, or not
doing what somebody
wishes they would. Tired of the whole
subject-verb-object paradigm. I'd
even like erasing
the prepositions in the poem,
deleting "beside" and "with." I want
only the barrow, feathers, and
water left from rain. Separate,
not even in relation, as
with the elements of a T'ang Dynasty poem,
the kind Williams loved,
the sort he and
Rexroth translated. Just
the Chinese characters
like drawings, the blank
spaces breaths, each one

itself: wheelbarrow, red, rain water, chickens,
white. There's
a quiet I want that won't happen
in this discussion,
a silence that comes after
long rain, the hush
when you swear you can
feel the swirl of
planets, the shifting
of rocks. I should lead
the class outside; we could
sit on the grass, look
at a red bud
tree, an empty
stone bench. But somehow
I end up telling a story
after all, the one about
Williams the doctor
having just explained to a mother and father
their child would die, or
was it the child
had died and
he had to break the news. Then
he walked down
the hall and stared out the window
at a wheelbarrow and a few
chickens. Now
the whole class is with me. I don't
remember where
I heard the story. I'm not sure
it's even true. The poem itself is
silent. You can't hear
any clucking.

AFTER SPRING BREAK, ARRIVING AT POUND'S "IN A STATION OF THE METRO"

I'm just home from five days of slogging through
overcoats and umbrellas and feet, cold
pavement in New York. Weary of crowds. "How can
this be a poem?" asks Jay, and—
though for years I've loved these two lines—I hesitate,
thinking: if Pound's "Petals on a wet,
black bough" are like faces in a crowd, they must be
wilted, bruised by the hammering
clamor of hustle and need. "It's about ghosts," Jennifer
insists, "or at least dead people, and
someone's putting flowers by a grave. The bough,"
she goes on, "is the casket, and the crowd's
the family, everybody's crying, so the bough's wet
with tears." But Graciela says she knows
they call the subway system in Paris "Le Métro," so
the poem is "a metaphor showing
how people in the dirty underground tunnel look fresh,
like flowers." Thirty heads lift and nod,
and for a split second I'm back in line at La Guardia's
Gate B5 waiting to buy a bottle of water,
my carry-on slicing into my shoulder, as the faces
around me swivel like sunflowers
toward the sun when a teenage boy whispers, "It's her,
it is, it's Halle Berry," and suddenly we're all
abloom, a petaled row leading to one specimen
rose, even as our feet cramp
into the tile floor. "I get it," says Molly. "This is
about the surreal feeling you'd have
in a subway, a rush of people, and you don't know
anyone. Still, you feel every human being
is delicate." I tell them that the poem grew after
Pound was stunned by the flood
of faces emerging from the metro at La Concorde,
how he struggled to compress
thirty lines into twenty seed-packed words. Molly's

right that we're ephemeral as
flowers, and Jennifer may not be so far off after all,
for none of us—not Halle Berry, not
this classroom, nothing, except perhaps the subway
tracks and colonies of rats,
and possibly, improbably, Pound's poem—will last.

ARRIVING AT WALLACE STEVENS IN THE 13TH WEEK

I borrow an apple from Amy, place it on the carpet, and ask
what's changed, as we stare at this red and yellow
freckled luminescence, our circled desks surrounding the mind
of nothing in our midst, altered by the various
blues of our various guitars. We agree "Study of Two Pears"
is about pears, but "The Idea of Order at Key West"
hums beyond the genius of these walls, and twenty pairs of eyes
puzzle over wide-open Nortons till Tony proclaims
the singer in the poem to be the moon, since it's always pulling
at the tides, causing the ocean's roar. But
tonight I stifle my irritation that he's found what isn't there
in the poem's portrayal of a woman's seaside
singing. For once I let Tony be artificer of his own notes,
even if dimly starred, as he strides alongside
the poem, thwarting my blessed rage for order honed by forty
years in classrooms. Yet I want him to slip
barefoot into the poem's curling surf, want him to swim out
into the noctilucent swell of it with no guiding moon
or pinpoint of harbor light, just the rise and fall of the waves
with their unpredictable lines, the undertow
of the water's elastic weight, though I don't want him to drown,
and maybe I'm the one who's deaf to songs
along the shore, to hymns that buzz beside my ears. Maybe
I can follow only one blackbird at a time,
blind to the undulate spangles of another's sense of things.

NEXT-TO-LAST WEEK IN THE SENIOR WORKSHOP

We're all chuckling over Brad's anti-football
poem, and awed by Meg's poem
on puberty rites among the Diegueno
of Baja, California, and, while everyone's
tuckered by this time in the semester, there's
a warmth in the room that wasn't here
in September or even October when the temps
hovered in the nineties, a comfort sewn
by fourteen minds bent over each other's
poems so that week by week we've all
knitted into each other, and now,
when it's time to end, it feels like layers
of skin being peeled. Sometimes, even
the best students won't bother to find me
in my office after winter break to retrieve
their portfolios. Most I'll never see
after finals. How I want to hang on, as if they're
my own children, say, "Keep in touch,"
"Don't get lost." And though after each
semester ends, it feels like sailing out
into open seas, unencumbered space,
fresh winds, I always fear it may be
me I'm losing, as if, without those voices
every week, I won't know what game
I'm playing, won't know what rituals
to follow, as if I won't find land again.

BOOKS, BATH TOWELS, AND BEYOND

After Gary asked, "Will we ever read
any normal people in this class?" and I quipped,
"No, of course not," and after the laughter had quieted,
we ambled through "Song of Myself," celebrating
our "respiration and inspiration," traveling along
with the voices of sailors, prostitutes, presidents, and tree-toads,
in sync with the poet's vision. No one
this time—not even Gary—grumbled about
Whitman's disgusting ego, and yet when we came to the place
where God is "a loving bedfellow"
who leaves "baskets covered with white towels
bulging the house with their plenty," I was the one who
wanted to stop. At that point, I've always
been puzzled. I get it that a lover could
be like a god. But *towels?* We'd just finished *The House*
of the Seven Gables, and I wondered if
Hepzibah or Phoebe ever sold linens in their shop. Yet
we never hear Hawthorne talking about blankets or sheets or
how anybody washes his face or her hands,
let alone armpits or "soft-tickling genitals"—leave
those to Uncle Walt. The store Hepzibah opened: a first step
in easing the grip of her cursed
ancestors, of joining the sunlit world. Last summer
when my husband and I moved back into our old house after
a massive redo, we gave away box after box
of sweaters and tchotchkes. We even disposed of old
books, including those with my neon markings in the margins
blunt as Gary's outbursts in class: "Ugh,"
"NO," and "Wow!" It was time to loosen the mind
beyond the nub of the old self. My mother used to huff through
the house every year like a great wind,
and when she settled down, not a doll over
twelve months old remained, not a dress, not a scarf, not even
lint wisping in a drawer. One year during
a flood, my husband's letters from lifelong friends
drowned in the garage, morphed back into pulp. I never hoped

the past would vanish into a blank, and yet,
when Holgrave in the novel cries, "Shall we never,
never get rid of this Past!" I, too, want it washed clean, to wake
in the morning released from echoes
of my father's muttered invectives, my mother's
searing tongue. I've now torn to rags the rust-stained towels
from my former marriage and
my husband's bachelorhood sheets, raveled
threads drooping like fishnets. How Hawthorne's Phoebe
opened that heavy-lidded house
to the light. I used to scorn her chirpy domesticity,
praying along with Emily Dickinson—whose balance
Gary had also questioned—"God keep me
from what they call *households*." And yet, after
my husband and I returned to our remade, renewed house,
what did I do but go shopping
for towels. Back and forth to seven strip malls,
bringing home only to return I don't know how many colors,
till finally, I settled on white. And as I
pulled out my MasterCard to pay for the contents
of my brimming cart, a gaunt, wizened man entered
the check-out line, hands pressing
to his chest two white towels just like mine,
eyes lifted to the ceiling as if in prayer. I doubt that Gary
would think it normal to greet the divine
while clutching terry cloth. But now I see
that Whitman knew what fresh towels could mean for a dazed
and puffy face, white towels unspecked by blood
or errant coils of hair, towels that spill from a basket
like sea-foam. Like cirrus clouds adrift while we're loafing
on tender, newly sprouted blades of grass
growing from the loam under our boot soles,
from graves of the old and decaying, all we've finally buried.

IN OUR CLASS ON ROETHKE

Jennifer's complaining he's really a wimp,
his endings don't grab her. "And what's more,
in 'The Waking,' he sounds drugged,
like maybe he's dying," says Jennifer, adding
she feels the poem is about death, since
it made her depressed, especially "that worm
climbing the winding stair." I almost holler out
she's got it wrong, that's not the poem I've loved.
But who can tell how light will take a tree,
predict the progressions of shadow shifting
into sun. We've just slipped back
into our chairs, after a trek across campus
to watch Tibetan monks tip grains of sand
around edges of the mandala that tomorrow
they'll efface, an illustration of Wallace Stevens'
mantra we've discussed, the only constant is change.
I'm grateful for Daniel, who says the poem
is about what the monks are doing, filling in
that space, grain of sand by grain of sand,
taking it slow. "And then, it'll all be gone," says Daniel,
adding, "It's hard to imagine
investing so much in something that won't last."
A measured way, the monks' design.
And one I've tried to learn to practice, studying
to forget the frantic hurry-skurry memorized
at my mother's knee. The last word she ever spoke
was "quick," and "quick" again, as if the dance
could never end too soon. Great Nature always
has that other thing to do to us—but
now I guess I must explain how Roethke
suffered from despair, yet how he also
learned to sing and whistle, romping with the bears
along the living ground. I say aloud,
"This poem is one I'd like someone to read
if there's a funeral when I die," and
Brittany says, "Oh please don't even think that way."

These students here beside me, every
Thursday evening, all semester. A week
till finals, then it's over. Our syllables
commingling, little speech-threaders. They keep
my shaking steady. Line by phrase,
word by breath, we learn by going, as we go.

ENDING THE SEMESTER IN AM LIT

The guy who served as a lighthouse
when discussions had grown so foggy I couldn't
steer us back on course—the one who never missed
a class, who camped in my office every
Wednesday afternoon obsessed with Bartleby
and Ahab, made all A's and wrote a dynamite final—
hasn't turned in his long essay. Is he
bleeding on a gurney in the ER, or moaning
by the freeway in a pile of smashed glass and mangled
chrome? I email, and he shoots back, "I haven't
written it." No apology, no excuse. I offer an
extra day. No response, not even to say he prefers
not to. I want to harpoon that essay and
splatter it onto my desk. I give him till
midnight, remind him, bold font on the syllabus:
"No essay, no passing grade." Still silence,
nada, no paper. Where *is* that essay? I feel
like Herman's wife Lizzie, nagging him, or Carlyle,
insisting, "Produce! Produce!" Melville's
narrator at least learned about his clerk's past
at the dead letter office, but I have no idea where
this guy works, or if he does. Is he playing
some kind of game, resisting like Bartleby,
forcing me to play Ahab, hunt him down? Why
can't I just give him an F? I've become
the narrator in Melville's story, his whole career
questioned by the scrivener's refusals. Maybe I'm
remembering my years as a grad student
when I skimped time with my son to write
all those essays, the dread dissertation, and, then, later,
meet deadlines for grades, committee
reports. Updating the CV to show every
minuscule pebble I cast into the scholarly sea. All those
sleepy post-Christmas days I missed—leaving
my boy and his dad in their jammies—to join
the tangled academic throngs at the MLA. On this guy's

final exam he added a note that said
our class had changed him, he'd been on course
to become like Ahab, netting every A in sight, but after
finishing *Moby-Dick* and then reading
Whitman, he decided to spend more time with
his daughter, who's just learning to walk, and he didn't
want to miss a single one of her
wobbling steps, he felt the pull to "loafe
and invite" his soul. But I'm left here anchorless,
like Melville's ship the *Rachel*
searching after her missing sailors, her lost children.

THE LAST TIME I TAUGHT ROBERT FROST

I shuddered when Olivia, who is writing her dissertation
on dialectics of the self in Gloria Anzaldúa, announced she found him
lovely. "Lovely?" I cried, professional composure shot,
my image of Frost collapsing suddenly as the Great Stone Face
on Cannon Mountain, the craggy Old Man fallen in shards
to the ground. True, this was not on par with the vandalizing
of his house in Vermont, Homer Noble Farm's wicker chairs,
wooden tables, dressers smashed and thrown into the fire to keep
the place warm while thirty kids swilled a hundred and fifty
cans of Bud with a dozen bottles of Jack Daniel's, and threw up
on the floor. After all, Olivia wasn't saying she didn't like
the poems, but *lovely?* A word my mother detested as phony,
like someone holding a pinkie straight out while drinking tea,
the sort of word my grandmother used when vaguely praising
a Bartók piece, or a play she didn't understand. Like people
saying, "How interesting," when what they really mean is, "Spare me
the details," or, "Could we change the subject." So when
I asked Olivia what she meant by "lovely" and she talked about
the lush, long vowel sounds, I wondered why I'd felt stabbed,
until I remembered my father's lying in the ICU, the fat respirator
tube jammed down his throat, the whoosh of forced breath
fogging the glassed-in-room, and my stroking his forehead while
my father, whom I'd never seen cry, began to leak tears down
his chiseled face. Finally, not knowing what more to do, I stood
by the window staring out at the New Hampshire pines
and began reciting one of his favorite poems: "I must go down
to the seas again, to the lonely sea and the sky." He started
to jerk, whole body spasms under the sheets, more tears carving
runnels down his cheeks, and I knew he wanted me to recite
"Stopping by Woods," his most-loved poem and maybe mine too,
but I couldn't. I couldn't turn from that window looking
out at the trees beyond the parking lot, the words to the one
poem I've known by heart for decades buried somewhere
below my throat. He died the next day. Maybe that was why
I asked the class if we could recite it, if perhaps some of them
even had it memorized, and Denise and Lupe and Nathaniel actually

said they had. So we chanted it, the other eight of us
reading from the Norton's crisp, white pages, but when we came
to the ending, not a single student needed to look down
as we sang the last stanza all together. I can't explain it, but for once
something dark and deep entered among us in the overly
air-conditioned room. As if we were all one self and yet still alone
in the cold, and wanting to stay. When we spoke again,
we talked until I had to stand up, open the door, and tell them
to leave, say it was past time for their dinners and
all the lovely, nagging promises waiting for them to keep.

(2019)

ON THE CHINESE SCROLL

a man in a boat
moves upstream toward
mountains—mist, with his
thin back bent, as he
faces the water
that flows from the hills
to the downstream pool
where he casts his thread-
slender line, alone.

OR DID I MISTAKE

the pole that pulls him
through the water for
a fishing line? Which
is it? The slant of
his hat, dark-coated
back—their angles as
he plies the current
show how he labors.

IT COULD BE THOSE

hills at the top
of the scroll aren't
rocky crags, but
rather ocean
waves cresting, and
the man's boat is
not aiming up-
stream, but down, to
the river's mouth,
which may never
murmur a sound.

I HADN'T SEEN

till now the small
thatched roofs rising
above the left
bank of the stream—
houses, where you
could stop, stretch your
legs on a couch,
a hammock, and
let the river's
current go on
its own dogged
pace without you.

EVEN TARNISHED

the sterling bowl's
repoussé iris petals swirl

across its rounded center, but
on the base, a crack somewhere,

so water placed inside—to hold
fresh-cut jonquils for a while—

leaks, staining the surface
of a polished table.

THE SILVER TONGS'

ends are shaped like bay scallops,
whose numbers have diminished in

recent years due to the loss of sea grasses
on which they fastened, and the overfishing of

sharks, who devoured the manta rays that gobbled
the scallops' predators. Such delicate, rounded pincers

are not designed to grasp anything heavier
than a cube of sugar. Scallops: ancient symbol

of the vulva, primal force within the earth. Around
an oval table at dinner, the way a guest's fingers

handled a pair of lustrous tongs could provide
the sterling moment of an evening.

THE HOLLOW

of a silver spoon, a palm,
fingers curling a shallow bowl.

To spoon-feed. Applesauce,
oatmeal, cream of wheat, chicken

broth. To enter the cave
of a waiting mouth. The bowl

up-turned, emptied of
the little it carries.

THE TRIVET'S

lacey silver ferns,
spiraling tendrils are encased

within glass that allows us to glimpse
the mahogany table's surface the trivet

is meant to protect: the cracks,
the gouged grain.

THE SILVER MILK PITCHER

on the granite counter
holds one wooden spoon

and three spatulas that rise from
the round opening like arms waving

from a narrow boat, or tongues
pulled from a mouth.

THE STERLING PLATTER

is engraved with patterns
of vines and leaves, florid

intricacies hidden when laden with
porcelain cups and saucers, sugar bowl

and creamer, tea pot, and white damask
napkins, so you don't notice the design

coils like a labyrinth with
no way in, or out.

MOM'S CREAMER

holds only a few
drops, just enough

to soften the bite of over-
steeped lapsang souchong

during late afternoon tea,
which she spent in her final

years alone, unless a daughter
happened to visit. The etched

oval on the side carries no
image—a cameo without

a face. The silver lip of
the creamer angles

to a point, sharp little
beak—peck, peck.

THE SILVER BASKET

was designed to grace
a small table, for passing

among guests to scoop a few
nibbles of sugared almonds or

walnuts from its shallow bowl, but
now it holds a cluster of polished

stones that for the Chinese mean
solidity, stability, the ground—

almost too heavy for this
dainty vessel to lift.

MOTTLED

as if with curdled cream or vitiligo,
the silver sauce boat's copper layer

underneath shows through like flesh below
the crackling skin of an oven-browned hen or

the torn hide of a roughly sheered ewe. A boat:
vessel for transport on water. Across the tablecloth

it floated gravies of our holidays. Thanksgiving—
turkey drippings, chopped giblets, white flour. Rivers

down mountains of mashed potatoes. Copper's less
precious than silver, but these days the baser

metal is stolen from alleys and back yards, a hot
commodity now it's used for fiber optics, plumbing,

and anything electrical. How a boat causes ripples in
still water, how the sun can shimmer through

clouds, sudden patches of shadow, light across
grasses of your own back yard.

THE SALT CELLAR'S

no bigger than a kinglet's
breast, one for each guest with

a tiny silver spoon alongside to dip
just a soupçon, a pinch, a smidgen of salt,

this element believed to excite desire,
a mineral that preserves, detested by evil

spirits, this covenant "before the Lord" in
the Book of Numbers, that derives from

mountains and ponds, that accounts for
most of the dissolved solids in oceans,

allowing us to float in the saltiest
seas, and not even drown.

THE SURFACE

of the small circular
silver calling card plate

is planished, little ripples
like a pond open for a friend

to drop in, or a heron's beak
to pierce the shimmer.

THE DRAGON BOWL

was the one piece I asked
my sister to send when she decided

to sell all Mom's silver, not because
it was sterling because it wasn't, only plate,

but for the sweeping creature, its tail, spikes,
fangs, claws reaching toward a bulbuous sun with

rays that spewed in every direction like the creature
itself spiralling round and round, looping its scaly

body etched and chased across the bowl's width,
this animal whose power for the Chinese lay

in its shedding skin, emerging as a new,
transformed being, able to soar, see

from a great height what has been
and what will come of it.

GLOSS

(2020)

WHAT SURFACES

Another chip in the white enameled sink, only three years old. How
I've tried to keep it pristine, and yet—
stainless steel pots scrape it till the black
cast iron breaks through. What's below a surface gloss. Now the flesh
on my hands has grown so thin
the layers underneath show through,
rivery veins and knobby metacarpals. Knuckles like pebbles—like
rocks. I've bordered my rose beds
with stones from Blanco Creek. How long
did it take to shape those irregular rounds and ovals? Our house, built
of blocks mined from the quarry only
five miles up the road—limestone
formed in the Paleozoic Era. My favorite paperweight: a fossilized
clam I found in the backyard, remains
from the time the land around us
lived under ocean. Something so pocked, wizened, holding my papers
in place. Arriving at the Grand Canyon,
we've all peered down at those
dozens of rock layers—granite, dolomite, sandstone, shale, basalt—
formed two million, maybe two billion
years ago. And who would want
to mend that great magenta-, purple-, blood-shaded rip in the earth's
surface? It's what we come for,
to gawk at all those layers, exposed.

ALONG A RIVER

you will know upstream
from downstream. Off these
sloped banks, clumped water
hyacinths, mossy
strands provide clues, no
movement other than
scarlet dragonflies
flitting the surface,
mosquitoes. Beyond,
a source you must find.

THE RMS QUEEN MARY

Docked since '67 in Long Beach, the same liner Mom sailed in '39 from England to marry my father. Relic of a past the well-heeled now are recreating, "cruise" being the upscale way for travel, like the tour labeled "Alaska's Glorious Inside Passage in 8 Days," or the one advertised as "Wonders of the Mekong, 10 Days Down South Asia's Amazing River." But the Queen Mary was not designed for this sort of travel, rather to get you from Southampton to New York in less than a week.

Or from one life to another. Within a year Mom had lost most of her Britishisms, but not all. "Oh, you Americans," she'd shudder at us daughters, though she carried on with Thanksgiving and the Fourth of July. The phrase "carry on" holds more weight than hand luggage. Alone on the Queen Mary. Not part of any migration. No soft-bosomed granny, no jocular uncles to keep her afloat. Those glossy first-class cabins were kept spotless. Then repainted, reupholstered, refurbished. Not a trace of her.

THE SILVER TUREEN (1)

It keeps slamming open, exposing the tangled roots of garlic I store inside it. How often my father quoted Lear's praise of Cordelia: "Her voice was ever soft and low, an excellent thing in woman." Better dead than loud. The tureen won't stay shut. Garlic smell throughout the house. And, of course, it's prettier when closed. Glossier, sleeker. The polished dome like a perfect loaf of risen bread, or a silky breast. Sleek, smooth, easy to run a hand over, no sharp edges.

TREADING THE BOARDS

What Great Granny Lilian Graves did before she became respectable. Or what she did after she'd been respectable, after her husband died of drink, leaving her penniless with four little ones. She farmed them out to relatives and went on stage. Ravishing, like Mom's mother and Mom herself, Great Granny danced, sang, and acted wherever she could. Even in America, in Tombstone, where she held the stage of the Bird Cage Theater with Buffalo Bill Cody, "a *charming* man," she once told Mom with a little smile. Where was it she caught Prince Edward's eye? London? Paris? After he tired of her, he set her up with Mr. Graves, who needed a research assistant. And why not a wife as well? The Bird Cage Theater to the British Museum. Later, widowed, she'd let my mother visit, served her tea. Mom would sneak up to London on the train, disobeying her mummy who'd tried to keep a daughter from this disgraceful woman who'd abandoned her children for a life of shame. "When you go out to Hong Kong, my dear," Great Granny told my seventeen-year-old mother, "you must buy black lace underwear. They do such things exquisitely."

"LITTLE PIECES OF STRING TOO SMALL TO BE USED"

Granny's label on a box in her attic. Four dozen cardboard boxes, filed alphabetically. And all tied with string. How Mom laughed about Granny, but when at bedtime I'd beg her to tell about her growing up in England, she'd brush my forehead with a quick, dry kiss, tuck the sheet around my shoulders, close my door.

Under the covers, with a flashlight, I read and reread the books Granny sent, about two West Berkshire kids in the '30s. Was Mom's childhood like theirs? The novels came in a parcel tied with knots so tight we had to use scissors, so by the time we'd unwrapped the box, bits of string littered the cement floor. I'd thank Granny on white blue-lined paper with my Parker fountain pen, and she'd answer on tissue-thin blue paper, stamps of Queen Elizabeth on the envelopes. I even wrote to Grace James, the books' author, and she wrote back on paper just like Granny's, telling me what happened to those children when they grew up, and explaining the stories behind the stories. I kept those pieces of thin blue paper, a tidy stack in my bedside drawer. But not wrapped with string.

Now in an old box, I've found a letter dated 1934, addressed to Mrs. Jacoby, Headmistress at Battle Abbey, Mom's "public" school. My mother's exam scores had been outstanding and could Mom's parents let her enter Cambridge, where, the letter writer was confident, Mom would "go far." But, as Mom told me once, no college for girls of her "class," no "bluestockings" in their family, and she needed to be presented at court instead, a distinction naughty Mom rejected.

My first trip home from college my bedside drawer was empty, all those blue letters gone. Have to get rid of old things, Mom said, her toes flapping the soles of her sandals.

That was after my father hadn't let me accept the scholarships I'd been offered from "good" colleges Back East. As a girl, I'd be a "bad investment" since I'd only be getting married anyway. I never kept the letters with those offers, not in a box or a drawer. Daddy did agree to pay for tuition and board at the nearby state school he'd always sneered at.

I don't remember when I carried all my diaries, notebooks, and stories out to the galvanized can in the garage. Ripped the pages into bits, everything I'd ever written. Little pieces. Too small to be used. Tossed them in. No amount of string could have held them together. Or me, at the end of my rope.

THIS FAR DOWNSTREAM

small leaves appear
distinct—pinnate,
alternate, whorled—
you can see how
they are joined to
the primary
vein, the leaf's mid-
rib, the patterns,
the direction
as they're facing
beyond the stem.

SUNDAY LUNCH AT MOM'S COUSIN DINNIE'S: JUNE 1969

I'd barely recovered from a concussive first year teaching ninth-grade English
in West Berkeley, from ear-shattering shrieks,
"Mothuh Fuckin Honky Bitch" rattling
steel lockers, but here we were, on my first trip to my mother's homeland, pulled up
in a rented Morris Mini at a gray stone, rose-trellised,
three-story house in Windsor. And here
they were, Dinnie and husband Jack in brown tweeds with their three grown kids
lined up by the arched entrance. I'd heard about Dinnie
for years, how, during the late thirties,
Mom lived with Dinnie's family in Hong Kong where the cousins crooned a breathy
Andrews Sisters knock-off act for the fellows in
the Royal Navy. Now this silver-haired,
brogue-shod, square-shouldered woman was striding up to my mother, murmuring
"Pamela darling," in a voice so exquisitely muted you
couldn't have known they hadn't seen
each other in thirty years. The two exchanged pristine pecks on the cheek. Lunch
was a limp white fish with hand-picked peas from
the garden and boiled potatoes
on gold-rimmed china. The conversation perked along politely, like water just
shy of a full boil. Asked about my students,
I tried to explain: a half mile
from the Black Panthers' headquarters, Telegraph Avenue, pimps, Black Muslims,
acid-dropping by the train tracks, but then
Penelope, Dinnie's eldest, just back
from her posh au-pair gig in Provence, asked: "What *ever* do you do about their
accents? They must be dreadful!" she moaned. I know
I came close to spitting a mouthful
of potatoes onto the linen table cloth. Now I think of the way Mom,
after sixty years in the States, still fussed about
British accents that didn't approach
RP standards. And I couldn't have told that young woman almost my age that
I'd spent years trying to flatten the lilting upper-crust
British intonations I'd learned
at my mother's knee, and that I'd begun saying "How ya doin," and "Gimme five,"
even grinning at "Sheee-it, Man" coming from
the coaches at lunch. And I couldn't have
explained that, as we hustled our students out of the building while hall guards
searched for the bomb reported in somebody's locker,

I wasn't fussing about accents. I've been
away from Berkeley now as many years as Mom had lived in the States before
our lunch with Dinnie, and after three decades
in Texas, I know I drag out my vowels,
multiplying diphthongs into triphthongs. In fact, a friend in Brooklyn has fondly
mentioned my "soothing Southern accent." Mom
would have been horrified. I'd like to see
Penelope again. Both our mothers are gone. I've heard her granddaughter's
dating a guy from Jamaica who's into trip hop.

IS HIS BOAT STRONG

enough to reach
up such a long
river with turns
beyond the first
rock ledge where all
the trees' branches
sharpen, before
the waters deepen?

SILK ROADS

Such a quiet act, the needle penetrating cloth. Loops of thread in coral, pink, fuchsia, teal, turquoise, forest green, lime, lemon, mustard, royal purple, brown, and black. The design dotted in crisp dark blue on the linen. A butterfly, a road.

The Great Silk Road. Overland. But by the time my great grandfather set off mid-nineteenth century to find more silk for Macclesfield's mills in Cheshire, he traveled by sea. The story goes he sailed up the Yangtze to ask the Chinese to trade. But how far upriver and on what sort of boat?

All from a worm, the caterpillar of a moth. Larvae of silverfish, wasps, mayflies, lacewings, and thrips produce silk, too, though not of good quality. Not used for textiles. And not for embroidery. Glossy three-ply filaments satin-stitching, chain-stitching leaves, wings, ridges in a winding path.

The prow of a ship cutting through water, the spray of droplets glistening in the light. A steel needle pricking the gaps between the woven linen threads, the needle emerging from underneath, poked back to the surface.

I don't know what Great Grandfather offered to trade for silk, only that the Chinese told him to go back where he came from. But overnight a typhoon ripped the current. In the morning, village elders boarded the battered ship, said they'd trade with this white devil, the spirits had willed it.

The pupas are dipped in boiling water or pierced with a needle. Then the cocoon is unraveled as a continuous thread. How a boat knifes its way through a current, lifting ripples, a wake. I want to slice through this story, unspool its lengths. Great-Grandfather didn't speak Mandarin. Who translated? Who traveled with him? Did trackers drag the ship through shallows, narrows of the Yangtze's Three Gorges, hauling that weight? And who paid whom for what?

Some embroideries are never finished. And even if we try to keep the underside tidy, to avoid messy knots and threads, it's hard to see a pattern on the back of the cloth, where the colors, even while shimmering, snarl.

THE SILVER TUREEN (2)

I never know when it will come crashing open, the domed lid swiveling back into the curved underside, like a pistol shot. Just shuffling past in my slippers as it sits on those four spindly grooved legs and *wham,* there it goes. I've never used it for soup, never for serving, only for storing garlic.

Which my mother hated. As she did "pasta" (which she pronounced the way she did "disaster") and anything Italian, though she'd sure cooked up plenty of macaroni and cheese casseroles when we were kids, when I didn't know a tureen from a cereal bowl. It was my New Jersey grandma's, round-bellied altarpiece of her high-ceilinged dining room, standing between the crystal candelabras atop her mahogany buffet. But I never saw it holding soup, either vichyssoise or Campbell's cream of tomato.

A lid like a mouth. Mouthing off. You and your big mouth. My father, sniping at Mom, "You don't know what you're talking about." Opening his mouth to shut hers. Keep your trap shut. That woman's got a mouth on her. There you go again, flapping your jaw.

I'm thinking of plants' stomata—"stoma," from the Greek for "mouth"—opening and closing as light and humidity shift, a silent way, inspiration and expiration, a breathing. All through the day. Not like this sudden, metallic crash. As if something no one wanted to hear is shrieked out loud. There it goes again. And I wasn't even close.

BELOW THE SALT

Granny's place before she married. A governess, helping the parlour maid polish silver before the house parties. At one of them, she met Grandfather. Sometimes the mistress let her join the grown-ups for supper, though mostly Granny nibbled buttered toast and a coddled egg upstairs with the children. Later, wife of the Chairman of the Board, she shrank from fancy dinners. From beaded, sequined dresses, from perfume and cleavage. Sent my adolescent mother instead. Grandfather escorted her on his arm, his stunning daughter, wrapped in silver fox and satin, her chocolate brown eyes, creamy skin—almost white as the salt.

IVORY CARVINGS

How it swelled in the bathroom sink, Granny's cardboard pellet. A basin full of water, and then, a slow unfurling—petals, a lotus. And more petals, rose, lavender, yellow, abloom in the chipped sink we spat in while brushing our teeth.

The lotus petals signal an expansion of the soul. Or were those paper flowers chrysanthemums? For Confucius, objects of meditation. In China even now, symbols of vitality.

For years on my living room wall—in intricate high relief, nine inches in diameter—a chrysanthemum made of ivory, poised on its stem, and set on a black background in a two-by-five-foot frame. Once it hung in Granny's high-ceilinged hallway in Hong Kong. Carved from an elephant's tusk.

How these creatures mourn their dead, circle the body, caress it with their trunks. Flap their ears, click their tusks, entwine their trunks when reuniting. Big money for those tusks, long, curved incisors. White gold.

Favorite bedtime reading, in Granny's voice, "O Best Beloved," how the elephant's child got his trunk, a painful stretching of his little nose by a crocodile. No mention of his tusks, although in Kipling's drawing they're right there, both of them, pointing toward a banana tree.

By the tenth century, not an elephant left in North Africa. Now from Kenya to Congo to Cameroon, mass killings daily. In Tanzania, villagers roll poisoned pumpkins into the road for elephants to eat.

Bananas—shaped like small tusks. Granny's collection of bric-a-brac included a banana carved from ivory. So clever, she'd say, the way the artist showed it half peeled, as if ready to eat. The petals of my ivory chrysanthemum—a mandala? Or a mouth forced open, jagged stumps, splinters of teeth?

ACCOUNTING FOR GRANNY

All the places she lived. First in Wales, Glagmorganshire, till her alcoholic father died. Then sent to South London—raised by an aunt who'd married the Vicar of St. Peter's Parish. Then at fifteen, hired as a governess. Even lived with her "family" in Shimla—she loved India, Mom said. Then Grandfather, China, and a succession of houses.

The one Mom showed me on my first trip to England: four stories, with a drive long as the street I live on now, past rows of beech trees bordering vegetable gardens, greenhouses, rose gardens, and kennels, swooping up to the manor's stone arched entrance. The whole top story, Mom said, for the servants. Twenty? A dozen? How many rooms, how many square feet? How could Granny have kept track? A person could get lost.

And how did it happen that, after Grandfather died, it was Granny all by herself in a ratty hotel before she rented her flat, a one-bedroom "efficiency," where, with Mom once, in my twenties, I visited her? What had happened to the bank accounts? She shopped in the village, carried her groceries up the stairs. Talked about "going aloft."

Easy for my uncle to find her that December morning she didn't answer the phone. No halls to wander through. She left the flat immaculate, clean towels folded, the kitchen trash emptied. Tidy to the end. Told everyone her heart would stop on the 16th, and so it did. She'd destroyed her account books, all her calendars. Left no tracks, no record. Only a bag of bread crumbs by the sink, labeled "For the Birds."

PERHAPS THE MAN

in the boat is
only looking
down, struggling
to pull his oar
through dark water,
arm over arm,
one lift, one dip,
no time to glance
at the distant
hills, wonder where
this stream began.

"ELEGANT," SHE SAID

My new friend was chuckling, saying she cracked up when I let fly
the "f" word while speaking to an audience
of five-hundred because, she said, I look so "elegant, a class act,
a knockout." I changed the subject. She doesn't
get it. In our family I'd always been the clumsy one, by sixth grade
inhabiting a close-to-six-foot, rib-protruding,
hunched-over frame, buck teeth in braces, wispy blonde hair, pale
bluish eyes. Called "Scarecrow," "String Bean,"
then in high school, "Boobless Bean." And with a regal-shouldered,
chocolate-eyed, russet-haired mother who
modeled for the fashion pages of *The Tucson Daily Citizen.* My little
sister, a brunette, "the pretty one," began
Flair Modeling School at fourteen. Those 1950s Clairol ads asked,
"Is it true blondes have more fun?" Not
this blonde. The time I brought my drawing of a girl to show
Daddy and his only comment was a clipped,
"She's not very pretty." Over my parents' Old Fashioneds, banter
about women: "pert little nose, a shame
about her piano legs"; "good-hearted, but that horrendous pitted
skin." Now the flesh of my arms droops like
crumpled silk. Yet my husband swears he loves my bones. Once,
when Mom was around my age, she spoke of
her granny Lilian Walker Graves, who sparkled on the vaudeville
stage. Men tripped on their shoe strings at
at the sight of her, Mom said. "And my own mother," she went on,
"had that same quality, just as I did, and—as your
little sister does," she added, looking at the ceiling. But then,
the year before Mom died in the retirement
home, as I walked beside her electric cart while she steered
past wheelchairs and walkers, a resident stopped us:
"Why Pam," she gushed, "This daughter of yours—no one
would question you're her mother! She looks just like you,
moves with your elegance, your grace." Mom jerked upright
and sputtered, "She *does?*" and pressed her foot on
the accelerator, whizzing off. I had to run to catch up with her.

MAYBE HIS BOAT

is drifting back
toward the mouth
of the river,
or he's grown tired
from the long push
and the banks down
farther lure him
with the fine silt
of easy slopes,
silky tendrils,
perhaps under
the mountains' mist
something hides he
fears he will reach.

MINING SILVER

Two hundred feet down, Catholic altars, shrines. Drilling into the rock, hard hats, face guards. Sometimes the molten magma is so rich in silver, the silver forces through the quartz crystal as silver wires. Looks almost like bent earrings, cheap, tired jewelry in the trash.

STIFF UPPER LIP

1.

Headlines in *The Evening Standard, Daily Telegraph, The Observer, The Daily Mirror, Sunday News, Daily Mail,* even *The Times:* "FIRE DESTROYS BATTLE ABBEY, 120 GIRLS AWAKENED BY ROAR OF FLAMES." And following: "Mrs. Jacoby, the headmistress, tells how, with splendid discipline, they tested new fire drill." Some young as eight, the oldest seventeen. January 1931. Mom would have been thirteen. The girls had practiced over and over. One girl would be tapped to wake the others, they'd all walk single-file downstairs and out the great front doors. "Clad in their nightclothes." Four in the morning. "Not one of them became hysterical." "The flames leapt to a height of a hundred feet." The fire burned on into the next day and the Abbot's Hall was reduced to a ruin. Built in 1066, Battle of Hastings. At six a.m., Mrs. Jacoby sent a telegraph to the parents of every girl: "All well."

2.

One hundred twenty girls in flannel dressing gowns crowding the courtyard, a January pre-dawn. One hundred nineteen girls' mummies and daddies coming for them the next day. Or the next—it would never do to leave Gladys (or Cynthia or Gwendolyn, or Edith, or Violet) in the midst of those horrid cinders, of course we'll bring the car, the poor dear, she must be dreadfully frightened.

But no one came for my mother. Because Granny was in Paris visiting a friend? Because Grandfather believed the telegram from Mrs. Jacoby saying "all" was "well"? No cell phones, no texting, no email, no way even to phone her daddy, ask him to please come, please. The tower fallen. All the mistresses returned home, even the one who taught French crossed the Channel back to Amiens. Alone with the housekeeper, the cook, and the gardener—the only girl left.

3.

How do you get back to the place above the staircase where the floor boards held? Where the wallpaper swirled with primroses, delphiniums, and petunias like the petals in your mummy's garden?

It was Wendy Flith, ten years old, who woke at four thirty, hot and thirsty, slipped to the bathroom for a drink of water, and smelled smoke. Thoroughly drilled, she blew her whistle, led the girls in her dorm room down the tower stairs. Meanwhile, Mrs. Hyndman had waked from the smoke, roused the rest. Timbers like bones, ribs protruding, the entire hall blazing.

4.

My mother rarely spoke of it. When she did, her accounts didn't vary, mirrored the newspapers.' Always, it was the girls' discipline she stressed, how they faced forward, eyes on the girl leading them down the stairs.

No mention of huddling with her favorite friends, no details of the nightclothes she was wearing (a red plaid robe? one with blue piping?), or the blouses, gone to cinders, she'd never wear again. Or how cold it was, so suddenly awake in the courtyard, waiting for the firemen. Watching flames pierce the Abbey's roof. Did she see the staircase crash to the stone floor as the last girl approached the open door? The papers' details were enough.

5.

Twenty years after Battle Abbey burned, the chair. Smoke in the night, my mother and father lifting the square wooden legs, tilting its bulk through the kitchen door. A cigarette dropped during the day, an ember bubbling through cloth and horse hair down to the metal springs. Out into the night. Her nylon nightgown, his seersucker pajamas, bare feet.

The smell stayed for days. They carried the chair back into the house, set it down in the living room, its blackened stuffing surrounding a ragged hole to stare down into—the padded arm a tangled chasm, its wiry innards coiled.

INTERIOR

Those Phoenix dust storms in the forties: a solid wall, brown mass hurtling toward us, as Mom screamed, "Close the windows, close the windows!" and we raced around the house, turning handles. Even so, after, a layer of dirt blurred the lines of every shelf and counter, every table, every cushion. Every book. The bathroom basin.

Where Granny on her visit helped me brush my teeth. Brisk little strokes around and around, up to the attic, she trilled, then to the nursery, down more stairs to the parlor, the drawing room, and, finally, all the way to the cellar. Rooms I'd never known existed.

What dust can do to the lungs—those fragile, spongy organs filled with alveoli. A struggle to breathe. These tiny spaces, miniature rooms within the duplex of the lungs.

Four rooms: two bedrooms, a kitchen, living room in that house. Smoke thickening the air. My father's five packs a day, my mother's half-dozen cigarettes with drinks before their dinner, when they talked and we were not to. In our cots in our room, strict seven o'clock bedtime for my sisters and me, no talking, no questions.

After Granny's visit, my own little mouth held polished hallways leading to rooms with windows glistening to moist lawns, a robin's-egg-blue sky. No dust. Or smoke. No need to open the rattling, rusted screen door to leave a choking house.

SILVER HANDLES, SPOUTS

Silversmiths form the pot first, then the handle. And of course, a pot needs a spout. Before the Ming Dynasty, people drank tea from clay bowls. The earliest teapots held only one serving, came from the Yixing region of China, fourteenth century, and you drank your tea directly from the spout.

Nobody ever says "born with a silver handle in her hand," though there's much fuss made about babies who slip into the world gumming silver spoons. Get a handle on it, we nag, handle it, get a grip. But no one mentions the necessity for handles on silver teapots. Without one, you'd burn your fingers pouring Earl Grey.

So much you shouldn't spout. The evening's dishes crashed on the kitchen floor, my mother's screaming, my father's raging, and the next day, not a word. The night my mother stood at the front door with a suitcase, nine-year-old me pulling at her skirt, sobbing, "Don't leave, Mommy, don't leave!" The next morning, over oatmeal, not a word.

It's complicated fitting a handle—or a spout—to a silver pot with bent shears, soldering and filing. How to move steaming liquids from interior spaces without harm? A slender trickle is always preferable to a torrid gush, especially if one is chatting in polite company. And how would you hold a scalding, heavy pot in your hand without a sturdy handle and a clear spout, a way to lighten the weight inside?

LATENT IMAGE

Before she died, Mom pulled that photo out of the album, tore it to shreds. The one that showed her at seven, naked, posed like a nymph, a statue on the lawn. Grandfather's insisting she strip in front of the servants and sit like that, her legs folded to one side, her head bent in the opposite direction. His little nymph.

Stilled, in that photo, caught by silver particles, the standard black and white photographic process introduced in 1871. A photo's final image: metallic silver embedded in a gelatin coating.

"Stills," we say, stopped action, a single frame of a film. Yet I never knew Mom stilled until she died, her trim body beneath a sheet. Always moving, vacuuming every crumb of dust to be sucked into the guts of the Electrolux, its bag emptied into the garbage and gone. After dinner, Ed Sullivan on TV, her hands working a needle or scissors, her feet joggling, toes wriggling. Daytime, her sewing machine's roar, her fingers zipping the fabric toward the needle, her foot pressing the pedal, full speed. And driving, always over the limit, as if to say "get me out of here."

Silver atoms, freed when silver salts meet the light, form an image that's stable. Once the film's developed, it's bathed in a chemical fixer. Clean water clears the fixer from the print, and the latent image becomes permanent.

The story she told me long after I'd moved away: how, when, at thirteen, she asked her mother what she should do about the black hairs spiralling in her armpits, Granny said, "Father can help you with that," and he did, in the shower, every week, shaving her.

BUT EVEN THESE

stones at the base
of the scroll may
be less rounded,
sharper than they
appear, jagged
edges may loom
underwater,
threatening this
too narrow boat.

SURGERY, A LITTLE HISTORY

Stunned by the god's "feathered glory," Yeats wrote
        of Leda, in one of my mother's favorite poems. How many
                painters have rendered this image, of a woman swooning
with a swan. But the trickery, the deceit of Zeus,
        disguising himself. And now, these doctors of mine,
                with their downy reassurance. Robotic surgery, they coo,
easy as slipping into and out of a pond. Not gods,
        but white-coated, so feathery-voiced I believe them,
                sign the forms. Their sleek offices, paintings of lakes,
of cool streams on their walls. Such calming
        waters I lie back, feet propped in the metal stirrups,
                till the speculum is pressed inside, probing for what lies
underneath: stems of water lilies, small
        fish. Scraping the silt. No "sudden blow," the surgeons
                promise, "minimally invasive, laparoscopic, tiny incisions,
needle-thin instruments. Nothing to fear,"
        they stress. But photos I've now seen online show
                massive silvery cones, spiked bills that angle like spears
toward the bull's eye of a belly. "Indifferent"
        beaks that peck around inside, pulling sagging
                organs upright, shoving them into new places, wrapping
them in mesh like the webs between toes of
        swans. "A month," they say. But it's more like
                twenty before my body's mine again, works again, though
I'm told I'm a lucky one, patients half
        my age may need a catheter for a year, even two,
                "post-op," and often, they add, women will need
the surgery redone. We say we're "put under"
        an anesthetic. And now that Mom's been gone
                ten years, I'm sinking down into murk to remember
the time during eighth grade when she
        picked me up, surprising me after school, my gray
                Samsonite packed in the Ford's back seat: "We're going
to the hospital, honey, just a little operation,
        so you won't have those awful cramps anymore." After
                the nurse stripped me and tied me into a blue robe that left

my bottom bare, she told my mother
to leave. They swooped in then, medical students,
checking for cancer, they said, and pulled aside the gown,
fingered my breasts. The next morning,
the nurse wheeled me down the hall for the little
operation. The doctor and his white-jacketed flock were
waiting, thought the anesthetic had
kicked in. I was awake all during their hooting,
their laughing. Spread-eagled in the stirrups, the clamp
inside, the scraping. No Yeatsian
"white rush." The blood that followed. Mom
never knew. Shortly before she died, she told me how,
the first year she was married, her doctor
insisted she come to the office Saturday morning. Got
her on her back, fiddled with her clitoris, diddled her, his
fingers pulsing inside her, experimenting, to
make her come. The same ob/gyn who delivered me,
who believed women should suffer in childbirth, no need
for an anesthetic while he rammed those forceps
deep inside to haul me out. The body holds these
incisions. For years. And genetic memory exists: we carry
molecular scars. No eggs from such visitations. Only
hard-boiled knowledge that you won't get the truth
from these hook-scissored beaks when what they do is tear,
rip into you, and maybe, maybe you'll recover,
put on new knowledge with your own power. Flap
back at them, beat your own wings against them. And snap.

HOW A SURFACE

can gleam in light,
a crystalline
slice, so you think
you can avoid
going under.

THE SILVER TUREEN (3)

Company coming, close it, push it to the back of the counter. All those papery shreds of garlic skins I should have cleaned out. Maybe place the old crystal vase filled with roses in front, so no one will even notice the tureen, ask about it.

All the photos, everyone lined up, arms around arms, mouths stretched in endless smiles. The albums we keep, the posing.

NOW I LEARN

The story about Great Grandfather sailing up the Yangtze: false. I've found a volume from Oxford University Press, as well as files in the London Metropolitan Archives setting the record straight. And in a cardboard box buried in a closet: a blue cloth-bound book my grandfather published in 1958, *The House of Dodwell.* It's even on Wikipedia.

William R. Adamson was the man who, in 1852, came back from China with a ship loaded with silk and the embryo of a fortune. George Benjamin Dodwell would have been only a year old. Later, at twenty, he signed on as a clerk in the Shanghai office. By 1899 he'd been elected Chairman of the Board, the company renamed for him.

How did I get this wrong? Had I embellished, exaggerated the tale? Had Mom? Because it had a more silvery sheen?

GATHERING BONES

Like a book, Mom said about life: you turn the page and go on. The same way she moved in and out of houses. Garage sale after sale. Each year like a chapter torn from a novel's spine and hurled.

But some of us go back, looking for patterns. The way a plot builds, chapter upon chapter, like a pelvis resting on the femur, femur on the patella, on the tibia and fibula.

That film I can't forget: *Aftermath,* story of a Catholic Polish farmer who discovers Jewish tombstones buried under the town's road. He's obsessed with digging them up, five-foot, rounded headstones, one by one. Doesn't know why. He plants them in rows, like corn, in his field. Learns Hebrew, reads the inscriptions, names and names.

During the months before she died, when I begged her to talk about her childhood, my mother changed the subject, demanded more milk in her tea.

Let sleeping dogs lie, the villagers, even the young priest, warned that farmer.

Years ago, Mom told me about a nightmare. She was racing, breathless, through a walled, labyrinthian garden to save herself from a gigantic man. How many houses had it taken to escape? New Jersey, Arizona, house after house, different towns, and finally, in less than a decade, three houses in New Hampshire. Each one repainted.

At the film's end, the farmer learns it was his father who'd led the villagers in a round-up of the local Jews, locking them in the family's cottage, which he set on fire.

The night before the family's ceremonial scattering of Mom's ashes on the lake she'd loved, I slept with the cannister beside me. Sunrise, I carried it down to the dock, opened the lid. I reached in, gathered a small handful, and over my arms and legs spread powdery flakes of crushed bone. I slipped then, into the water that carried them, glittering, in the light.

Once I'd dreamed of myself as a toddler, walking down an unlit hospital hall with closed doors on both sides. I was holding my mother's hand. But no, she was gripping mine.

FOLDINGS

Packing for his return to England, Grandfather showed me how to roll socks into little fists, tuck them into shoes, fold shirts into rectangles tidy as sealed envelopes. I was three. His suitcase a marvel of geometric shapes. Key twisted in the suitcase lock.

I'm folding sheets now, smoothing squares into smaller squares so they'll nestle at right angles on the linen closet shelf. I was six when Granny showed me how to iron without an iron, "finger pressing," she called it. How to smooth the wrinkled, still-damp fabric of a skirt or blouse with the flat of your hands.

That July when Mom called, took a half hour to tell me what she'd stuffed so deep in a trunk it had taken decades to uncover. She said she'd finally remembered: nighttimes, in the big bed, her little-girl self folded between them, her daddy played with her, taught her to play with him, her mummy, wide awake, right there.

How you can fold yourself in on yourself. The toes of the socks curl innermost, the tops wrapping around them. How you can take your own layers and tuck them into creases.

Grandfather's origami—on his second visit, he showed us how to press plain white paper into tiny triangles, and then—voilà!—open a flower, a bird.

A different kind of folding. And unfolding. The way you shake a clean sheet till it sails over the bed, billows. The way a white-winged dove folds her wings close to her rounded middle, then opens them out, lifts off. Unfoldings, the way a flock of swallows makes pin pricks in the sky, openings.

Last summer in Paris, at the Centre Pompidou—the paintings of Simon Hantaï, wide white walls with his room-sized unfoldings. He'd crushed the canvases, folded the cloth so he couldn't see the whole surface while he brushed the paint. Pliage. Said he didn't want to know where the edge was, where the canvas stopped.

HER LISTS

Four times in my life I saw her. And can't forget the way, afternoons, Granny sat upright on the sofa doing her "accounts." Checking items off lists. Long lists, though she was a guest, not even housework to supervise, no shopping needed, no doctors' appointments while away from England.

Both my sisters and I make lists—we'll even add an item once a chore is completed, simply for the pleasure of crossing it off. Little checks, like sketches of birds in flight.

For years Granny would have had much to keep track of—the sprawling hilltop mansion in Hong Kong, another house in Shanghai, a country manor near Windsor, a London townhouse. Scores of servants to oversee. Laundry lists. With every move, the ivory, the china, and the silver all properly packed, accounted for in the next new place. Lists upon lists.

And a list of lessons for her daughter: The best way to thread a needle, how to mend a rip in a silk skirt. How to wear a veiled hat, arrange the feather so it cocked enticingly.

Were there lists under the lists? Items like: "Write Cousin Stanley in Hong Kong, inquire whether we could send dear Pamela for a year or two."

Was it she who encouraged her own child to do with Grandfather what she couldn't bring herself to, so he'd leave her, his wife, alone? Or did she think a little girl should be trained in the arts of the bed, be prepared for what would follow? Or—was it that, as his wife, she knew her duty: to satisfy a husband's desires.

And which one of them insisted Mom leave for Hong Kong when she turned seventeen?

When Granny used to faint during fancy dinners, Mom told me, guests thought she was just being dramatic. Yet when the list you can't write down constricts your spine, how do you stay upright? Check marks like wings. But no feathers could carry such weight.

INCEST

This story has a hundred beginnings. The best old British tradition. No horses were frightened. There were no horses.

BIRD SONGS

Turned into birds, those sisters: Procne, Philomela, a nightingale and a swallow. Oh swallow swallow, hovering as the dark drops, nesting in the rafters, hidden places. How Philomela's threads told the story. Without a tongue.

My mother's sewing, her foot clamped on that pedal, racing the Singer's steel needle through the cloth. The skirts she made, heavy with braid, rows and rows of rick-rack, silver, copper, black. And her jewelry that clanked, metallic, like armor.

These stories no one speaks. How we're silenced, mute. Procne unaware her husband raped her sister, till Philomela's weaving told the tale.

Mom's skirts, voluminous. Yards and yards of her own seaming. And necklaces that roped around her throat and chest, jangling. While lying in the sun, slathered with lotion. All covered up one way or another. High-necked blouses, stiletto heels that clanked on the concrete floor.

Even smothered, a story won't die. Centuries, characters shift, but not the plot. How you know and you don't know. Enough for now to say: my sisters and I—grown daughters of that mother, all skilled with colored threads, with embroidering our own patterns on cloth, and each of us harboring birds. No nightingales in our country, but oh, the swallows, nesting, safe among the wooden bones, timbers of an old, old house.

§

PERHAPS UPSTREAM

the water grows
calmer, cleaner,
perhaps there you'll
see down into
the riverbed,
where small fish might
flicker among
crevices, moss
wisping among
cold granite stones.

BEYOND A CERTAIN AGE, I LOOK FOR PARIS IN PARIS

I know about le Syndrome de Paris, triggered when a greenhorn's
rosy-lensed image turns muddy, but I'm no wistful
Francophile neophyte, so why am I
feeling like my British uncle who'd sniped as I left for my first trip
to Paris: "Why bother with that filth?" When
my friends heard I was heading
again for the City of Lights, they said "Paris? *oh! yes!*" in a breathy,
pre-orgasmic voice, as if they were picturing my
lounging outside a café on
the Boul'Mich over a café au lait or glass of chilled Sauvignon Blanc
as prelude to a blissful night with my husband in
a cramped but oh, so charming
chambre double, forgetting that I can't do caffeine or alcohol, and
that, as I'd also forgotten, in mid-July the sidewalks,
the Métro, and the galleries would
be chock-a-block with chattering Brits, Italians, Yanks, Germans,
and Brazilians, along with—since it's the week
of the Tour de France—clusters
of steel-bodied cyclists, so we're jostled by tee-shirts emblazoned
with slogans like "Endurance Conspiracy" and
"Tourminator." The outing we'd
planned to Giverny is canceled, too much traffic, when for months
I've been yearning to peer down into the waters that
spawned Monet's *Nymphéas:*
those rounded walls in l'Orangerie, depths that lead to more depths,
dissolving boundaries. Where is the Paris of my mother's
rebellious cousin who painted with
Max Ernst, or the Paris of my grad student and her new husband,
noses nuzzling before la tour Eiffel on their
Facebook post? Or the Paris
of my twenties, when I first floated into Monet's water lilies, when
the Seine glimmered like a thousand liquid candles
as I sauntered across Pont Marie
at midnight. On l'Avenue de Clichy, on Rue de Rivoli, I see only
dog poop, crumpled plastic bags, and unfiltered
butts. A two-hour wait to enter

Notre Dame, the façade blocked by tawdry bleachers. Pebbles
from the Tuileries have collected in my sandals
though I keep jiggling my feet
to shake them out. Maybe I have actually become my British
uncle. Samuel Johnson said if you're tired
of London, you're tired
of life. I'll bet he'd put Paris in the same category—after all, didn't
he say French faces shine with "a thousand
Graces"? I can't begin to
keep up with my mountain-goat, marathoner husband who'll
cover seven arrondissements on foot at
a greyhound's trot. Yet
now, on the day before leaving, I'm fueled by a breakfast of hard
boiled eggs, and he says, how about Sacré Coeur,
it's only a ten-minute walk,
we'll take our time. So we do, and the hill with its rounded, gleaming
white cathedral is washed with breezes. Inside
les Jardins Renoir, we are
alone in the courtyard, red poppies brimming at green edges of
stones, a silence glistening through sudden empty
space. And here it is: not Giverny,
but a round pond, and, *oh! yes!* pink and white water lilies, their
shimmering pads like clean hands open to sky,
stems trailing into the barely
visible muck, and tiny speckled fish burbling to the surface, then
spiraling back down to the silt, murky depths,
the dirt that underlies us all.

THE SCROLL'S LANDSCAPE

is black and white,
the foreground trees'
thin strokes like scars
creasing the shore,
while only from
a distance will
the high mountains,
adrift in mist,
appear silver.

(2022)

IN THE GALLERY

All the faces on the canvases, and all
the moving fleshy faces facing the ones flat and framed
on the walls, the living faces shifting
to a glimpse of a hooked nose, wrinkled chin, or one black
eye with a drift of braided hair covering
a cheek, and others full-faced, but never for long, as these
gallery-goers move about, facing one
frame and then another, as I sift among them, just another
face, and then, suddenly, before me:
the largest canvas in this wide room, one of Monet's early
Nymphéas, the water lilies' petals seeming
to shift among rounded leaves, their stems submerged in
layers of murky water, almost as if
moving the way we are, the way faces from the past sift
into my dreams at night, of some
people I'd rather forget, and of people whose loss I grieve,
like the woman I sat beside in this same
museum five years ago, the two of us never shifting while
speaking of our long dead mothers,
and now, that woman, decades younger than I, has died
too, and how her face drifts to me
late in the night, and now, right in front of my own face,
a portrait of a man who looks so like
a man who once held me, his face engraved in the frames
of my mind, his brown eyes sifting
through this space of so many gallery-goers drifting in this
white room, the way water lilies, their
colors, shift across a pond's surface, before they go under.

ON SALT

Neruda says the salt sings. But how about
Lot's wife, turned into salt for looking back? I can't
imagine she was singing. Maybe she turned her own
self into salt, so she'd never forget
the kitchen where she simmered lentil stew,
the bed where she suckled her babies. We always
look back at what we've left. The past
won't stay put. I can never forget my son as
a toddler, his little chuckle. And I'm still grieving
the loss of my friend whose cancer
invaded her intestines, liver, kidneys, and finally,
her pulsing brain. Could salt from tears harden to
a stone pillar? And I wish I could erase
moments when I've been bullied, flattened
by comments that sliced through my skin. At times
those tauntings attack me in dreams,
like salt stinging a wound. Before refrigeration,
salt kept fish and pork flesh from decay, preserved
our food. Easy to know when to dump
rotten meat, that stink. But not so easy to know
when or how to dump a memory. How we work
to hold onto silvery moments, take selfies,
post on Facebook, print photos and slip them
into leather-covered albums. And the way we hate
forgetting, losing names, dates. How we
fear Alzheimer's, the brain's wiring gone
awry. But if we remember too much, we might be
paralyzed, turned into a salty rock-hard
column. Is that what happened to Lot's wife? It's
a metabolic process: our brain's designed to forget
most details. That's how it forms impressions,
makes good judgments. The case in the 1920s of
"S," who remembered every single detail of his life,
though he understood nothing. And now,
suddenly, I'm remembering: later in his poem,
Neruda says the salt plain near Antofagasta is singing
of grief. That entire plain, I've read, is ringed
by mountains and volcanos, cone-shaped, composed
of hardened lava and ash, some of them active, alive.

ONE WEEK AFTER THE ELECTION

—November 2016

I'm in the ER with my husband,
        a kidney stone, it turns out, stuck up there,
no seed from which anything
        but pain can grow. Stone sober, they say,
and is he ever, grimacing between
        a rock and a hard place. Too bad he doesn't
drink—a little bourbon might
        help. For days I've been rereading Yeats,
"Easter 1916": "All changed,
        changed utterly." Stony, rocky. But no rock
to lean on. The doc now says
        my husband's kidney stone might be too big
for him to pass. "The stone's in
        the midst of all," says Yeats. Nectarine,
apricot pits: seeds like stones,
        swallow one of those, you're in trouble. But
planted in good dirt, seeds can
        press down furry white roots, send out pale
green stems, leaves, then flower,
        fruit again. Sweet flesh surrounding the seed,
the pit. I need to focus more on
        fruit, stop keening over this election. Can't
let it harden me to stone. How
        I wish I could inject some kind of power-
packed seed into my husband's kidney
        stone, let it sprout roots, stems that would
unfurl, splinter his stone into
        minuscule motes to drop out of his sweet
body, join the pebbles and stones
        we'll step on as we walk to the car for me to
drive him home, where we'll munch
        on peaches, biting gingerly to avoid the pit.

ABOUT CHOCOLATE

Hurricane Irma is hurtling into the Caribbean
and on into Florida, as India, Nepal, and Bangladesh sink
under water with 1,200 already dead. Meanwhile,
our friends in southeast Texas are mopping up in the wake
of Hurricane Harvey, so why am I reading
about a new kind of chocolate, red chocolate, as if dark,
milk, and white chocolate weren't enough. Ruby
chocolate we've got now, but all these come from the same
cacao plant the Olmec people used even before
the Mayans. I grew up on it. Hershey bars, Snickers, and
brownies, in my lunch box, after school, and
after supper. Cocoa before bed. Chocolate, like touch,
releases oxytocin, the "love hormone" that reduces
stress. Easter Sundays my sisters and I would hunt down
chocolate eggs, peeking behind bookcases and
the TV. Candy bunnies, fluffy chicks. And all the chocolate,
oxytocin. But how much could a carton of Mars Bars
help folks floating in their front yards? And truckloads of
Baby Ruths couldn't rescue little kids harvesting
cocoa beans in West Africa who, I've now learned, are
routinely—even with "Fair Trade"—kidnapped,
handed machetes to cut bean pods from the trees, often
slicing their own flesh. They couldn't have
seen the ads for chocolate: "Comfort in every bar." "Get
the sensation." I just finished Sacha Batthyány's
memoir. In 1945, during a party with Gestapo bosses
in a castle near the Austro-Hungarian border,
at the nearby train depot two hundred Jews were digging
a pit. After dinner, the guests were handed
guns. Some drove, some walked to the station. They filled
the pit. There had been wine, followed by
cognac, with chocolate. Now I'm remembering the time
when my sisters and I were visiting our
grandparents, they served us a chocolate cream pie that—
we found—swarmed with black ants.

THE DIRT

A neighbor across the street has paved over his
		whole front yard. Easier to hose off the dog shit,
he says. No dirt in the house, no need to scrape
		his feet at the door. But dirt isn't only filth, nasty
stuff. It's the soil our spinach and potatoes
		grow from. In the Bible, the first human's name:
Adam, meaning earth. And the latest "dirt" on
		dirt—we're running out. That's the skinny, our
dirt's grown skinny. From the Koran: "They
		tilled the soil and populated it in greater numbers
to their own destruction." All this year our own
		neighborhood's been surrounded by earth movers,
clanking, beeping machines: wheel loaders, dump
		trucks, bulldozers, back and forth over acres of
former woods, native grasses, the live oaks
		and juniper already chain-sawed down and hauled
off. Flattening the ground to make way for
		another pharmacy, another body spa, nail salon,
more storage units. Scrape it up. Skin of the earth,
		soil. The interface between rocks and plants and
animals, including us. The poet Roethke: "God
		bless the ground, I shall walk softly there." I guess
my neighbor's never read Roethke, would think
		his poems just "horse pucky," not realizing how
animal feces nourish the earth. In 1916,
		Vladimir Simkhovitch argued that lack of dirt
caused the decline of the Roman Empire. Even
		Lucius Junius Moderatus Columella, writing in
AD 60, noted that Rome's agricultural
		problems were due to farmers' poor treatment
of the soil. I remember the mud pies we made
		as children, feet sloshing in sloppy dirt. And our
parents smiled. Shall I tell the neighbor
		about the new process called "earthing"? Simple
enough, you let your bare feet walk on

some bare ground. I need to do this. Dirt, we've
now learned, contains antidepressant
microbes that cause serotonin levels to rise, is
better than Prozac, and with no side effects.

THAT BELL FOR ETHEL

Small brass dome under the edge of the round
mahogany table, or oval, with leaves if they
had company. Like us, for instance, in seersucker
shorts and blouses, flown in on Grandpop's
nickel from our cramped Tucson tract house
and scratchy Bermuda grass to this upscale.
Jersey suburb, with acres of manicured lawns
between neighbors, with beds of blossoming
dahlias, roses. That bell, upside-down dome
with its black nipple of a button for Grandma
to press when she wanted Ethel to bring more
biscuits or Parker House rolls, more buttered
corn on the cob, more mashed potatoes—
or to tell Ethel we were ready for the lemon
meringue pie. That bell with its cord attached on
the table's shadowy underside running down
one carved leg, then under the "Oriental"
rug leading through the pantry and into
the kitchen, where Ethel spent hours preparing
menus miraculous to me, so used to my
mother's TV dinners, hamburgers, Bird's
Eye frozen peas, macaroni and cheese. But
oh, Ethel's kitchen! With its polished Revere Ware
and lead-heavy cast-iron skillets, a cupboard
smelling of ginger and cinnamon. After
lunch, dinner, dishes cleared, the china and
silver washed and dried, the kitchen scrubbed,
she climbed the back stairs—barely wider
than her starched-white-uniformed body
and lit with a single hanging bulb—to
a 7′ × 9′ room under the attic. They allowed her
one weekend a month to take the train
into the Bronx to see her sisters
and sons, people I never met, never
learned anything about. But I wish I did know
who they were, could find them, tell

them how I hated the way the grownups,
over their ice-chilled highballs, made fun
of Ethel, how they guffawed at her notion that
crops would thrive if planted in sync with
cycles of the moon. Ethel, who
responded to the dinging of that little
brass bell in a half-minute, was "colored," and we,
of course, were not. Today that bell
dangles from a fragment of cord
under the table that's mine now, the table
I sort and fold laundry on, a job Ethel did for
Grandma (who couldn't open a can of
Campbell's soup). Decades since
that bell's been disconnected, though
its sharp edges now hang down so far below
the table's lip that if we sit right under it
and lift a leg too quickly, our jeans
or skirt will be sliced through to white skin.

AFTER THE SHOOTING IN TUCSON

—January 2011

Minute by minute how we stared from our cushioned room
at the breaking news, crowd gunned down
outside a Safeway. Catalinas' brown-purple crags a backdrop
for the TV's gloom about the bullet shot
through a congresswoman's skull. Over and over her name,
Gabrielle Giffords. And then, that night, as
President Obama's voice urged us to act with good will,
quoting from Arnold's "Dover Beach,"
I quivered with the electric rush I'd felt as a girl when Daddy
read Keats to us after dinner, his tattered
high-school anthology in one hand, a long-ashed cigarette
in the other. The sight of those mountains,
the sound of a poem out loud, and I was thrown back
to the first year I taught, not far from
the Catalinas, when Sally, Lizbeth, and Gwen lingered
after school and we'd read Eliot together,
puzzling over his "muttering retreats," wondering about
that "overwhelming question." But little
did we know as we sounded those luscious syllables,
on the Salt River Pima-Maricopa Reservation
barely a mile away, kids younger than our little sisters were
pulled from their homes and crowded
into dorms at the Indian School in Phoenix where matrons
shaved their heads and showered them
in kerosene, stripped away their names, dressed them in
new ones like "Bobby" and "Susan." Where
songs of the saguaro, the dove, names of grandmothers,
mountains, the river were erased. Replaced
with electric clock alarms. Before he died, I asked
to record my father's voice, his voice
I couldn't bear to lose. "Fled is that music . . . Do I wake
or sleep?" he'd murmur, as I sat upright
in my chair, as I did when Obama recited, "Ah love,
let us be true / To one another!" To think
that, all along, I'd believed we were learning how.

ON STAIN REMOVAL

My old washer's rubber gasket catches
the new sheets in its maw, black goop
staining the white, the beige, and even
when I bleach them, dark traces remain,
the way I've never cleaned out my old
guilt, bone-aching pain from the time
I said spiteful things about my dying
mother in the hospital bed, thinking
if she couldn't talk, she couldn't hear,
a notion corrected by the nurse who
came in and whispered to my mother,
mentioning to me and my sisters how
hearing is the last of the senses to go,
or from the way I once read a poem
making fun of my ten-year-old son
when he was trapped in the audience
and I don't blame him if he's never
forgiven me. I know even dry cleaners
won't get the stains out of my new
sheets, and other than these dark gashes,
they're still functional, like me, with
age spots, snaking veins, and distended
joints defacing my hands as I'm
once again making the bed, trying to
straighten, smooth these sheets
under the weight of mended blankets.

SOUR TAKE

Folks sure do love their sugar. Especially
godly church folk, their pot lucks with all
those desserts, cookies, cakes and pies
and everyone saying, "Oh I really
shouldn't," then helping themselves
to more. All the while chirping and
cooing to each other. Oh, how we
crave peachy sweet lives, have another
slice. "Sugar in the morning, / Sugar in
the evening, / Sugar at Suppertime," sang
the McGuire Sisters in 1958, as I was
growing up on popsicles, ice cream,
chocolate chip cookies. Years later, I'd
overload my Visa card following
Julia Child's recipes in *Mastering the Art
of French Cooking:* Charlotte Malakoff, Soufflé
Rothschild. What was dinner for friends
without a heavenly dessert? But no sugar
for me any more—my blood sugar levels
soar, only to plummet, not into a fiery,
but a limp, paralyzed hell. In a restaurant,
everyone begging me to order
the chocolate cream pie, the cheesecake,
and they don't get it when I say I really,
really don't want even a single
slippery bite. Sugar highs, sugar
lows. Reminds me of the low-down on
the history of sugar, sugar cane,
a tropical grass discovered in India
by the Persians between the 6th and 4th
centuries BC. Columbus first brought
sugar to the Caribbean, where slaves
were shipped and forced to hook their
backs over the fields. And in our own
country's Southern colonies: slaves
fed the sweet tooth of good white

folks, who loved their Red Velvet
Cake, their Ultimate Hummingbird
Cake, their Coconut Cake. Sweets
for the sweet. And those plantation
owners fed their slaves sugar, one way
to keep them going. Eight times
more addictive than cocaine, sugar. And
what about candies folks love to suck on
today? Milk Duds, Malted Milk Balls,
and Sugar Babies: all coated with a glaze
made from beetle shit. And what's that
turbulent smoke in Brazil looking like
a nuclear bomb's been detonated? Every
May through November, sugar cane
fields are set aflame to burn green and dry
leaves off the stalks so harvesting takes
less labor, owners get more bang for
their buck. Air so bad people's lungs
clog. Of course, I've got to admit,
when my friend calls me "Sugar," and
my man calls me his very own "Sweetie,"
I lap it up. "Be my little sugar, / And
love me / All the time," sang that famous
trio of sisters. But since my body runs with
the metabolism of a hummingbird, I burn
calories like crazy, need fatty red meat
to keep from descending into sourness and
worse. Come to think of it, I'd rather
be somebody's fat—or solid protein—
neither heavenly nor hellish, but sticking
to the ribs, with staying power for
a good long time. Yet I can't forget how
cattle are rounded up, prodded onto trucks,
run through chutes to have their
throats cut, their bodies hung from
steel hooks and carved into pieces to fit
between shrink wrap and styrofoam.

WHY CAGES

So we can peer in. So a creature
can't hide. Zoos keep jaguars in 9-gauge
chain-link pens. Wild, these cats
race across grasslands faster than a bicyclist
with the Tour de France. Parrots
fly a hundred miles a day, but caged,
they'll bite their feet, bellies, till
they bleed. "Zoochosis": psychosis caused
by confinement. Our ancestors
lived in caves, but that's not the same as
being locked up. "Give me land,
lots of land, under starry skies above, don't
fence me in," crooned Bing Crosby
in 1943. How much open space do we
humans need? A student of mine
signed up with a college group volunteering
to be jailed for a week. She said
before long, they all began sobbing, raging,
and none of them was even
confined in solitary. I've never stepped inside
a prison. But I've been kept
alone in a medical ward, electrodes taped
across my body, one small
window for interns to peer in at me, a loud-
speaker over my head, a voice
booming in at random moments. I seldom
scream, but I did, again and again.

ON SCISSORS AND MATISSE

In old age he used scissors to create
Jazz, the cutouts everyone raves about, those
primal colors. All done by a man
in a wheelchair, post-colostomy. Can't they see
how in those red, green, yellow
shapes, hearts fan into flames, stars shatter
into grenades? His "Sword Swallower":
no exuberant circus performer, no songster
with notes springing from his mouth,
but a head wrenched back, jaws forced open
as swords pierce his throat, knives
slicing a tongue. At three, my tonsillectomy:
a phony promise of ice cream before
waking in a ward with a hundred children
lined up in cots, parents forbidden
for a week, no touching permitted, screams
at night, constant sounds of gurneys
rattling, glare of the yellow-lighted doors
into surgery. What kinds of blades were
used for tonsillectomies? I think of my prized
nickel-plated scissors that cut
through white space around the figures
in my paper doll books. 1940s, with
WWII exploding, the bedridden Matisse
learned his daughter had been
tortured by the Gestapo, forced onto a cattle
train to Ravensbrück. Not much
older than three when I saw *Life*'s photos
of Buchenwald's survivors. Bodies
shrunk to papery skin stretched over
jutting bones. What fractures splayed
behind those eyes? Impossible to see inside
the paper dolls' figures, their pink-toned
flesh. Matisse's daughter Marguerite jumped
from the train before it reached
Ravensbrück, hid out in the Vosges Mountains'

pine forests till fellow resisters
rescued her. I'd take care with my scissors
never to slice a paper doll's
arm or hip. How old do you need to be
before you discern the forms
under the forms of Matisse's cut outs? Before
you learn of the friend who watched
from her bedroom window as her brother
set himself on fire, of the sister
who saw a man drop from twenty stories,
a lake of blood five feet from
her Capezio flats, and of the friend hauled
by a crazed Nam vet into his bedroom
and raped in the ass for two hours, his loaded
.45 beside her head. Before you learn
the muscles, bones, nerves of Ravensbrück's
inmates were cut out, implanted in
other prisoners' bodies, the incisions injected
with bacteria, wood shavings, ground
glass. How to speak of a tonsillectomy? After,
my mother said, I was never the same.

IN MY SEVENTY-SIXTH YEAR

We need a new roof. No gale force wind has
ripped it off, it's a matter of age. The skin
of our house has thinned,
like mine. No crisis, no dearth of power or clean
water as in Puerto Rico after Hurricane Maria,
no walls blackened or splintered
like those from California's wildfires. At least
newscasters label these "catastrophes," not
"issues," a word everyone
uses now for a neighbor's fuss over fence lines
or a three-million-gallon oil spill. We don't
need anything fancy, no
dome or mansard, no gambrel or skillion, I just
need a well-braced shield to keep me from
lung-flattening news, from
the fact that our poor world reels and not from
issues but from calamities, and from the way
my own past blunders
leak through my ceiling like the rancid blather
of some politicians. I'm grappling with how
old age can make us
porous, unable to pull into the hard-muscled shell
of a younger, stronger self. These fissures in
my roof let thoughts of my
dead seep through, what I said, or didn't say,
and wish I had. Portuguese have the word
saudade, a longing for what
once had been, for those no more alive and
chattering beside us. Roof above the head:
shelter, insulation, a basic
need. But no tightly seamed roof, thick-shingled
with sword-sharp edges, can fend off all
the squalls, the hitches,
crises, issues that might be swirling nearby,
can guard the tissue-thin skin of my walls.

IN PRAISE OF STUMPS

Dumb as a stump, they say. My neighbor
hates stumps, and, after sawing down half
the trees on his manicured acre, wants all
the stumps removed. Eyesores, they take
up space on his lawn. Not an easy job,
stump removal. Grinders cost at least
a hundred bucks a day to rent, and he'd
need goggles, a chain saw, a pick mattock,
digging bar, and a shovel. Potassium nitrate
works, with a drill and kerosene. Years ago,
I'd planned to rid my yard of its scraggly
stumps, till I learned the roots of trees feed
each other, pump sugar into a stump
to keep it from dying and the stump will
send out new sprouts that can lift into
saplings, and then, in time, into full-sized
trees. I hadn't known that stumps offer
nesting sites for chickadees, titmice, owls,
and woodpeckers, shelter for chipmunks,
shrews, salamanders, and foxes. But my
neighbor's not the only one in this
suburban enclave with codes more rigid
than a concrete slab: grass over six inches
high bordering the street and you're in
for a big fine. I'm thinking of Hopkins'
"Long live the weeds." I like our grasses
tall enough to ripple in the wind,
so native salvias can bloom and feed
the butterflies and hummingbirds. Sick
of tidiness, the desire to emulate British
country estates with our faux scaled-
down mini-mansions floating on green
carpet no one ever touches, other than
a hired man on his ride-em mower who
keeps the outdoors outside, keeps anyone
from taking too deep a breath, from any

Whitmanesque desire to go live with
        the animals, which I'm fantasizing I might
want to do, but right now, I'll go out,
        speak to my dead trees, tell them I know
their roots are alive, connected to all
        the leafy trees nearby, and I know they're
signaling each other through an
        arboreal internet, their intricate fungal,
mycelial network, maybe warning
        about our thick, dumb-as-a-ditch skulls.

RILKE TO ROETHKE ON ROSH HASHANAH

"Lord it is time"—past time—for
    our country's political bombast and vitriol
to end, for the South Texas heat
    to drop, for my crammed Inbox to clear,
for relief from knowing my old friend
    who's not even old has only a few weeks left
on this over-warmed planet with oceans
    so littered with plastic bags, bottles, duct tape,
balloons, six pack rings, drinking straws,
    and rubber duckies that dolphins and whales
choke, suffocate, and end up beached
    on our coasts, but it's Rosh Hashanah, Jewish
New Year, time for reflection, renewal,
    time for believing earth will go on—so maybe
when the oaks, mesquite, hackberries bare
    their branches, while, as Rilke says, the "dry
leaves are blowing," there'll be room to see
    stars as well as the branches, stems, nodes that
birthed the leaves, to study the furrows
    of the cedar elms' underpinnings, so I turn from
Rilke to Roethke, to the "urge, wrestle,
    resurrection of dry sticks," that "sucking and
sobbing" of "cut stems struggling
    to put down feet," and then, finally, I remember:
"In a dark time the eye begins to see,"
    and I know, if this is Roethke's "purity of pure
despair," it's time, past time—on this
    day that resounds with a ram's horn—I struggle
to lie down, rest, grow from the dark.

ON DELTA FLIGHT #2164 FROM JFK

I'm headed home from a stint at Long Island's
Walt Whitman Birthplace, a day after
visiting Dickinson's Amherst Homestead. With
her thread-laced fascicles, Emily liked
to see a train "lap the miles," but at jet speed,
we're hardly lapping. Along with Walt,
I find crowds "curious," and, as an introvert
with an extrovert bent, I always want to
know everyone's stories, since we're all part of
the "eternal float of solution." But right
now I'm jammed in a middle seat among 524
passengers, and the silent man on my left
drapes his hairy fingers over the armrest. His
thick head blocks the window. I'm hardly
floating. Whenever I'm in a plane, part of me
is stuck in 1947, not yet five, waving
to my sobbing grandma at La Guardia before
flying with my straight-backed mother
and toddling sister across the United States all
the way to Phoenix. Clouds rippled
beyond the window, billowing threads. But then
I didn't see my East Coast grandma
for four years. The way she'd held me in her lap
while dropping stitches from her
rumpled knitting. Who was I without her blue
eyes meeting mine? Even now, whenever I
leave home, I fear I won't return, will lose touch,
become "Nobody." Maybe that's why I'm
always bantering with strangers in our tangled
strands as we board and deplane. If they're
chatting with me, I could be somebody. Yet I
must keep my own skin intact, and though
I wish, like Walt, I could be "loos'd of limits and
imaginary lines," I must hold to a few
limits or I'd lose my whole self. "The Soul selects
her own Society," says Dickinson, but

who am I in this crowd? Always, as Emily laments,
"the bewildering thread." I need to fasten
my own threads the way warp strands on a wooden
loom are tightened, so the weave will hold.

NOT MONTALE'S EEL

These fluttering creatures brushing
        our windshields, littering our highways and lawns:
snout-nosed butterflies on the move
        this fall for a solid month, drawn by the dangling
fruit of hackberries, trees tidy folk
        call "trash," but with perfect fuel for these twenty
million headed to the Rio Grande—
        and somehow I start thinking of Montale's eel,
la sirena infiltrating *gorielli di melma,*
        vast "pockets of mud," though I'm embarrassed
to remember how, when first translating
        the poem, I assumed the eel was male, like a lone
sperm making his determined journey
        upstream only to die unless he'd beaten all the other
guys to the ovum, and of course
        I can't forget Monty Python's hilarious "Every
Sperm Is Sacred," so then I wonder about
        the millions of migrations from the first time
a single cell from the ocean drifted
        to land, beginning a series of transformations
leading to our own species that's spread
        itself across the globe, often, like butterflies,
struggling to find food, or sometimes
        to wipe out neighbors and lay claim to silver, oil,
or fertile loam, and of course, thousands
        of these butterflies are devoured by the chickadees
and titmice that normally empty our
        backyard bird feeders, though I guess it's always
about moving from one place to another,
        each of us food for someone else, or there wouldn't
be life at all, and I know we don't want
        existence to be a stagnant pool with no whirligig
beetles or dragonflies, but I sure don't
        feel like "sister" to that gleaming eel of Montale's—
some days I'd like to stay put on solid
        clay that will hold my feet steady, but I guess it's all

a matter of motion, the release
    of CO_2 so oxygen can travel through capillaries;
migrations, even the poet's
    l'iride breve, "brief iris," won't flower without roots,
tentacles swimming through dirt.

IN THE GALÁPAGOS

Though Melville called these islands
a pile of "Cinders dumped here and there"
with "a wailing spirit," I don't want ashes
of his morbid mental state to smother
my memory of bobbing in a fiberglass
panga where at first I saw only the garua,
the stratocumulus hovering over tips
of volcanoes, mist that drapes the rocks
in a whitened haze, so I wasn't even sure
we'd reached a place that's real. It all
shifted, the way for an instant we'd
see a whale's flukes, a tail flashing above
the ocean, and gone. Then, straight
ahead, splatters of bird droppings
like paint streaks on stone, but the paint
moved, the rocks teeming with
white-feathered, blue-footed boobies,
their beaks and outsize feet a brighter
blue than any sky I've ever seen
as we anchored off Isla Fernandina
and hiked a hummocky field of ropy
pahoehoe lava, when I almost tripped
on a rock-black tail, no, hundreds upon
hundreds of iguanas warming like soft-
bellied dollops of stone, the only
sound besides our whispering the hiss
of brine spewed through their nostrils,
salt-caked, white as the guano
under them. And beyond, palo santo
trees, holy sticks so laced with lichen
their whiteness shimmered at noon
as if by moonlight. Not Melville's end
of the world, but a beginning, air so fresh
I felt I'd grown new lungs. When
I walked on Isla Isabella's sand alongside
a Great Blue Heron, and sat down to rest

in the midst of a dozen nursing
sea lions, I didn't spot any of the creatures
our kind have carried with us, the rats
pigs, dogs, cats that eat the eggs
of the giant tortoises. I remember
that, while exploring Chatham Island,
Darwin noted he'd met an "immense
Turpin" and was mesmerized. But
did he know, in the years surrounding
his voyage, crews like his—and
Melville's—hauled off thousands
of those tortoises, stacked them flipped
on their backs in the ship's hold,
where they survived for months
without food? I keep thinking of the flightless
cormorant—steady on her nest
of marine grass and algae over
rock, on an island where nothing has
ever been mined, hammered, or
soldered, where the lava hasn't
been crumbled to pebbles—who sits
within a circle of her own
shit, above a cloud-gray chick
and one still whole, unbroken egg.

AFTER READING BAUDELAIRE

With sky a tight-fitting cast-iron lid,
        humidity and temp ninety-eight, rain stalled
over the next county, I listen to Edith
        Piaf, her raunchy, chutzpah-laden contralto—
je ne regrette rien, she growls and purrs,
        as if she actually believes she has no regrets,
although I sure do, have never eased
        the ache of leaving my baby boy with sitters
so I could keep on with grad school,
        how some nights I'd come home to a bundle
of shuddering sobs till I held him
        and nursed him, but now of course, he's grown,
a solid forty-one, and I'm proud as
        any proud mom can be, yet I can't shake free
of those tangling webs, while I know
        the spleen isn't what Baudelaire and his cronies
thought, rather a neighbor of the stomach
        churning out antibodies, blasting worn-out red
blood cells, not the seat of down-in-
        the-mouthness and foul temper as medieval
physiologists believed, so maybe I'm just
        cleaning away forty-plus years of regret, because
I'd sure like to sing along with Piaf
        that I regret nothing, and, after all, I wasn't as
bad as other mothers I've read about,
        even Martha Sharp, who during the SS Nazi
years left her own offspring for months
        at a time to rescue Jewish kids and bring them
to the U.S., saving them from Auschwitz
        and Treblinka, saintly to be sure, but I wouldn't
blame her children for feeling some
        pretty sour spleen about a mom's not being
there to hug them for winning archery
        medals at summer camp or battling measles
or bronchitis, so I hunker down again
        with Piaf—her *laissez-vous faire, Milord*—in awe

that, decades after a girlhood in
her grandmother's brothel, this "Little Sparrow"
is even now clearing my gloom,
the way currents of rain end a drought, the way
milk lets down from a breast.

IN LIGHT OF THE ECLIPSE

Three celestial bodies it takes, the sun,
moon, and our earth. And now, in a single day:
visits by two old friends who propel me back to selves
I inhabited decades ago, and by my grown
son, who's returning portraits of ancestors he hasn't
room for. How these gilt-framed nineteenth-century
pastels spiral me down to the year
I turned five when my parents moved us away
from my silky-skinned Grandma, East Coast red oaks
and flowering dogwoods to the prickly
Phoenix dustbowl of the forties. We're not even
in the direct path of the eclipse, but all these orbitings
from years back shift the way I see
my own face in the mirror, and what I see is
not what I'm used to seeing. A red-tailed hawk has
swirled around the house and lands
on a branch inches from my window, hunches
there all afternoon. Not a glimpse of the finches,
wrens, cardinals that always flutter
around our yard. The room is breathing an odd
shadow. But the moon only appears to cover the fire
that gives our planet life. The orbits that
govern us, circles within circles, one sphere
moving into another. Now in this uncanny light,
I find a bird's nest cradled on a sumac
limb, a woven round of leaves and twigs,
and I wonder if it's waiting to be filled. Or if a clutch
of eggs has hatched and nestlings have
flown—or if the dark circle in its center
means it's been abandoned. The word "eclipse": from
the Greek "to vanish." Yet today I'm
recovering vision all these years have clouded
over. How the bustle of a sunlit life can eclipse earlier
selves within us. Is the moon
over the sun's orb a closing? Or an opening.

LIFTED

Cardinals, finches, chickadees flock
  to our feeders. Up to four thousand feathers
on each bird's little body. On a tundra
  swan: twenty-five thousand. "Light as a feather,"
we like to say, as opposed to "this
  too too solid flesh," or my stiff and creaking
joints. But even dry feathers aren't
  so light. Headdresses Las Vegas show girls
wear will hold two thousand plumes,
  weigh twenty pounds. All the rage, feathers,
especially for hats in the late nineteenth
  century. Women's toques were even topped
with stuffed whole birds. In 1886,
  on the streets of New York, Frank Chapman
counted over forty species of feathers
  on bonnets, caps, cloches, down brims. I guess
we earthbound humans have always
  yearned to fly. I'm no Icarus, but oh, how I wish
I could transform my flabby arms
  into wings. Last June as I stepped onto a Gulf
Coast pier, I stopped. Two yards
  down on the wooden slats stood a great blue
heron. We stared at each other for,
  I swear, ten minutes, before he opened wide his
long wings and, shrieking, flew off to
  a hill beyond, a sight staying with me wherever
I drop my feet. Sometimes when I'm
  happy, I'll flap my arms. Just feeling that motion
makes me smile. During Brahms's Fourth
  Symphony last night, as I leaned my aching back
against the concert hall's padded seat,
  the violinists' bows rose like feathery quills, and
a thousand listeners sprouted wings.

CIRCLINGS

—In memoriam, Jeannine Keenan

~

Pacing across the bamboo floor,
I stop inside each sunlit circle cast
by seven skylights in my roof,
marveling that all day these disks drift
across the room, and how
she would have loved to know of my
little ritual, but I can't tell her,
she's been gone for months, and for
months before, she couldn't even
step from her bedroom by herself,
her sentences so garbled I had to
guess at what she was laboring to say,
but I wish I could tell her
about the way light travels through
the day, and how I try to step
within each single round as if I could
hold onto the light, as if she
could fit within one of these spheres.

~

Sections of a grapefruit sliced
in half, fibrous rays fanned from its core,
a yellow glimmer she would
have relished, and now, six garlic cloves
around their stem, spokes of
a wheel, plump white bulbs nestled into
the center; and I see that an
apple core, sliced crossways, resembles
a rose window like one she—
as a child—would have knelt beneath.

~

In the parking lot of our
neighborhood grocery store, a grackle,

with its round eye, catches
            mine till it lifts above the cracked asphalt,
and I think of Stevens, whose
            lines she'd often quote, with his blackbird
flying beyond sight, marking
            "the edge / Of one of many circles."

~

The shock—the way she went,
            together with her husband of sixty years,
the pair encircling their sagging
            bed with photos of daughters, grandkids,
favorite books and the tigers and
            lions she'd sewn, stuffed, plush creatures
she'd brought almost to life from
            chenille and thread, and then—he gave
her the pills, and only after he
            knew she'd left, sent one shot to his head,
leaving only a small circle of blood
            on the pillow, but not before he'd called
911 to report what he'd done
            and was about to do, and then—the news:
even on TV, and the phone
            calls among those of us who loved her, circling.

~

The star jasmine vine outside
            our front door, a spiralling around
the porch, filaments clinging
            to an upright post, and I'm swung
back to years when her sturdy
            arms cradled a new gift, a woolen
shawl, a wooden bowl, a basket
            she wove from reeds of a pond she
once loved but left, and
            now her leaving tangles the coils
of my body's core, till I'm
            left leaning on any post I can find.

~

I try to peel an apple so the skin
          remains in one unbroken spiral,
but it breaks in pieces, as my blunt
          knife, that she would have known
how to sharpen, slips from its path.

Under the lines of the cross,
          beneath a horizontal slash through
a vertical stripe, far below
          the towers of those medieval cathedrals
she'd visited so often,
          the labyrinth, spiraled path mirroring
the old circles of our long
          journeys, seeming repetitions, endlessness
of our steps, and yet, how
          we keep on, one foot, the other, not
wandering, but a gradual
          swirl to the center, small place to rest.

Always sunflowers she wanted,
          for birthdays, any occasion, even saying
that, if somehow she could
          return after she'd died, she'd be a sunflower—so
after she left, we scattered
          sunflower seeds over her ashes, and now,
by the roadsides on our drive
          to the coast: acres and acres of seed-packed
heads swiveling throughout
          the day, each round with its seeds following
Fibonacci's sequence, which
          she knew, as she knew of Yeats' gyres,
the way things turn, return,
          a phenomenon—I'd almost forgotten—
she labeled "the spiral surprise."

THOSE ROADS, THESE MOONS

(2023)

THESE ROADS

Not a straight and narrow track, but open
sky all day as Steve and I cruised South
Llano River State Park, thickets of live oaks,
mesquite, buckeyes, and juniper, the river
glistening at every turn. No WiFi, no TV,
no bad news blasting. After we parked,
Steve hiked into the river, whose current
dragged him fifty yards downstream
before he could clamber out. But nothing
like the Honduran mamá and her toddler
son who drowned while trying to cross
the Rio Grande. I think of my amigo Miguel,
who, at two, with his familia, fled Durango's
Sinaloa cartels, the piles of severed heads.
His papá held him, whispering this was only
a game, but then, at the river, the border,
they were locked under fluorescent lights till
he felt, he said, like a flattened rat. Sent back,
but years later, enough saved to pay a coyote,
they trudged at night through desert, stars
splattering the sky, then daytimes, hiding
in dark holes. No roads. His red Converse
sneakers turned brown. Finally they crossed
the Rio Grande at Anapra, met by Tía Mela
with her Green Card. Miguel's shoulders
shook when he told me that story—and after
forty years. But no passports or papers
needed for us today, driver's licenses, credit
cards tucked in our wallets, water bottles,
lunch packs safe behind the front seat as
we sailed under cerulean skies, feathery clouds.
A galaxy of difference between exploring
and escaping. On our drive to the river and
back, sometimes Steve leaned on the gas till
we soared ten, even twenty miles over the limit,
but we were never once bothered by a cop.
As we headed home, a full moon rose
over the hills, the sunset bleeding behind us.

COCKROACHES

(June 2020)

Phoenix in the fifties, and my British-bred
square-shouldered mother smashing roaches
with a fury that, even as a kid, I knew must
have come from somewhere else and long
ago, as she fumed against the filthy creatures
invading her spotless house. These insects do,
of course, spread germs, will invade your nose
or ears while you're sleeping. And now my own
house crawls with the damned pests, so I smash
them every chance I get, flushing their carcasses
down the toilet. But what is this new anger that
engulfs me now? With their tough exoskeletons,
spindly antennae, they skitter across floors and
counters, into the room where the TV blares
reports of more gunshots, more Black killings
by White cops, knees on necks, choke holds
blocking blood to the brain. The police are
protected by their own kinds of exoskeletons,
riot gear, helmets, chest shields, as they taser,
pummel, and shoot. I've read that cockroaches
wriggled onto slave ships leaving West Africa
and packed with kidnapped, naked, branded
women, toddlers, men. The insects gobbled
food and multiplied as they slithered over
bodies crammed on planks, covered in shit,
piss, gasping for clean air. So roaches reached
our own shores, rampant ever since. And I
know my mother, shipped alone from England
as a teen (though sailing first class all the way),
would—if she were alive today—join me in
pounding the soles of our shoes onto every
roach we spotted. My own anger is not enough.

PANDEMIC ROAD

Upended. Glasses nowhere, couldn't
see. Sudden kind shoulders to lean on.
Oil slick, they said, not my fault. Then
flashing red lights, the cops, a tow truck.
Car totaled. As Karl Shapiro wrote, an
auto wreck "Cancels our physics with
a sneer." And now, housebound by
the worst pandemic in a century, cities
thick with thousands retching blood
from a virus that leapt from animals
to humans and from human to human
in a process scientists call "slippery,"
like the road that wrecked my poor car.
I think of Yeats: "All changed," and
"utterly." When every rhythm of the day
is erased, when boundaries have circled
so tight we're starving for human arms
and the open gestures that allow us to
gesture back, we might as well be facing
a wall like the one I crashed into, unable
to see beyond the upended hood of a car
which no longer can take me anywhere
I'd thought I'd always wanted to go.

DRIVING WHILE WHITE

Tarantula eyelashes in my twenties, fluttering
above a miniskirt. And the seraphic smile I'd
give the cop who'd pulled me over, speeding.
Again. The time I was hitting 80 in a 60 mph
zone, and lowered my eyelids, bent my head
to the officer, confessing I'd just learned I was
pregnant, so happy I didn't even notice I was
speeding, and he grinned, "You be careful now,
little lady." Dozens of times: "Oh, officer, I'm
so sorry! I just didn't realize!" "Oh my gosh,
I'll slow down, I promise." And the response:
always a kindly "You do that, ma'am." These
days, still blue-eyed, no longer blond, silver-
haired, I'm a nice old White lady, and when
my bike-tanned husband is driving, I will
lean across him, tilt my head, smile, gush
to the cop who stopped us. Never ticketed.
In the Sixties, when I asked my Black lover
why not get married, I wanted his babies, he
said, "You don't know how hard it could get."

DIAGNOSIS

1963, at twenty-one, I saw little men dancing around
the bedroom, guffawing at me, like humanoid pustules
popping out of walls. My husband took me to a doctor
who sent us to a shrink. "Plain as day," he said, "piece
of cake," pointing to a page in a fat leather-bound book:
"schizophrenia." As if easy to diagnose as chicken pox,
smallpox. "Crazy!" we shout, thrilled at something's
being so odd it might as well be "insane!" In a delightful
way, we mean. But not so delightful if committed to an
asylum. I'd known the history of women confined to
loony bins for reading novels, grief over a child's death,
masturbation, or marriage trouble. Outspoken women
became "hysterics," and were locked up. "I'll commit her,"
said the shrink, "And we'll start electric shock treatments.
She'll probably need a lobotomy." He charged us $700,
but my husband lied, said he'd forgotten the checkbook.
Called my folks who took me to an old physician friend,
who listened as I explained that for asthma, I'd been
prescribed Marax, which made me jittery. So then I was
given Phenobarbital. That combo, those dosages: lethal,
this medic said. A couple more weeks, and I'd be dead.
A pox on that shrink. At least the lesions are invisible.

UNDER ROADS

Australia aflame, creatures
in the thousands burning,
but the wombats are saving
wallabies and echidnas, lizards
and skinks, by ushering them
into their burrows, tunnels.
Temps rising here at home.
Last week we hurried through
downtown Austin, at one point
following a woman hunched
over a shopping cart loaded
with ragged clothes, plastic
bags, sackfuls of food. No
burrows tunneled under her.
On our border with Mexico,
thousands crammed behind
scorched barbed wire, kids
yanked from mamás and papás,
hungry, groped, beaten, raped.
Now in my own front yard,
some creature has been digging
a hole, every day wider, deeper.

KNOTS IN THE WOOD

—April 2020

All these patterns in my hardwood
floors, curl and swoop of the grains,
sporadic umber circles interrupting
the parallel lines of the boards. Before
sheltering inside for a month, I'd head
straight for the kitchen or bathroom,
not even glancing down at the oak's
polish. Today I'm staring at the nodes
and knurls in these planks, learning
that knots are formed from branches
that died. Some of these resemble
the pockmark on my left arm from
childhood's smallpox vaccination.
Now they remind me of the spherical
shape of the virus forcing us to
stay home. Tens of thousands already
dead. COVID lacerates the lungs, air
sacs plugged with fluid. When I look
into my yard, oak leaves fluttering,
I remember: Trees are the planet's
lungs, breathing out oxygen, moisture,
swelling rain clouds that feed us all.
I glance down again at my own floor,
its planks sawn from trees once
living. No surprise these knots don't
remind me of rose buds or pearls,
but blisters, scars. And accusing eyes.

SABBATH ROAD

Curling through the Catskills,
beeches, oaks, spruce, maples,
pines, leafing, glistening around us.
We hadn't seen a car, truck, or bus
for miles, when suddenly beside us
on the one-lane dirt road: two dozen
full-bearded, black-hatted men,
women in long skirts, hair hidden
under scarves. As if we'd traveled
back to eighteenth-century Belarus
or Galicia. Of course, since this
was Saturday, Shabbos, these Hasidim
couldn't drive. But where were they
headed? We hadn't seen a synagogue
anywhere. No one smiled or waved,
and I remembered riding a bus through
Jerusalem's Mea Shearim, enclave
of Haredim and Hasidim much like
the families close beside us, when I was
glared at, a goyish whore, they must have
been thinking, with my uncovered head,
no loose skirt covering my bare ankles,
and my husband beside me, wearing
no kippah. Men turned their heads
from the front of the bus to glare.
I'll bet I'd been staring too, never
having seen men with curly sideburns
long as the beards trailing their chests.
But now, at home, a fresh outbreak
of anti-Jewish venom: the Monsey
stabbings, mass shootings in Pittsburgh,
Poway, men and boys chased, punched
in Brooklyn's Borough Park. Could
be our strolling neighbors are trying
to avoid this savagery against Jews,
even those without wide-brimmed
velvet black toppers. In the car,

as the leaves whispered above,
we tried not to stare at the families
so close to us, knowing that, just as
crowns of trees don't encroach on
each other's space, allowing each
tree access to light and air, we
shouldn't intrude, but still wishing
that, like trees, with underground
networks endlessly messaging,
we could just reach out through
tendrils of our twisted human roots.

ANOTHER WAY TO LOOK AT FALL

This fluttering, this slow wafting
of golden leaves softening air
seems a voluntary act, yet
I've just learned that leaves don't loosen
and drop of their volition, but
get sliced off by the branches—with
winter weather on the way, trees
can't afford to nourish their leaves,
so they scissor them, severing
them, and wind does the rest. Now I'm
thinking how this pandemic means
forfeiting affectionate hugs
with closest friends, symphony seats
where we'd be thrilled by violins,
even visits to my one son
who lives across the continent.
So I've let go, and like a tree,
guard my body, stick to basics.
But then I think of other ways
we let go: leaving a toxic
friend, job, or marriage, all the pain
these ruptures can cause. "Tear yourself
away," we say, but sometimes, like
jaundiced leaves, we hang by a thread.

UNDER FRIGID SKIES

Frozen pipes, power
out across the state.
We're lucky, still with
heat and water, while
all over Texas,
folks shiver under
piles of quilts, blankets.
People sleeping in
furniture stores, sprawled
on couches and chairs.
One family died
when their chimney caught
fire, exploded.
Sleet coated roads closed.
In the yard, grizzled
branches disappear
under white crust, leaves
weighted with ice clumps.
I'd thought white contained
all colors, but now
it's blindingly no
color, a solid
Melvillean blank,
impenetrable,
while a scene outside
from last week still looms:
on the ground, dozens
of vultures flapping
and pecking, ripping
a dead buck's carcass.
A tearing into
flesh to feed all those
black-brown wings able
to fly beyond this
ceiling's stifling white.

A WANING MOON BRINGS

Time to declutter,
remove the old stuff
that's been jangling chords
while clogging your veins
as outdated cans
clink on pantry shelves
and clothes you never
wear cram your closet.
Now darkness gathers
from all corners of
the sky, so our rooms
will turn toward new
silences without
the clatter of more
news carped on TV
or toxic emails
from hostile colleagues
or a harrowing
thought I can dwell on
far too long till I
want to crawl under
blankets and not pull
out till the sweet man
I know loves me will
reassure me that
it's okay to go
dark, quiet for a time,
since silence can be
the most musical
sound, and darkness may
reveal what glaring
lights might be hiding.

MERITS OF COVID

Sometimes I forget
about the virus
when I'm home and hear
myself humming tunes
from childhood until
I remember news
about the bridge with
traffic lessened since
the pandemic, so
quiet now the songs
of white-crowned sparrows
have grown softer, more
melodious, with
the males attracting
more and more females
so nestlings will soon
orchestrate new songs.

END OF OCTOBER

Four nights of full moons
culminating on
the thirty-first, when
a veil the Celts called
Samhain opens and
brings us all closer
to souls of the dead
than on other nights
during this event
that has not occurred
for seventy-six
years, and won't again
for nineteen more years,
by which time I could
be dead. But on this
night I'm not thinking
of my long-gone mom
or dad, but on light
shimmering in my
own room, gleaming in
once-dark corners so
I'm seeing my own
house radiant with
what is here right this
minute, and with no
minutes left to lose.

THE PINK MOON HERALDS

Blossoming season,
cherry blooms, wild phlox,
primroses dazzling
our yard, an ocean
of pink rippling all
the way to the street.
A frilly color,
often found on young
girls' fancy dresses,
pink also carries
bad vibes. A pink slip,
or an epithet
hurled at anyone
suspected of views
too leftist: "pinko
commie"—not quite "red,"
but close. Nothing like
feeling "in the pink."
The phrases that slip
from our tongues (always
pink whatever our
skin's shade). Strange not one
of our ten thousand
books in this house have
pink covers, when all
the tongues forming those
words, no matter what
land, seas, the writer
had crossed, would have been
some tinged shade of pink.
All the blooms birthing
from our supple tongues.

DURING JUNE'S BIRTH MOON

After three days bound
to a hospital
room with no windows
and blank walls, on IV's,
unable to eat,
my arms constantly
poked by needles, blood
samples for who knows
what, finally back
home to the TV
bellowing today's
headlines I silence
so I can relish
our windows, these views
of old oaks and shrubs,
leafy undergrowth.
Just now I'm spotting
a racoon heading
a trail of her kits.
One even peeks in
at me, its eyes wide.
Then a bit later,
a white-tailed red fox
leads a rumpled pup
across the tall grass.
And now, I notice
vines under the porch
begin to quiver,
hiding a young doe,
uninterrupted,
nestled, safely, here.

NOTING NEW MUSIC

There's no longer a piano
in my house, the ivory and
ebony keys sold to someone
else's hands—can't press my fingers
for chords, trills that resound beyond
these rock walls, and I'm bereft with
no crescendos, fortissimos,
but wait: now I'm hearing other
notes I'd not noticed before, soft
clunk as my careful husband shuts
his sock drawer, steady thud of his
shoes on wood slats of the floor as
he rustles plastic bags to take
for recycling, while my rumpled rag
swishes over the counter, with
the washer tumbling through its spin
cycle as egg shells crackle in
my fingers, and outside tonight,
the buzzing of crickets, and just
overhead: symphonies of stars.

UNCOLLECTED POEMS

CRASH

You thought it was
the road home, and
it was, till it
wasn't, pavement
slick from splattered
rain, and flash, crash,
you're smashed against
a pole—car tilted,
eighty degree
angle, air bag
flattened against
your chest, glasses
nowhere in sight,
until kind hands
open your door,
"Are you okay,
Ma'm? Now just breathe,
here's a blanket,"
and someone wraps
your shivering
shoulders as you
stutter, quiver,
never having
thought the road that
normally leads
straight home could end
with your car totaled,
towed off before
you had a chance
to thank all those
tender human
faces, but now
that wool blanket
is being used
to cover the pipes
outside our house

since tonight will
be the season's
first hard freeze
but no blankets
are warming me,
still shaking from
every pore,
not a single
road seeming safe
even with no
rain. My muscles
still tangle, tipped
against that pole.

ALONE WITH WOLF MOON

The New Year's first full
moon was named because
mid-winter, wolves howl
more often, to send
an alarm, gather
the pack, to signal
their locale, or, at
times, simply to wail
from pure loneliness.
I too want to howl,
though can't match Ginsberg's
elegy, but my
own howls are grieving
with this pandemic
that's murdered masses,
including a star
student I once taught,
and also I'm howling
over the pillage
of our Capitol,
rioters fed by
a crazed president
who, thank all the fates,
has been replaced. If
only we could join
an ear-piercing group
howl, but we're alone
these days, unable
to hug together,
and I'm hungry to
rally all our pack,
having seen only
two humans since last
spring, and I wonder
if I howl long and

loud enough, raising
my chin to this bright
orb, some one will know
I exist, not lost.

THE BONES KNOW

It's the time of year—September nights cooling—we dropped our father's ashes into the lake. They weren't what I'd thought of as ash. Too many bits of bone. Twenty-five years ago he died, same age I am now, about to turn seventy. "How old would you be if you didn't know how old you are?" said Satchel Paige, but most of me feels every bit of seventy, though my doc says I've the bones of a twenty-year-old. James Weldon Johnson's song: "Them bones them bones them dry bones." My father played that Mills Brothers' 78 over and over, along with "Lazy River." What happens to bones in water? Last summer during the monsoon, I plodded through Cambodia's Killing Fields, stumbling over bones. A femur beside two pebbles on the path, and, in a pool of muddy water, metacarpals—metatarsals?—and, further along, clearly, a rib. "Them bones them bones gonna walk around." Bones surfacing still, after even a light rain. Centuries, it can take, for bones to decompose. Hired crews collecting them.

BONE ASH, BONE CHINA

From whose bones? Horses, dogs? Pets put down? Muscle shreds removed and sold for pet food. From pets to pets. Then they're heated, the raw bones, 1,000 degrees centigrade, sterilized, and ground with water.

Extremely hard, intensely white, fine bone china allows light to pass through. 50% bone ash, the rest, clay and stone. My grandma's "gold band" pattern: Lenox Westchester, introduced in 1915, about the time she married. A solid gold rim circling that shimmering white surface. White as white can be.

The ash left when bones burn can also be used as fertilizer, high in calcium phosphate. Food for a field of corn, or spinach, broccoli, or tomatoes, color to pile on those plates along with porterhouse steaks, lamb chops, pink flesh still attached to bone.

THE MAKE-UP OF BONES

Without them, we'd be slugs, sliming through grass. Helmet over the brain, chest plate for lungs. Storage for calcium, phosphorus. It's bone marrow that makes our lymphocytes, blood cells.

Long, short, and cube-shaped: the wrist and ankle bones. Flat bones: the sternum. A fetus begins forming bones about the tenth week. At birth, an infant's body contains over 270 bones. Then they fuse, their number reduced by a quarter, our flab, protruding veins, our discolored flesh masking the framework within.

All this pulp I carry, this enveloping epidermis, these muscles that cramp and twinge. Some days I'd like to get down to the bone. If I could be rinsed clean of all these messy casings, face daylight, the sun's glare, with a clean, white, solid edge

AND I THOUGHT I KNEW WHERE I WAS GOING

—Tranquilo Bay, Panama

After two flights on 737s followed
by a third in a plane barely bigger than my Honda
before an hour on an outboard motor
boat rippling froth as it arced around inlets and
islets and onto the open sea, I felt
as though I'd inhabited Frost's "Directive," with
a guide "who only has at heart your
getting lost." And more kinds of trees in one place
than I'd ever seen, surrounded as
I normally am by South Texas live oaks, mesquite,
juniper, none tall enough to keep
from seeing sky. Rainforest trees so high, so dense,
I couldn't tell which way the sun rose
or set. Nothing like Frost's white pines, birches,
spruce, or maples. Not a single right
angle, no streets, no cars. No TV or WiFi. Aerial
roots, vines, leaves tangling till I could
barely stumble through the steep slosh of a muddy
path someone had cleared between
the towering kapok, guanacasta, black oil palms,
gumbo limbo, the massive strangler figs,
trumpet trees. Who was I in this place where all
the greens of this world melded
into one vast green, where waters beyond the boat,
beyond the bay, merged cerulean,
azure, turquoise, ultramarine, into one unbroken
sheen of wide open sea. And thousands
of birds above, around us, all seeming to know
where they were headed, unlike me,
who, for once in my life, was simply holding still.

ROAD TO A CANDIDATE

—February 2020

GPS leads us to the east side of town,
to the Galaxy Theater, but not the right
place at all, so I walk on in, ask a slim
brown-eyed man at the snack bar
how to find the Cowboys Dance Hall
where the candidate is speaking, and
the guy writes directions on the back
of a cancelled receipt. But no dice,
left lanes, right, on ramps, off, then
stopping to ask at a 7/11, three gas
stations, wondering whether to just
go home, but decide to keep on,
till we park at a sporting goods store
where a silver-haired woman tells us
it's a straight shot from there, so in
minutes we find the dance hall, cars
lined up roadside for over a mile.
We slide into a parking spot someone
has left and plunge into a crowd of
five thousand folks for the last
minutes of the candidate's speech
in this echoing hall, elbows brushing,
knees colliding, everyone tangled in
the crush to find the way out. All
the wrong roads to see just one of
the half dozen hopefuls running for
President of our fractious country,
the turn arounds, exits, entrances,
flashing lights blinding our eyes.

WHAT BLOSSOMS

"A White Sport Coat and a Pink Carnation," Marty Robbins,
oh yes, *doo wah.* Those 1950s high school dances, a boy
decked out in pressed trousers, polished shoes, arriving
at the front door with a corsage, always carnations, which
my mother despised as tacky. Not that she didn't like
flowers—she spent hours on her knees planting zinnias
in our Tucson desert yard. But she never knew her own
great grandfather bred carnations. Ephraim Syms Dodwell,
from Buckinghamshire, in 1886 published his life work
in *The Carnation & Picotee: Its History, Properties, and*
Management, which I found by chance on Amazon. Mom
had no idea. And I'm sure she'd never heard the legend
claiming carnation petals sprang from Mary's tears
as Jesus wilted on the cross. But how I'd melt when that
fifteen-year-old boy, sporting a frilly pink boutonniere,
his crew cut slick with Brylcreem, offered me a cluster
of carnations, probably with no idea they symbolize
passion. Also courage, a fact I wish my mother had
known. At eighty-seven she simply stopped eating
and drinking, left on her own time, her own way. We
didn't take carnations to the service, but daffodils,
her favorites. And the boy whose timid hand
placed into mine a carnation corsage: I learned
he died three months ago. I didn't know where to send
flowers, which would have been, of course, carnations.

ON SILVER SPOONS

The Golliwog spoon, we called it, the handle shaped like a head with heavy-lidded eyes and a thick-lipped mouth. Coddled eggs, cream of wheat in that spoon. And someone gave me a Golliwog doll—kinky black hair, clown-red mouth.

A second silver spoon: simple, ridged lines leading from the handle to the shallow bowl. "Tiffany & Co.," "Sterling" stamped on the back.

Two baby cups: one upright, sterling, from Tiffany's, straight-sided, no decorations. The other: urn-shaped, graceful, flowers twining around the handle, leaves spiraling the circumference. Orange juice, chocolate milk from both.

Bridge club friends of my New Jersey grandparents gave me the plain spoon and cup. But the others came from Tony, my father's devil-may-care best friend who'd waltz double forte down Broadway, bouncing my cautious father out of his Presbyterian gloom. Both were besotted with my mother, but dependable Daddy won out, while Tony joined the diplomatic corps, moved to Bogotá. Colombia: a country I'd never heard of till years after that silver had been packed away.

No sterling stamp on the flowery cup or the Golliwog spoon. Golliwog. A caricature of a caricature. My mother and father read me the books. "A horrid sight, the blackest gnome," ran Bertha Upton's prose.

I never met Tony. Not worth squat if it's not stamped sterling, says the jeweler. When was it I unpacked the Golliwog spoon? And realized it was probably an image of a god, maybe a Dolmen from Pre-Incan times. Or the San Agustín jaguar god—square nose, slanted eyes.

Two spoons, two cups, gifts for my birthing. Better than the spoon-like forceps that dented my scalp as I struggled into air. Forceps, a pair of spoons that molded me. Spoons: the Spanish, Greeks, Russians, Turks, and even North Americans make music with them, like silvery castanets. The clink of two metals against each other. It took a long time for my head to reshape itself.

DISTANCES

—In memoriam, Rodolfo de la Garza, 1942–2018

I could see them from my bedroom window,
Catalina Mountains north of Tucson's downtown YMCA
where we kids met for dances Friday nights,
Rudy and I swaying cheek to cheek, the Platters' "Only
You" and Johnny Mathis' "It's Not for Me to Say"
on the turntable. We'd double date in Ronnie's dad's
Chevy, French kiss in the back seat, nights too
dark to see the mountains, no lights back then sprinkling
the foothills covered in creosote, octotillo, and
palo verde. Rudy's muscled arms around my skinny back,
his sinewy chest pressing against my 32A
padded bra. The two of us, both stars in Miss Alice Butts'
Advanced Latin class. So a decade ago, when
I met Rudy again, and learned over lunch in Manhattan,
catching up after half a century, that he taught
at Columbia, I wasn't surprised. Then I discovered his
dozen-plus books on immigration and the border
with Mexico. Every time I visited New York, another
lunch, more details of our messy divorces, our
flourishing remarriages. But when I joked about his
dumping me for my friend Patty, his face drooped
as he confessed he'd always regretted our splitting up,
but she was eager to "put out," while I didn't know
what "going all the way" meant. The last time I saw him,
he choked back tears, said he'd really loved me
then. And he sure was the best of the bunch of boyfriends
who followed. No mountains around our
Gramercy Tavern lunches, only skyscrapers, as we
kissed cheeks before he hailed me a cab
and sprinted to catch his train uptown while I returned
to my husband in our cosy hotel room. Ray
Charles' "I Can't Stop Loving You" came out in 1962,
long after Rudy and I had broken up, and
though I adore my husband, I can't stop thinking back
to the time I was fifteen and a handsome
brown-eyed boy liked me so much he gushed over my

soft arms and legs. "Remember When,"
    the Platters crooned. After the first stroke, his wife
emailed, he was never the same. Now he's
    gone, and only one of the original Platters is still alive.

IN THE ENDOSCOPY CENTER

I'm led into the cubicle and instructed
by prim little Kristin to "lay down" on the cot,
at which point I reveal my inner grammar
cop and explain that she means I'm to "lie down"
unless she wants to lift me up and plop me
down herself. "Oh," she blurts, "I didn't know,"
rushing out before I can pull the stinger. Then
Fred comes in with the IV to put me under for
the gastro doc to probe my entrails, and with
a grin calls me "professor," adding he's glad to
see I'm "lying down." How long had my
inner bitch lain dormant before growling into an
outer bitch? I should have scoped the lay
of the land before going all English prof on this
poor girl. Best to let such sleeping dogs
lie. But my grammatical husband, sitting with me,
chuckles and nods. I sure wouldn't want
to shock young Kristin with a tale from memory
lane, how in college we joked about who'd
just gotten laid, since I'll bet she'd be more comfy
if I quoted the old prayer, "Now I lay me
down to sleep," and I would not want to lay on
her the fact that this beloved man
of mine is, amazingly, still eager to lie with me.

ANNUAL ANGUISH

Always, October,
I forget that wrens,
chickadees, titmice,
don't need our feeders
stocked with safflower
seed, thistle, peanuts,
because the snout-nosed
butterflies streaming
across town provide
more tasty food than
we'll ever offer,
but I'm bereft, left
wondering if I've
been needing all these
feathered visitors
more than they've needed
me, their fluttering
wings lifting, soaring
beyond places I'd
like to be leaving.

THE VISITATIONS

Cooped up, unable
to see any friends
in the midst of this
pandemic shutdown,
every morning
I stop work to watch
my window frame, as
a Bewick's Wren pecks
at the screen, cocked tail,
twitch, twitch, its belly
silvery against
the background of live
oaks that keep their leaves
all winter, under
which I've now spotted
a huge doe strolling
our yard, followed by
an even larger
buck, rack of antlers,
both right outside my
back door, close enough
to reach out and touch.

ALMOST ALONE DURING COVID

Nine months without hugging any
friends, no one in the house but us,
though in the yard we're surrounded
by junipers, mesquite, sumacs,
Mexican persimmons, leafy
presences I count on—so I'll
wrap my arms around a low branch,
but when it grows dark, as I turn
on lights inside, I notice how,
while trees outside fade in the night,
our living room lamps cast their glow
on your skin, and I can leaf my
fingers through your hair, let my hand
stroke your sturdy back, your solid
trunk my shoulders lean against, and
then I remember the trees' roots,
connecting beyond these strained eyes,
the limits of our outstretched hands.

THE FALL, 2020

Six months now unable to hug friends, only my sweet-
muscled husband here with me, and I thank September's
crescent moon for his company while we're addicted to
the Netflix series *Un village français* with English subtitles,
so I've brushed up my college French as we're beginning
the seventh season with the characters our buddies, lovers,
or enemies, in this saga of a village in eastern occupied
France taking my mind off Facebook, Twitter, and TV
news that spike my blood pressure, with these characters
more alive to me than faces I see flattened on Zoom,
while the post-war chapters grow more and more
bleak, with the kindly village doctor who treated a few
Germans jailed and his rival facing a firing squad,
and the doctor's flamboyant wife who'd slept with the SS
commandant carted through bellicose crowds,
every thread of her flaming red hair shaved, and the naïve
school teacher, who'd had a baby with a young German
officer, attempting suicide, and I can't stop thinking about
these lives I've been following, since at night in bed
their faces whirl in my head, and I wonder why I'd always
thought WWII was so clear-cut, Nazis bad, French
good, not realizing that the ethical village mayor ended up
choosing twenty on the list of hostages to be
sent to camps since if he hadn't, SS officers would have
carted off sixty, and while our sick nation's reality show
can't compare with the terrors of Vichy France, still I'd
like to enter the series myself, become one of these
folks, like the rotund schoolmaster, or the grizzled farmer
Anselme, or Sarah, the sweet, efficient Jewish maid,
all now more vital to me than any news anchor, though
I could never be brave as the curly-haired resistance
heroine Susanne, who leads the gaggle of guys camped in
the forest plotting against the SS, yet under a harvest
moon I could at least carry notes hidden in my sleeve, and
oh how I long to right our American wrongs,
neo-Nazi shootings, cops' knees on Black necks, caging

of migrant kids, while I'm wishing I could enter
        that long-ago era, where embraces could follow a *café,*
a *baguette.* Where we know—now—the outcome.

HOPE

. . . the thing with feathers. . . .
—EMILY DICKINSON

Sometimes I forget
about the virus
when I'm home and hear
myself humming tunes
from childhood until
I remember news
about the bridge with
traffic lessened since
the pandemic, now
so quiet that birds,
white-crowned sparrows, are
singing more softly,
more musically,
with males attracting
more and more females,
so nestlings, windfalls,
will be fluttering
the skies with new songs.

ON ELECTION DAY

(2020)

Live oaks breathe outside
the house, yet the shapes
of their leaves drift in
our rooms, a dappled
light and shadow more
enticing than art
pieces hung static,
two-dimensional,
while these fluttering
forms take me away
from ceilings, worries
while we're all waiting
for the results of
this year's election
with its wall-crushing
possibilities
I cannot bear to
ponder, determined
to ignore, focusing
on these shadowy
traces quivering.

WHEN THE SPRING IS NOT RENEWING

Too many friends without water
a month after our long freak freeze
when nights dropped near zero right here
in South Texas, ice piled on leaves,
branches. So I'm in need of spring
more than ever. Yet wandering
around our yard, I find mostly
gray twigs spiking air, few swelling
green sprouts that normally this time
of year would be lacing branches
with "darling buds" poised to blossom.
But not now, no joyful paeans
to the season with all these boughs
brittle as my bones, bark rough, cracked,
wrinkled as my skin, reminders
that this place has been home almost
forty years, about half my life.
So I am wondering if I
can hang on even another
ten, let alone twenty. Though I'm
not sure I want to, the Arctic
Circle drifting south, which may cause
another sharp freeze next winter,
bringing another springless spring,
no blooms to feed butterflies, bees,
hummingbirds, or my grieving eyes.

TEN MONTHS NOW, NO FRIENDS VISITING

And by the time we'll finally
be able to gather again,
my hostessing skills will be so
rusty I'll have forgotten how
to carry the tray with tea cups.
Good thing I'm not made of metal,
since if I were, I'd be encased
in a red-brown crust. How will I
remember the way to welcome
a visitor at my front door
swung-wide, not just cracked half open
to bring in a package? Or, hug-
starved, will I squash the bejesus
out of the plumber, the guy who
comes to trim the trees, or the sweet-
faced woman who delivers
my meds, let alone my oldest friend?
Open armed I'll be, like our country's
Statue of Liberty, greeting
all comers, but I remember
how she once was so covered in
rust she had to be closed down for
a year, and I wonder if I'll
need to be drenched with vinegar
before inviting folks inside
where I've been hunkered down, wearing
the same dreary mouldering robe.

FOUNDATIONAL

Layers of a life. Pressed down like compacted rocks.
    But wherever I've gone, I'll remember earlier eras
when I'd lived in other states, geographies, geologies:
    New Hampshire's granite mountains and white pines,
the caliche of Arizona's deserts, the tumbleweed.
    But none of these were riveting as the outcroppings
now before me, deep within the Chisos Mountains.
    How the land rises and juts, rocky red-brown crags
scalloping horizons. No WiFi, so I forget emails,
    lists, the brain-searing news. And then, one vivid
memory: nineteen years old, just married, living
    in a 10′ × 48″ trailer facing the Dragoon Mountains
north of Tombstone. Sixty years ago. First thing
    we'd see every morning, those jutting rock mounds.
Hired to be the school district's accountant,
    I barely knew how to balance my own checkbook.
Now, here I am, alone with these mountains
    circled around me, their balanced rock sculptures
hovering, lifting amid uncountable vastness.

STRUGGLING TO FIND HOPE

Hundreds of thousands crammed
        at our border, families escaping gangs,
rape, murder, terrors I can't even
        fathom, but I'm helpless to act from
my comfy two-story house. Now I hear
        a thumping coming from above, so I
trudge upstairs and realize there's
        something banging against a high window,
so I climb onto the step stool and
        find that flinging itself against the glass is
a tiny bird, black and white. I fear
        its toothpick bones will shatter against
the pane, so I try to scoop him up,
        but he flutters away from my grasp. I miss
and miss before I manage to hold him,
        taking care not to crush his fragile talons.
Ruby-Crowned Kinglet. Smaller than
        my palm. Slowly I step down, carry my
rescued migrant to the open balcony
        door, and open my fingers. Off, off,
he flies, to the sanctuary of the tall
        oaks' bright leaves. Minuscule miracle.

WHEN RIOTS ARE HARDLY A HOOT

"They're rioting in Africa,"
crooned the Kingston Trio back in
Nineteen Fifty-Nine, when all
the barbarity and terror
of that "Merry Minuet" seemed
oceans removed from my teenaged
suburban eyes glued to the glass
screen of our sixteen-inch TV
where those harmonizers wowed us
on the Jack Benny show. Even
black and white footage of Martin
Luther King's youth rally down to
the Sylvan Theater rippled
with hope. But last week, riot on
our country's Capitol Building—
not the kind where we'd say "Wow, what
a riot!" "what a blast!" "cracks me
up!" since our whole country sure is
cracking while we're in the midst of
a pandemic with case numbers
spiking above twenty million,
deaths three-hundred fifty thousand,
and no room in Arizona
morgues for any more bodies so
they're stored in refrigerator
trucks, and meanwhile I'm hunkered down
in my threadbare bathrobe, reading
Yeats again, "mere anarchy" now
loosed upon us with those thousands
of rioters in Washington
unmasked, waving Confederate,
Nazi flags, and I'm wondering
if our lungs are breathing in
this Twenty-First Century air
or are somehow gasping back to
Ireland in Nineteen Eighteen or

Germany, Nineteen Thirty-Eight,
and I want to escape from this
glass-shattering waking nightmare
splintering, crashing down on us.

SIZING

Don't sweat the small stuff, folks say,
                    always wanting bigger, higher. Pull
to rise over land, build the tallest
                    tower. Whose new steel and glass
skyscraper trumps whose? But isn't it
                    the small things that bring us down?
A bee sting, a splinter in the ball
                    of the foot that even a needle can't
wiggle out. A tick bite followed
                    by rashes, also fever, even paralysis.
The cause of my young mother's
                    dysentery, her hundred-thirty pounds
shrunk to eighty: an amoeba less
                    than half an inch. And this pandemic
we've been living through, resulting in
                    almost a million deaths, from a virus
smaller than a dust mite. And now, fury
                    over abortions in Texas outlawed after
an embryo is six weeks old, size of a rice
                    kernel. And a single sperm: a fiftieth
of an inch. In each milliliter of ejaculate,
                    up to two million sperm, all competing
to trump the others in the race
                    to pierce the ovum—small stuff indeed.

TURNING EIGHTY, RUMINATIONS

"She's not very pretty," Daddy
said, when at nine I showed him my
drawing of a curly-haired girl.
I guess I'd made her nose a bit
bulbous, and I hadn't shown her
in a frilly dress. "Pretty as
a princess," they'd say, and I had
sure been gazing at photos of
the two little princesses my
British granny air-mailed me. And
now that the elder princess, who
grew up to be Queen, has died at
ninety-six, I'm reminded of
the fifties' fashions we girls were
required to follow, ruffles and
lace—always, the goal: be pretty
as a picture, and a silent
one, no one wanted a loud-mouth
twit, just let those hair ribbons float
around soft twirling curls (formed by
a Toni permanent wave). And
I will never forget the time
Daddy scoffed at Mom when she voiced
her thoughts about an election,
his voice incredulous, "Good grief,
you don't know what you are talking
about, just stick to your sewing!"
Now I know why my being loud
has meant more than being pretty.

TRANSITION

Almost eighty, I'm needing
a new computer and skills
I'm not sure I can even
learn at this point in my life
as I'm left, after last month's
surgery, with only half
my insides, so I'm living
with a fraction of my old
get up and go, a gutless
wonder, helpless to offer
the smallest amount of aid
to my neighbor whose husband
barely survived a car wreck,
and though the news right now is
chock-full of stories about
England's queen who, ninety-six,
just died, I can't imagine
living that long and shaking
thousands of pairs of hands, but
then I remember Ruth Stone
on her Vermont farm where she
dashed out dazzling poems till
she died in her late nineties,
so maybe I'm not done yet,
even if left with half a gut
I can digest any breeze
that may waft toward my ears,
my open eyes, eager tongue.

AFTER THE WORM MOON'S ARRIVAL

COVID infection rates across
town plummet. We're feeling almost
normal. No touching anyone
for over a year, so webworms
(each no bigger than an eyelash)
slithering across our yard and
inching all over my cotton
shirt feel bewitching. Then today,
a thrill when seeing an old friend
the first time in months, and learning
we'd both had the vaccines, we closed
arms around each other, rocked back
and forth. Even better than curls
of just-born worms tickling over
my body. Now I remember
the Good Gray Poet, who gloried
in touch, so I'm singing my own
breathy alto "yawp" to rejoice
in the return of warm flesh on
flesh, as the webworms begin
their transformation into moths,
translucent wings fluttering air,
caressing our sequestered skin.

HOW CAN I EVER FORGET

My mother's high-heeled clacking
over concrete floors, nothing
ever quick enough, never
time for kisses or chit-chat,
too busy for such nonsense,
but these days I relish my
man's measured steps across our
wooden-slatted floors as he
reaches his firm muscled arms,
our flesh uninterrupted.

YOU INSIDE ME

I'm lifted tall
as the live oaks
lining our drive,
branches reaching
over the street
and up to clouds
as leaves caress
walls of our house
till all the rooms
are cushioned with
muscled sweetness.

HE MAY APPEAR A SMALL MAN

But his words travel across
continents, oceans beyond
our rooms, while adding music
to the silences held in
our walls, nothing like the way
a pot-bellied man I once
knew would holler, roar over
the blast of the football game's
announcer, ripping throughout
the house, shattering any
peaceful breath, while the voice of
my husband these days would calm
wild monkeys, even howlers.

I HAVE NEVER SEEN HIS HANDS

Clenched, unless you count his grip
on a tennis racquet, or
gripping my fingers in his,
until I know I am safe.

STUFF

Who brought these pieces here? Somebody making the shift
to assisted living? Someone's sixty-something kids after
Mom or Dad had finally "gone aloft,"
as my English granny would have said? The tchotchkes
cramming this antique shop I stroll through with my son:
ivory-handled button hooks, cameo pins,
tureens with porcelain peacock tails for handles. Before she died,
my husband's mother begged him to take the claw-footed,
eight-foot-tall armoire he hated. At seventy,
my mother labeled every object in her house, color-coded
for each daughter. She wanted to know which one of us
would wear her ruby ring, jade necklace,
turquoise bracelet. Where will my granny's silver trays,
salt cellars, tea pots, go? What about my mother's copy—
tattered, water-stained—of *Just So Stories,*
"O Best Beloved?" The 1924 collection of poems my father
cradled when he read aloud at dinner—will those end up
on my son's shelves? At Half Price
Books? A garage sale, eBay, landfill? A friend says we spend
the first three-quarters of our lives accumulating, the final
quarter, disposing. As a kid, I treasured
my doll-sized china tea sets, which, packed with crumpled tissue
in a taped box, fell off the back of our truck while leaving
one house for another. Like my photo albums
of the '60s the movers never found. No pictures left of my black
mascara eye-lashed, mini-skirted, leggy self, no images
of my tennis-playing lover. I've read about
the bower birds, who attract their mates with shiny
pebbles and trinkets rescued from trash bins. Did one
of my tiny tea cups end up in some
bird's bower? Sometimes I crave bare walls, windows open
wide to sky, the oaks, mesquite, and sumac. But who
am I without my journals of the past
twenty years, my embroidered needle case, the filigree
glass vase my husband gave me? Empty as if coming
into this world? Or preparing to leave.

AFTERWORD

STEVEN G. KELLMAN

"Every house needs someone to watch the swallows," wrote Wendy Barker. And, for more than twenty years, I was privileged to share a house and two acres with a virtuosic watcher of swallows, clouds, trees, flowers, and human singularities. For both her readers and her students, Wendy was a wise and generous teacher. She taught me how to be attentive to the natural world, and how to love.

When Wendy died, abruptly, on March 11, 2023, she seemed on the verge of a new, exciting phase in her career as a poet. She had recently published *Weave: New and Selected Poems* (2022) and had finished compiling the chapbook *Those Roads, These Moons* (2023), destined to be published posthumously. Days before her final hospitalization, she returned, euphoric but exhausted, from a triumphant stint as visiting poet at Arizona State University, her alma mater. After her death, I found a postcard in her university mailbox that she never had a chance to read. It lacks a return address but is postmarked Phoenix. It reads: "Dear Wendy, I'm grateful that you're the first poet I've ever met. Your readings, imbued with passion and excitement and life, moved me. Thank you for the chance encounter with your art and spirit. I'll keep at it!"

Wendy herself kept at it until she could not. Although she was eighty, she seemed endowed with a new burst of creativity and had just begun a book of love poems centering on our marriage. In *Poems' Progress* (2002), a fascinating volume in which she recounts how she came to write each of nearly two dozen poems, she recalls: "Someone once asked after a reading I had given, 'What do you consider your best poem?' I answered without a breath of hesitation: 'I haven't written it yet.'" If I had to choose a favorite among the collected works it might be one of the *Poems from Paradise* (2005), written after our rapturous first trip together through India. She made a point of including "If a God" whenever I was in the audience for one of her readings. But, a fellow professor, I am also partial to the teaching poems in *One Blackbird at a Time* (2015), in which a classroom becomes the arena for epiphanies, not merely about the literary text at hand. However, I also wonder what might have been written had Wendy lived even a few more months.

This volume collects the poems Wendy was working on during her final weeks as well as all of her earlier published poetry. Of all the many books and journals I have edited in my career, no project was as emotionally wrenching as assembling Wendy's life's work into this astonishing valedictory collection. Many of the poems date from before we became a couple, even generations earlier, but many others reflect our domestic lives together in Texas. Others recount our travels to destinations including Paris, Jerusalem, Costa Rica, India, Panama, Cambodia, Bulgaria, and the Galápagos. One even memorializes my bout with kidney stones. Like her messages on my iPhone, all preserve the distinctive voice of Wendy Barker. She was an accomplished and popular reader who mesmerized audiences from Berkeley to Hyderabad, and most of her poetry was written with an eye toward the ear.

Because of the remarkable range of her work, it is hard to define a "Wendy Barker poem." It could be long or short, metrical or not. While some could span several pages, others aspire to the condition of haiku. A spare eloquence ignites "Full Moon, Zenith":

> You have opened your door
> and answered my questions.
> Even at midnight, leaves
> of the oaks, persimmons.
> Seven deer on the lawn.
> We could read in this light.

In her final years, Wendy drew inspiration from the ancient practice of quantitative verse—lines measured by the number of syllables, not stresses. The autobiographical *Nothing Between Us: The Berkeley Years* (2009), which she liked to call a novel in verse, consists of linked prose poems.

She is almost always inviting the reader into a conversation, one whose ostensible casualness masks labored craft. "A line will take us hours maybe," wrote William Butler Yeats. "Yet if it does not seem a moment's thought, / Our stitching and unstitching has been naught." Although a Wendy Barker poem might seem like a spontaneous overflow of offhand remarks, it is the handiwork of multiple revisions. She was fond of advising her students: "You must kill your darlings." And many of her own precious lines ended up, after deliberation, in her study's recycle bin. A stringent critic of her own work, Wendy conjured art out of self-doubt. In “Exorcism of a Nightmare,” she imagines someone asking: “Why no poems these days?” The questioner continues:

> Actually none of them are any good,
> just more fifth-rate clutter
>
> robbing the woods of their bones again.

She piled up dozens of specialized volumes beside our bed—on nephology, chromatics, dendrology, and other disciplines. Her poetry was a product of intensive research as well as inspiration. “Sour Take” is spiced with the history, economics, and gastronomy of sugar. For “Silk Roads,” she studied how the delicate fiber is produced and how it has been brought to market. For the sequence “The Bones Know,” “Bone Ash, Bone China,” and “The Make-Up of Bones,” she boned up on osteology.

Among Wendy’s papers are as many as twenty versions of a single poem. She would regularly invite local poets—Cyra Dumitru, Joshua Robbins, Stephanie Schoellman, Zach Sokoloski, Darrell Stafford, Natalia Treviño, and Alexandra van de Kamp, among others—to our house to workshop new texts. Through lucent picture windows facing the trees and birds that Wendy loved, they would often spot a deer skittering past while they quibbled over images and syllables. Wendy also relied on a far-flung network of fellow poets—Ralph Black, Kevin Clark, Alice Friman, Bonnie Lyons, Alicia Ostriker, Joel Peckham, Barbara Ras, and Hannah Stein, among others—to provide feedback on works in progress. I was the final reader before she sent her poems out into the world. Wary, if not of her worth, then of the fickle literary marketplace, she usually ignored my plea to aim for venues with the widest circulation and greatest prestige.

In her iconic *ars poetica* “I Hate Telling People I Teach English,” Wendy both mocks and affirms her literary calling. When a repairman asks her what she does and she replies that she writes poetry, he quips: “Ah— / fluffy stuff.” Nevertheless, though her lines sing of buntings and junipers and hyacinths, this is not Hallmark greeting-card verse. There is nothing fluffy about the natural and unnatural disasters that figure in many of these pages. In “Closeted Indigo,” she notes: “There are ways of bludgeoning so the bruises / don’t show.” In Wendy Barker’s poetry, the bruises do show.

“I know poetry’s got to breathe / with the fumes of its time,” she writes in “Truth, Beauty, and the Intro Poetry Workshop.” The fumes that befoul *Nothing Between Us* come from a time in which interracial romance was taboo and dangerous. Behind the radiant, ingratiating smile that so many remember about

Wendy Barker was also a tough intelligence and keen moral sense that looked askance at gibberish and recoiled at cruelty. She had no patience for doltish movies and novels and became irate over public mendacity and misdeeds. Although she did not think of herself as a political poet, she was passionate as a citizen participating in a representative democracy. We worked together as volunteers on several election campaigns.

Wendy sometimes—as with "After the Shooting in Tucson," inspired by a mass murder in Arizona—addresses contemporary horrors head-on. More often she approaches them by indirection. While some of her poems might appear to begin as fluffy stuff, they soon acquire devastating gravity. Much of "About Chocolate" seems an innocent recitation of facts about the confection—first cultivated by the Olmec people, varieties of candy bars, the gastronomical chemistry—until the startling revelation that kidnapped African children often maim themselves harvesting it and an abrupt segue to a scene from the Holocaust.

Although he discouraged her from applying to elite private colleges, telling her she should instead set her ambitions on someday being "a great man's secretary," Wendy adored her banker father and mourned his death in several poems. In one, she wrote:

Before he died, I asked
to record my father's voice, his voice
I couldn't bear to lose.

As Ronsard, Shakespeare, Marvell, and others have proclaimed, the poem survives the poet, though rarely by much. Even if art is immortal, it is meager compensation for personal extinction. For those who knew and loved her, Wendy Barker's death was a grievous blow. The beguiling voice that lingers in these stunning poems is one we could not bear to lose.

INDEX OF FIRST LINES

ABOUT THE AUTHOR

Born in New Jersey in 1942, Wendy Barker (née Bean) grew up in Phoenix and Tucson. She received her BA and MA from Arizona State University and her PhD from the University of California at Davis. She taught high-school English in Scottsdale, Arizona, and later in Berkeley, California. She joined the faculty at the University of Texas at San Antonio in 1982 and served as its poet-in-residence and the Pearl LeWinn Chair of Creative Writing until her death in 2023.

In addition to publishing more than a dozen books of poetry, Barker co-translated a collection of the final poems of Rabindranath Tagore. She was also the author of *Lunacy of Light: Emily Dickinson and the Experience of Metaphor*, and she coedited a book about Ruth Stone. The many honors she received include the John Ciardi Prize for Poetry, the Rockefeller Foundation Residency Fellowship at Bellagio, the Mary Elinore Smith Poetry Prize, and the Distinguished Citizen Award of the City of San Antonio. She was beloved by several generations of students.